Late-Breaking Foreign Policy

LATE-BREAKING FOREIGN POLICY

The News Media's Influence on Peace Operations

Warren P. Strobel

UNITED STATES INSTITUTE OF PEACE PRESS
WASHINGTON, D.C.

Cover photograph: News cameras confront U.S. troops who have just hit the tarmac at Port-au-Prince's airport on September 19, 1994, to begin Operation Uphold Democracy in Haiti. Photo by Alex Webb; used by permission of Magnum Photos, Inc.

United States Institute of Peace
1550 M Street, NW
Washington, DC 20005

First published 1997

Printed in the United States of America

The paper used in this publication meets the minimum requirements of American National Standard for Information Sciences—Permanence of Paper for Printed Library Materials, ANSI Z39.48-1984.

Library of Congress Cataloging-in-Publication Data
Strobel, Warren P., 1962–
    Late-breaking foreign policy : the news media's influence on peace operations / Warren P. Strobel.
        p. cm.
    Includes bibliographical references and index
    ISBN 1-878379-68-2 (hardback). — ISBN 1-878379-67-4 (pbk.)
    1. United States—Foreign relations—1993– 2. Press and politics—United States—History—20th century. 3. Television broadcasting of news—United States—History—20th century. 4. Foreign news—United States—History—20th century. 5. United States—Armed Forces—Developing countries—History—20th century. 6. United States—Armed Forces—Civic action. I. Title
E885.S82 1997
327.73—dc21   97-9626
                                                                           CIP

Contents

Foreword *by Richard H. Solomon*   vii

Acknowledgments   xi

Introduction   1

1. Fighting the Last War: A Brief History of Government, the Military, and the News Media   19

2. Driving Fast without a Road Map: The News Media and Foreign Policy Today   57

3. Reporting the New Story: The News Media and Peace Operations   91

4. The Push: The News Media and Intervention   127

5. The Pull: Public Opinion and Peace Operations   165

6. Assessing the Gap: Conclusions and Recommendations   211

Notes   235

Index   265

Foreword

When Ted Turner launched the Cable News Network (CNN) in 1980, he foresaw the potential of a worldwide audience with an interest in round-the-clock news from practically every corner of the globe. He may not have envisioned his new venture as a media phenomenon that would come to have a significant impact on foreign-policy making. Since its first mention during the Persian Gulf War, however, the "CNN effect" has been the subject of considerable media commentary and scholarly analysis, linking it to everything from governments' loss of control over foreign policy decisions to a very public "back channel" for heads of state who seek alternatives to communicate their intentions to current and potential adversaries.

In Warren Strobel's important work, a media professional examines the CNN effect through the perspective of the numerous post–Cold War crises around the world that have led to U.S. intervention. Unlike previous studies of the media and U.S. foreign policy, which typically addressed the way American public opinion influenced a president's decision to go to war, this analysis explores the media's influence on the decision to deploy U.S. troops as part of peace operations. Foreign policy officials make the decision to deploy troops on such peace missions (or "operations other than war," in military parlance) under public pressure generated by televised images of human suffering, but often without a clear, vital national interest at stake—usually to restore order in failed states and to protect vulnerable populations. When the missions go badly, resulting in casualties or deaths of U.S. peacekeepers, the same officials often feel even more pressure to withdraw the troops quickly. Does the CNN effect—the notion of the news media as a force that drives foreign policy decisions—threaten to remove statecraft from the domain of experienced diplomats and policymakers?

Specifically, how much of an influence can be attributed to the CNN effect in the decisions to deploy—or withdraw—U.S. troops on peace operations to Somalia, Haiti, Bosnia, and northern Iraq? This is the main question Strobel attempts to answer in this study. Were these interventions the result of deliberate policy decisions by the president and his advisers, or hapless responses to the public's demands that something be done about the emotive images as they played on millions of television screens? Despite the appeal of the CNN effect's putative power, Strobel demonstrates that there are some crucial conditions that must obtain for the CNN effect to influence foreign-policy decision making.

In the course of this study, Strobel also reveals the impact of tremendous advances in communications technology not only on specific foreign policies but on the *process* of policymaking as well. The pressures of accelerating deadlines and rapid communications have made thoughtful analysis a relatively scarce commodity in the high-speed information marketplace. If real-time television has diminished the broadcast journalist's already precious few moments to sift through the blur of details and conflicting accounts of a foreign crisis, the same pressures have serious consequences for foreign-policy officials, who often must respond to the pressures of the crisis with little time for considered judgment. The real-time televised images of starvation and clan warfare in Somalia, ethnic cleansing in Bosnia, brutal political repression in Haiti, and waves of refugees fleeing mass slaughter in Rwanda have suddenly made foreign policy a very public process, as citizens demand some sort of instant response from their government. These images have also made foreign-policy decision making much more reactive and intuitive: crises in a remote corner of the world are no longer hidden from view, and foreign policy officials have less time to assess intelligence and analysis before having to decide whether or not to intervene. While diplomats are certainly not "relics of the days of sailing ships," something can be said of the power of the CNN effect when the occupants of the State Department's top floors stare intently at the images of a crisis on their office televisions while awaiting the arrival of an embassy's cables that analyze the visual impressions.

Strobel's vantage point is that of a working print journalist who has relied on his official contacts during his years covering the State Department and the White House to give his newspaper's readers a daily look at how decisions are made at the highest levels of government. During his yearlong stint at the United States Institute of Peace as a Jennings Randolph fellow, he visited his government contacts again—not as a reporter on deadline, but as an analyst—and he has synthesized their recollections in a reporter's conversant style. He also knows the television side of news gathering and describes in a reporter's detail not only what drives the broadcast journalists who "parachute" into the midst of crises around the globe (and their producers at the network headquarters who dispatch them to such situations) but also the imperatives of technology that drive the increasing rush to "go live" with the story. Strobel also explores the impact of the communications technology revolution on his own special medium—print journalism. The author's observation that television's ubiquitous "headline news" roundups have created a more analytical niche for the next morning's newspapers testifies to both his acute sense of how the media industry is going through a significant shift in its division of news-gathering labor, and his reflective approach to this complex subject.

The technological revolution in communications has indeed transformed the foreign policy machinery as well, and this book serves as one important effort of the Institute of Peace to address the major changes now transforming the practice of statecraft. This year, the Institute devoted its biannual conference to the impact of information technology and the telecommunications revolution on conflict management—an event entitled "Virtual Diplomacy." The conference built on a related gathering in 1996 on the theme of "Managing Communications," which examined the issues surrounding the coordination of information among the myriad governmental and private-sector organizations involved in humanitarian-relief missions.

Journalists, it is often said, provide the "instant history" of problems that academics will grapple with for generations to come. Indeed, reporters have a heavy burden: they observe, investigate, interview—and then must compose an accurate story that includes not only the salient facts of *what* has happened, but *why* and what its implications will be. Warren Strobel has brought the best of both worlds to this groundbreaking work on contemporary foreign-policy making in an era of vast change driven by the revolution in communications technology.

Richard H. Solomon
President
United States Institute of Peace

Acknowledgments

Writing a book, especially one on the elusive and occasionally mind-numbing topic of the media-policy relationship, can be a lonely experience. I was fortunate beyond words to have friends, family, and colleagues who helped ease the loneliness and ensure this project came to a successful conclusion.

First, my profound thanks to the United States Institute of Peace for giving me not just a bounty of time and resources but an intellectually stimulating atmosphere to conduct the research. Lou Klarevas was far more than a research assistant. His lively mind and enviable ability to rapidly find needles in haystacks of data were instrumental in forming my thinking, although I take sole responsibility for my conclusions—and any errors. My editor, Peter Pavilionis, worked tirelessly and carefully to help mold a very rough first draft into a much improved final product. Dan Snodderly supported the project from its early days, and offered encouragement to a first-time author. Joe Klaits, for whom the word graciousness must have been invented, makes the Jennings Randolph Program a fertile home for me and many other scholars. Chet Crocker, Ambassador Solomon, and all those in the front office took an active interest in my work. I am forever grateful that they found this labor worthy of publication. Thanks also to Pamela Aall, Sally Blair, Sheryl Brown, Wilson Grabill, Kay Hechler, Scott Hibbard, Brook Larmer, Susan Collin Marks, Jerry Schecter, John Torpey, Frederick Williams, and many others.

The *Washington Times* has always supported me in this and other work. Josette Shiner encouraged me to pursue this opportunity and then wooed me back to the newspaper. No one complained when, upon my return, my editors and I discovered there was much work left to be done on the book. My partner on the White House beat, Paul Bedard, rearranged his schedule to accommodate mine on numerous occasions. Major Garrett, a fellow journalist-author, provided inspiration and friendship. A special thanks to Adam Christmann in the *Times'* library for cheerfully fulfilling each of my many research requests.

Many individuals in government, the military, journalism, and academia took time out from their busy schedules to help. No one was more generous than U.S. Army Maj. David Stockwell, who not only helped me navigate through the fact and myth of what happened in Somalia, but shared his personal views of that difficult time, provided a sophisticated analysis of the military-media relationship, and encouraged me at every turn. Michael McCurry helped in many ways, and read portions of the manuscript, as did Mary Ellen Glynn. Former secretaries of state James A. Baker III and Lawrence Eagleburger, and Brian Atwood, Kenneth Bacon, Sandy Berger, John Bolton, Richard Boucher, Sandy Charles, Hank Cohen, Col. Jim Fetig, David Gergen, Barbara Francis, John Hannah, Dee Dee Myers, Andrew Natsios, Bob Oakley, Stanley Schrager, Brent Scowcroft, Jim Steinberg, Margaret Tutwiler, Sir Brian Urquhart, Col. Barry Willey, and Warren Zimmermann were among those who readily shared their experiences and analysis.

While it was at times awkward for one journalist to be interviewing another, my sessions with fellow reporters were vital to understanding all sides of the story. Ralph Begleiter of CNN helped sort out my already clouded memories of the Baker State Department, as did Reuters' Alan Elsner. Roy Gutman helped ensure I got the story of Bosnia right. Don Oberdorfer's journalism is history in its own right, and he gladly supplemented it with recollections, both written and oral. Thanks, too, to the *Washington Post'*s Keith Richburg, Art Pine of the *Los Angeles Times,* and Tom Gjelten of National Public Radio. I am indebted to my many friends at ABC, including Mark Brender, Laura Logan, and John McWethy. Three other journalists who tried their hand in the academy, Barrie Dunsmore, Nik Gowing, and Johanna Neuman, were first-class models to follow. After completing my own work, I got up the courage to read Johanna's—and was pleasantly surprised to discover we had reached similar conclusions via different journeys.

Many top-notch scholars had already expertly plowed much of this ground, giving me sure paths to follow. Many are cited in the text, but special thanks to Steven Livingston and Todd Eachus of George Washington University, RAND's Eric Larson, Colin Scott of the Humanitarianism and War Project, Adam Clayton Powell III of the Freedom Forum, and Daniel Hallin of the University of California, San Diego.

My parents, Carl and Shirley, have been life-long sources of generosity, encouragement, and wisdom and gave me the greatest gift of all: curiosity. Neither this book nor much else would have been possible without the love and support of my wife, Terri, and our boys, Mitchell and Adam. Companion, copyeditor, and much more, Terri is the strongest person I know. She somehow pursued her own career, kept hearth and home together, and rarely complained during the difficult presidential election year of 1996, when she mostly saw me packing bags for yet another Clinton campaign trip, or the back of my head at the computer terminal.

Introduction

KISLOVODSK, USSR, April 25, 1991—In the aftermath of the Persian Gulf War, Secretary of State James A. Baker III hoped to use the defeat of Iraq's Saddam Hussein to push Arabs and Israelis into peace talks.

Baker traveled to this resort in the southern Caucasus region of Russia to meet with Soviet Foreign Minister Aleksandr Bessmertnykh. Baker's goal, telegraphed to reporters beforehand, was to extract the Soviet Union's endorsement for the new Arab-Israeli negotiating effort. This would strengthen his hand as he traveled on to the Middle East to pursue his diplomacy.

For journalists in the State Department press corps accompanying Baker, this, then, would be their measure of his success or failure that day: could he win over the Soviets, whose goals in the Middle East since World War II had been opposite to Washington's? As journalists waited outside the guest house where the meeting was to take place, Bessmertnykh appeared and began chatting with them. The reporters asked him if Moscow would support the U.S. proposals for new Middle East peace talks. Bessmertnykh was noncommittal. Later, before the meeting, Bessmertnykh and Baker appeared before the cameras for a photo opportunity. Same question to Bessmertnykh. Same answer. After the meeting, the two ministers held a formal press conference. Surely all would be clear now, the reporters thought. For a third time, they asked the question in various ways. To their surprise, Bessmertnykh still declined to give a clear endorsement of the American proposals.

When the press conference ended, reporters headed for the telephones to report the story that Baker, en route to the Middle East, had failed to gain the USSR's unequivocal endorsement. Given the speed and scope of worldwide

communications, the story would soon be all over world capitals, where atten-
tion was on the future of the Middle East following Operation Desert Storm.
Baker's diplomacy would be more difficult.

Baker's spokeswoman, Margaret Tutwiler, caught wind of what the press
corps was about to report. Suddenly, reporters were recalled from their work.
Baker and Bessmertnykh were going to hold another press conference. If the
picturesque but run-down spa of Kislovodsk had been a movie set, this would
have been "Take Two." But American reporters, having already given Bess-
mertnykh ample opportunity to answer the question of the day, conspired
among themselves not to ask any further questions about the Middle East. If
the Soviet was going to change his tune, he would have to do it on his own.
The reporters asked about anything else they could think of—Afghanistan,
arms control, and so on. Finally, one of Bessmertnykh's aides whispered in the
ear of a Soviet reporter and—surprise!—the foreign minister called on him.
The Soviet reporter asked this "incisive" question: "Mr. Foreign Minister, have
you anything further to say about the Middle East?"

Hitting that "softball" out of the park, the Soviet official finally did endorse
the U.S. plan, completely reversing the headline of the day . . . and in the process
facilitating the remainder of Baker's diplomatic mission in the Middle East.[1]

I open with this anecdote because it offers a view of the relationship
between the news media and foreign policy officials that differs from the
popular image of distance and confrontation. It is a view that undergirds
this study. The relationship, examined up close, is so intertwined that at
times it is all but impossible to determine who is affecting whom—who is
setting the agenda and who is following it. Was it the news media that set
the course of events that day in Kislovodsk? After all, to Baker and Bessmertnykh, the perceptions of the assembled press corps, with their cameras and notepads, were vital to the success of their policies. The persistent
questions and the whirring videocameras meant they had to conduct their
diplomacy far more publicly than they would have liked. Bessmertnykh
said words—in effect, etching policy in stone—that clearly he had been
reluctant to use. Did the news media force a change in Soviet policy—or
merely in rhetoric? Or were the officials using the media? In the end, the
journalists reported what Baker and Bessmertnykh wanted them to. They
had no choice. After the second press conference was over, members of the

press corps tore up their radio and TV scripts or put a new, more positive lead paragraph on their written accounts of the day's events. The story appeared, with some caveats, in a way that helped Baker, who was legendary among the Washington press corps for using the news media for his own purposes.

These questions, and others addressed below, are not simple ones. But attempting to answer them is vital in an age when information and images move around the world instantaneously, seemingly affecting the lives of millions, the outcomes of wars, the foundations of states.

The role of television in affecting American public opinion and the policies of U.S. administrations has been the subject of scrutiny and anxiety at least since the Vietnam War. This concern has grown over the past decade, driven by events such as the uprising of Chinese students in Tiananmen Square, the Persian Gulf War, two coup attempts in Moscow, and the horrors of Bosnia, Somalia, and Rwanda, not to mention assorted dramatic acts of terrorism or the fall of communism in Central and Eastern Europe. This period roughly parallels the creation and astonishing growth of Ted Turner's Cable News Network (CNN), which has made twenty-four-hour-a-day global television news a reality and turned live broadcasting from around the world into a humdrum occurrence.

Various commentators have ascribed sundry new powers to the miniaturized cameras and satellite dishes employed in modern television news gathering—and to the men and women behind them. Some of these observations are accurate; many are not. Understanding properly the role of the news media is vital to the future of American foreign policy and, without exaggeration, to the American way of governing. Getting it right opens the possibility that reporters and government officials will be able to work better together, carrying out their similar, if often opposed, tasks for the benefit of American society. It also will ensure that officials, when they formulate policies that determine the nation's future and put American lives at risk, better understand the potential impact of the news media on themselves and those who voted them into office. Getting it wrong has high costs. Whether the media are the culprit or whether the fault lies in government policies, a public that is pushed into each (televised) instance of tragedy somewhere in the world, only to be pulled out when the (televised) costs become too high, likely will soon tire of the exercise. As of this writing, the nation's mood offers evidence that precisely this is happening.

This book attempts to document and understand one small, but vital, slice of the news media's impact: its effect on U.S. military intervention in an era when full-scale war seems to be, at least temporarily, a phenomenon of the past. The 1990s have seen the proliferation of limited military operations where less than "vital" interests, as traditionally defined, are at stake. These are peace operations.

The view that the news media's influence has usurped the traditional function of government policymakers was perhaps stated most starkly by the dean of American diplomacy, George F. Kennan. Writing in his private diary as U.S. troops landed in Somalia to combat mass starvation, Kennan worried that if such momentous decisions are made by popular impulse stirred by fleeting television images of horror, "then there is no place ... for what have traditionally been regarded as the responsible deliberative organs of our government, in both the executive and legislative branches."[2] Variations on this view have also been stated by personalities as disparate as billionaire presidential candidate H. Ross Perot and former UN secretary general Boutros Boutros-Ghali. During the 1992 presidential campaign, Perot declared on the ABC News program *20/20* that the advent of instantaneous worldwide communication has made embassies and their inhabitants "relics of the days of sailing ships."[3] More recently, Boutros-Ghali has said, "For the past two centuries, it was law that provided the source of authority for democracy. Today, law seems to be replaced by opinion as the source of authority, and the media serve as the arbiter of public opinion."[4]

This book argues that these concerns are misplaced, and the observations behind them are in error. Collectively, the comments above implicitly accept the existence of what has come to be called the "CNN effect." And to complicate matters, the term is understood differently by commentators both inside and outside the news media. Some use it to describe the "diplomatic ping-pong match" that occurs when world leaders use the network to send messages to one another during an international crisis such as the Persian Gulf War.[5] Others use it to describe the shrinkage of the time in which foreign policy officials must respond to world events that are nearly instantaneously displayed on their, and many others', television screens. Former assistant secretary of state Rozanne Ridgway has spoken of a "CNN curve," which she describes as CNN's ability to prompt popular demands for action by displaying images of starvation or other tragedy, only to reverse this sentiment when Americans are killed while trying to help.[6]

A much narrower definition of the CNN effect, one that is implicit in Kennan's diary entry, describes it as a *loss of policy control* on the part of government officials supposedly charged with making that policy.[7] This definition asks whether there is an independent effect on the foreign-policy making process by media such as CNN, which virtually wrest control from policymakers, who in turn can do little or nothing about this transformation. While this definition comes closer to the policymaking process itself, its presumption that the news media either have or do not have this powerful effect is too stark a distinction.

This book shows that the CNN effect implied by Kennan does not exist. It disappears under the examination that follows of numerous incidents in which the media supposedly played a major policy role. But to say that the news media do not steal policy control from foreign-policy decision makers is not sufficient. One must look at why the media, especially television, sometimes seem to have such power. How, when, and why do media reports inject themselves into the policymaking process, and what, if anything, can officials do about it?

A detailed look at the modern news media and foreign-policy makers, seen through the prism of peace operations, reveals a relationship like the one that played out in Kislovodsk. The relationship is far more complex, situational, and interwoven than the above definitions imply. As stated above, the news media are rarely, if ever, independent movers of policy. In hundreds of hours of interviews with people on both sides of the camera, and in a close examination of four peace operations, I found no evidence that the news media, *by themselves*, force U.S. government officials to change their policies. But, under the right conditions, the news media nonetheless can have a powerful effect on process. *And those conditions are almost always set by foreign-policy makers themselves or by the growing number of policy actors on the international stage.* If officials let others dominate the policy debate, if they do not closely monitor the progress and results of their own policies, if they fail to build and maintain popular and congressional support for a course of action, if they step beyond the bounds of their public mandate or fail to anticipate problems, they may suddenly seem driven by the news media and its agenda. They may discover what has been called the "dark side" of the CNN effect, a force—as sudden, immediate, and powerful as an avenging angel—that can sweep them along in its path.[8] This seemingly random, but in fact predictable, exercise of media influence was described graphically by a senior diplomat at the U.S. mission to the United Nations:

> It is very difficult to work out and anticipate how the CNN factor will come into play. It is like waking up with a big bruise, and you don't know where it came from and what hit you.[9]

The central point of this book is that the very nature of peace operations, as described in chapter 3, opens policymakers up to these sorts of potential influences. Peace operations thus require a more sophisticated understanding on the part of military and civilian officials of news media behaviors, and a more intricate melding of military, political, and public affairs objectives.

This more nuanced view of the CNN effect helps reconcile starkly competing visions of the news media's influence. On one hand is the view that CNN in particular can be an awesomely powerful, even frightening, tool in the hands of government officials, even in a democratic society. This view was frequently articulated in the aftermath of the Persian Gulf crisis of 1990–91, which saw an extraordinary effort by the U.S. military to formally control the news media, and the determined use of the media by civilians in the Bush administration. On the other hand are the almost plaintive cries of Kennan and Boutros-Ghali just a few years later.

In truth, the news media's impact is almost invariably due to the conditions that officials themselves (or other policy actors) create. The impact depends on the type of crisis involved—whether it is warfare or a peace operation, and, in the latter case, whether the operation is primarily humanitarian in nature or primarily peacekeeping or peacemaking. And, as described below, in peace operations, at least, a great deal depends on which phase the operation is in. Yet these findings preserve a greater potential role for officials than that seen by many commentators.

The chapters that follow have an additional purpose. They attempt to disentangle the effects of modern communications technology from the effects of geopolitical changes on the news media–policy relationship.

First, technology. Much of the impact of the increased speed of communication—I focus on global real-time television, but facsimile machines, the Internet, and other technological advances can illustrate the point just as well—falls on the conduct and processes of making foreign policy, rather than on the policy itself. According to the dozens of officials with whom I spoke, real-time television can accelerate the governmental decision-making process, sometimes for good, sometimes for ill. It can force government officials to spend far more time than they used to explaining and selling their policies to the public(s) and worrying about how those policies will be received. Dramatic real-time reports can prompt rhetorical adjustments by the president and his lieutenants. If allowed, these reports can exercise a powerful agenda-setting function, forcing a sharp and sudden change of focus at the upper levels of government. In short, they make the conduct of foreign policy and the use of military force more transparent, subjecting diplomats and military officers to a level of democratic review that has little, if any, historical precedent. For this reason, many officials do not like these changes.

Many years after that day in Kislovodsk, Baker would say the effects of technology are two: temporal and spatial. By the term "spatial," Baker meant that the camera now can bring crises from virtually anywhere around the world onto the television screen and thus directly into officials' in-boxes.[10] Before, the true extent of civil war, famine, or anarchy might go unknown—or, more likely, be hotly debated—for decades. I heard much the same from many other top officials of the Bush and Clinton administrations.

Temporal effects have already been discussed briefly. The important point here is that what has really changed is officials' margin of error. It has narrowed considerably. To sympathize with the U.S. official quoted above, what seems to be a placid policy course on one day can seem to drown in a media frenzy the next. As discussed in chapter 1, even during the Persian Gulf crisis, generally seen as a model of official handling of the news media, there were several points at which the Bush administration very nearly let control over the characterization of events slip from its grasp and into the news media's.[11] Again, the very existence of these risks further indicates that official prerogatives do remain.

For all its wonders, modern communications technology has left many important variables unchanged. Even those media effects that do exist become absorbed or diluted over time. There is evidence that government officials are becoming more adept at dealing with the temporal pressures associated with the CNN effect and, sadly, in spatial terms, that both they and the viewing public are becoming increasingly inoculated to the humanitarian horrors from afar that they see on television.

More important, when deciding whether to send U.S. military forces into harm's way or whether to withdraw them, officials look far beyond the realm of portable satellite dishes, laptop computers, handheld video-cameras, and the like. The evidence strongly suggests that they examine the same constellation of factors they always have: the risks of intervention, the likely benefits of the mission, the stakes for the country, the depth of congressional support, the state of public opinion. The public, for its part, continues to weigh the real costs of a military mission against the perceived U.S. interests.[12] If those costs—chiefly American combat casualties—are shown on television, it may have a temporal effect, speeding the end of a mission that already lacks public support. But television has little effect on the public's basic calculation of costs and interests.

A final question concerns how technology has altered, if at all, the day-to-day relationship between reporters and the officials they cover. CNN and its brethren have had one impact in this regard, one that has been little noted outside some journalistic circles. The task of reporting basic facts—the traditional who, what, when, and where of journalism—has increasingly fallen to CNN and other instant news outlets, which range from new cable television-and-Internet hybrids to personalized electronic wire services. They deliver the news hours before the morning newspaper. For this very reason, an increasing portion of the newspaper has become devoted to journalism's why. Many officials felt newspaper coverage of them and their policies has become more analytical and interpretive—less objective, less a mere recording of the day's facts. Beyond the scope of this study, but worthy of further investigation, is the impact of the Internet and related electronic communications on objectivity. Much of the information that floods the Internet is unmediated, in the sense that it may come from non-traditional sources, is not subject to traditional journalistic filtering, and has a high emotional or subjective content.

Notwithstanding these developments—and the ravages of Vietnam, Watergate, and even more recent history on reporter-official relations—here, too, less has changed than would seem at first glance. Reporters' reliance on "official news," the statements and actions of high government officials, remains strong. Their relationship with government officials remains largely as it was described more than thirty years ago by Bernard Cohen in his seminal study of State Department correspondents and officials, *The Press and Foreign Policy*.[13]

Officials, however much they might bemoan the fact, cannot conduct modern foreign policy without explaining it to, and building support among, the American public. This they do through the news media. At times, policymakers, and especially the president, through their powers of governance, can string along the news media and the American public, or deceive them about their course. But if government officials stray too far from their public mandate, the news media will sooner or later make this fact transparent, and those officials will find public opinion in open revolt, demanding, usually without great specificity, a change of policy. Thus, more than passing similarities can be found between what eventually happened in Vietnam and what happened in Somalia in the summer and fall of 1993. Somalia lacked a geostrategic rationale such as the containment of communism, which persuaded Americans to sustain costs in Vietnam long after they otherwise would have, but it had real-time television to bring the costs to the American people for evaluation much more rapidly.

By the same token, it is virtually impossible for the news media and public opinion to take policymakers in a direction that is 180 degrees from their intended course. Surveying U.S. foreign policy as it pertained to peace operations from 1991 to 1995, I found not a single instance where the news media, with their dramatic images and words, their pervasive reporting, their persistent questions, were the sole cause of a reversal of policy. Rather, the news media had an impact on policy when that policy was weakly held, when it was in flux, or when it did not have congressional and public support. If policymakers are inattentive or unsure, then someone else will determine the direction. When policy is clear and strongly held by the executive branch, is communicated well, and has congressional and public backing, the news media tend to follow. Indeed, the media's very nature and the still-powerful tyranny of "objectivity" ensure that it can do nothing else. These observations are not mine alone, of course. They were stated perhaps most eloquently by Daniel C. Hallin in his study of print and television coverage of Vietnam, *The "Uncensored War."*[14] Historian Michael Beschloss, award-winning television journalist Ted Koppel, and others have made similar observations.[15]

Chapters 4 and 5 will show repeatedly how the news media are not the independent actors in the foreign-policy decision-making process they often are described to be, but rather a part of the process itself.

If modern communications technology provides only part—indeed, a small part—of the explanation for the *apparent* growth in the news media's power, then we must look elsewhere for the rest of the explanation. This search is complicated by the fact that the technological developments already noted occurred at roughly the same time the international system was undergoing fundamental changes.

The initial change that concerns us is the demise of the Cold War. If, as Hallin states, the news media's impact is inversely proportional to the level of consensus in society, then the existence (or belief in the existence) of a Soviet threat can be seen as the geostrategic glue that bound officials, reporters, and public together for more than forty years. As discussed in chapters 1 and 2, journalists often challenged the specific tactics and policies that presidents used to fight the Cold War. But they were more supportive of the strategy of containment and the notion that the Soviet Union was a mortal threat to the nation than is usually remembered. Today's headlines reveal the lack of a similar raison d'être for American foreign policy around which society—and journalism—might form a consensus.

The waning of the Cold War led directly to the second major change discussed in this study, the addition of new missions that the U.S. military is called upon to prepare and conduct. These peace operations differ radically in many aspects from traditional warfare. But for our purposes, the most important difference is in the relationship between the mission on the one hand and the news media and public opinion on the other. In war, the nation is mobilized, major news media often follow leaders and public to the point of jingoism, the enemy is known, and the desired goal (if not the means to it) is clear: victory. None of this is true during peace operations. While peace operations are arguably a legitimate part of U.S. security policy, they do not invest the nation's attention and resources as does war. The nation's physical or economic survival is not at stake. Mass public opinion is not mobilized in the same way. For this reason and because of the distinct nature of the new "battlefields," *the news media cannot be restricted in the same way*. Indeed, as discussed in chapter 3, the traditional wartime relationship between reporters and officials is turned virtually on its head. Rather than controlling reporters, in peace operations military commanders and their civilian bosses desperately need them to help build support, to explain what may be a complex and indistinct picture, and even to gather useful information for them in the field. In return, they must offer access and independence that allow reporters to distance themselves from their would-be chaperones in the U.S. military. The different nature of the "combat," terrain, and policy actors in places from Mogadishu to Port-au-Prince further tips the scales in favor of reporters. Finally, as a peace operation comes to an end, its outcome is likely to be much less clear-cut, less easily explained to the media and public, or even less satisfying than that found in warfare.

This changed nature of U.S. military operations accounts for much of the news media's apparent growing influence in helping determine American foreign policy. While reporters' tools have changed, the world as we knew it has changed even more. Yet these nonmedia factors have generally been given little attention in discussions of the CNN effect and the like.

For reasons of simplicity and analysis, I have roughly divided the life cycle of a peace operation into two phases. The first encompasses the administration's diplomatic and political response to a crisis, culminating in decisions on whether and how to deploy U.S. armed forces. If independent news media pressure drove the decision to intervene, the news media can be said to have exerted a *push* effect. The second phase includes the entire time during which U.S. forces are deployed, as well as the decision for and manner of their withdrawal. If news media coverage of a peace operation (especially any setbacks it encounters) independently contributes to the decision to withdraw, the media will have exhibited a *pull* effect.

These effects describe what is widely thought to have happened during the Somalia operation: Televised images of starving children forced President Bush to dispatch American troops to the Horn of Africa in December 1992. He was "pushed" into action he would not have taken otherwise. In this view, that same medium, television, by reporting the tragic costs of the Somalia mission in October 1993, forced President Clinton to withdraw. He was "pulled" out. Although there are grains of truth in both these accounts, this book demonstrates that what really happened in Somalia and the other operations examined here is far more complex, and the role of television and other media was much less influential than is often cited.

Nevertheless, this push/pull division remains a useful tool for analyzing the news media's role in peace operations. The media's behavior and the relationships among the nation's leadership, the public, and news media are quite different when decisions are being made about whether to intervene from when decisions are made after U.S. troops and prestige have been put at risk. I argue throughout this study that the media have greater potential effect once an intervention is under way, even if it is the policy equivalent of sticking a toe in the water to test the temperature. Many who make foreign and national security policy in the U.S. government understand this, with the result that the news media (or more precisely, fear of its effects) can be a negative influence on intervention decisions.

At times, this book uses the term "peace operations" in a generic sense. When so used, it refers to these operations in the broadest context. I take my definition from the Clinton administration's 1994 policy on multilateral peace operations: the entire spectrum of activities from traditional peacekeeping to peace enforcement aimed at defusing and resolving international conflicts.[16] Excluded from this definition at one end of the spectrum is warfare as traditionally understood by the U.S. military and, at the other, quasi-military operations such as drug interdiction that are included under the Defense Department's broader terminology, "operations other than war."

However, the study itself and the interviews I conducted were built around four major cases of peace operations, with a fifth minor case sometimes used for reference. The first case is the international response to the civil wars that broke out in the former Yugoslavia in 1991. The second is Operation Restore Hope, the Bush administration's dispatch of nearly thirty thousand U.S. troops to establish security for humanitarian relief efforts in Somalia, and the subsequent activities by the United States and the United Nations in the second UN Operation in Somalia (UNOSOM II), which was under nominal UN control. The third is the international response to the mass slaughter and refugee crisis in Rwanda in spring and summer 1994, particularly Operation Support Hope, the huge U.S. logistics effort in support of the UN High Commissioner for Refugees (UNHCR) and other relief agencies. The fourth is the U.S. intervention in Haiti in September 1994 to restore the elected government of President Jean-Bertrand Aristide, and the follow-on UN Mission in Haiti (UNMIH). Finally, from time to time I refer to and analyze Operation Provide Comfort, the mission to sustain and protect Iraqi Kurds following their failed revolt at the end of the Persian Gulf War.

These cases obviously do not constitute a complete, nor perhaps even balanced, selection of modern peace operations. Left out are arguably some of the greatest successes of the United Nations and its member states: Namibia's peaceful transition to independence, the holding of elections throughout most of Cambodia and the establishment of a recognized government in Phnom Penh, and the ending of fratricidal bloodshed in El Salvador and Mozambique. These latter operations, while garnering some press and television attention, have not been the subject of media frenzies. Like the news media I write about, I am guilty of focusing on the dramatic, the bloody, and the controversial. I picked the four cases of the former Yugoslavia, Somalia, Rwanda, and Haiti because each dealt with an actual or prospective U.S. intervention with military force and because each raised at least the appearance of media impact on U.S. government policy or public opinion.

This study focuses almost solely on policy processes (both executive and legislative) and public opinion in the United States. Again, while I hope this approach gives a clear picture of this one subject, it leaves out many others. This approach also risks leaving the reader with the impression that U.S. troops did more, and U.S. policy played a greater role, in these missions than was actually the case. It is not my intention to diminish others' contributions. In Bosnia and throughout the Balkans, troops from Europe, Asia, and elsewhere at first bore the brunt of the frustrating and dangerous work to contain the conflict; in Rwanda, as in many places, volunteer relief workers were the first to address the horrible wounds and were still there long after the television cameras moved on. In terms of news media, I also have focused primarily (although not exclusively) on the U.S.-based media. Of course, this line is harder and harder to draw as mergers, news-sharing, and other cooperative arrangements blur the distinctly national character of many news organizations.

The reason for this focus is twofold. First, my own experiences, occasionally found in the book, are with the U.S. foreign policy machinery and journalism as it is practiced in the United States. Second, the project had to be circumscribed somehow. All the same, this focus points the way toward further areas of useful study. It is a reasonable hypothesis that press coverage of, and public and governmental attitudes toward, peace operations differ around the world. Delineating these differences and the reasons for them would aid in a more comprehensive understanding of the subject. It might enable government leaders to better understand the sources and limits of public support for peace operations and the impact of national and global news media on both.

My conclusions are my own, but they are based in the first instance on hundreds of hours of interviews with over seventy individuals. I interviewed people from five basic groups: policymakers from the Bush and Clinton administrations; U.S. military officers (particularly from the Army and Marine Corps), including many military spokespersons; UN officials; representatives of relief organizations, both intergovernmental and nongovernmental; and journalists, primarily from television and newspapers. The interviewees were not chosen in a strictly regimented fashion; however, I sought out those individuals I believed were in the best position to determine how the news media had affected them and those around them and to give a perception of public opinion at the time. I purposely tried to interview officials at different levels of policymaking—the military spokesperson in the field and the desk officer at the State Department, as well as the secretary of state and the cabinet department spokesperson. The interviews with fellow journalists were particularly useful in further understanding their interactions with these various groups, as well as their assessment of the impact of their own work. The interviews themselves did not include a standardized set of questions. Rather, I sought to probe each individual's personal experiences, the view from their particular place in the policy "food chain," and their insights into the news media's influence on peace operations. Some government officials, both current and former, and other sources agreed to share their candid views on the condition that their names not be used. While unsatisfying for both the reader and the journalist, I agreed to respect their wishes in the interests of describing the various decision-making processes that surround peace operations as fully as possible.

Other sources of data include a review of the copious literature on the news media, the military, and foreign policy; a survey of newspaper coverage, primarily in the *Washington Post* and *New York Times*, of the events in question; videotapes of some of the most dramatic events recounted; opinion polls; and data on television coverage of the cases. Some data analyses were performed to determine patterns of television coverage. However, in most cases when I use numerical data, either regarding media performance or public opinion, I draw on others' work. I made no attempt to characterize media coverage in a mathematical fashion, such as through coding for story content or counting the use of particular words or phrases (bibliometrics). These skills do not come easily to a journalist. This study, then, is not scientific in the purest sense of the word. Rather, I have tried to lay out an understanding of the news media's impact on peace operations that is both analytical and practical. The words of those on the receiving end of that impact speak for themselves.

A few other definitional matters need to be cleared away. As noted in chapter 2, when I use the term "real-time television," I employ the definition provided by fellow journalist Nik Gowing. Real-time television refers not only to images that are broadcast as they occur (that is, live), but images that reach policymakers and other audiences within a few hours of the event.[17] There does not seem to be a substantive difference in impact associated with this brief of a delay in broadcast.

How to disaggregate the effects of the different media that make up the "news media" is always an analytical challenge. When I use the term "news media," I refer collectively to all the major branches of modern journalism —broadcast and cable television, newspapers and magazines, wire services, and radio. At times, particularly if a single story dominates the news, the combined pressures that these media bring into play are a phenomenon in their own right. Most of the discrete examples of supposed media impact examined in this book involve television, and I have tried to make it clear in the text when I am discussing that medium's particular qualities and impact.

My vantage point, of course, is that of a lifelong print journalist with intimate knowledge of the story-selection and news-gathering processes; a decade of experience reporting on U.S. foreign policy and national security; and, even before my research began, a more than passing acquaintance with the work of my colleagues in television news. At the risk of sounding defensive, it is my view and the view of those I interviewed that the printed word and photograph continue to have a distinct impact of their own, notwithstanding the growing dominance of television and the emergence of CNN and its brethren. That newspapers continue to have a substantial impact on the policymaking elite—although perhaps less so on mass public opinion—is clear from several of the stories told here. Dramatic newspaper accounts of the famine in Somalia and the horrific human rights abuses in the former Yugoslavia influenced the U.S. government decision-making process on whether to intervene. Another medium, radio, helped spur the bloodshed and exodus in Rwanda and played a role in Somalia as well. A study of the news media and peace operations that limited itself to television would be incomplete.

Chapter 1 presents a brief history of the U.S. media's coverage of warfare from the Spanish-American War through the Persian Gulf War, pointing out certain phenomena and relationships between media, military, and public opinion that will be examined in more detail later in the book. Chapter 2 analyzes the changes wrought in the relationship between news media, policymakers, and public, first by the collapse of the Soviet Union and the end of the Cold War, and second by the emergence of new communications technology. The last section of this chapter begins my detailed examination of the CNN effect. Chapter 3 examines the mechanics of how reporters cover peace operations and interact with different groups on the ground. It shows how the relationship between the media and the military during peace operations differs in several fundamental ways from their relationship in wartime. Chapters 4 and 5 are the core analytical chapters of the book and contain my specific conclusions about the news media's impact on peace operations. Chapter 4 examines the *push* effect: the media's influence on U.S. government decisions about whether to intervene in a crisis by initiating or joining a peace operation. Chapter 5 examines the *pull* effect: the media's influence, once a peace operation is under way, on the conduct of the mission itself, on overall policy, and on public support. Chapter 6 summarizes my conclusions and offers some recommendations for policymakers.

The book's structure is intended to reflect the dual nature of the subject matter as explained above. The chapters are interconnected and can be grouped in two sets. Chapter 1 and, even more so, chapters 3 and 5 focus on military operations that are in progress and on the media-military relationship. Chapters 2 and 4 focus more on diplomacy and the relationship between the news media and foreign policy officials. Like the subjects themselves, these are proximate, not exact, delineations.

A final, somewhat personal, note. This book may be seen by some as an apologia for the news media and its many faults written by a member of that profession. It is not intended as such. I have tried not to gloss over the many failures of the news media (especially those of television, in my view). These include failures to aid officials and the public in spotting emerging problems before they become crises; to convey the complexity of international events that go beyond the black hat–white hat stories to which television seems inexorably drawn; to sustain coverage of peace operations after the initial drama is past, returning only when new bloodshed or suffering occurs; and to focus enough attention on international problems that lack the drama and "good video" of Bosnia, Rwanda, Somalia, Haiti, and the like. Rather, I tried over and over to pin down the news media's precise impact on *policy*. Although I did not begin my research with a detailed thesis in mind, I assumed the media's impact was substantial and direct. I have found otherwise.

I also have written under the assumption that the nature and mores of the U.S. news media are unlikely to change significantly, given the political and economic nature of this society. Government officials, I believe, will have to learn to deal with the news media as they find it, and can do so. Effective policymakers and military commanders understand this. Others, who see only the news media's potential negative effects, try to block out or hide from it, losing important opportunities to build support for their policies and thus govern.

1

Fighting the Last War

A Brief History of Government, the Military, and the News Media

> "The military is finished in this society, if we screw this up."
> —*Defense Secretary Dick Cheney, before the Gulf War*

> "The Gulf War was quite a victory. But who could not be moved by the sight of that poor demoralized rabble— outwitted, outflanked, outmaneuvered by the U.S. military. But I think, given time, the press will bounce back."
> —*Secretary of State James A. Baker III, after the Gulf War*

The fundamental questions I pose in this book cannot be answered without the benefit of historical perspective. This chapter offers a brief, but necessary, tour of how the press (and, later, the news media) have reported on, and sometimes participated in, the nation's past military engagements. The survey that follows is far from a comprehensive review of the milestones in media coverage of the nation's wars. Rather, it will show common threads in the media–government–public opinion relationship that ran through the previous century and are useful for a study of the relationship between the news media and contemporary peace operations.

Specifically, this chapter will show that the news media's impact has always depended on what the nation's leaders say and do when the nation is at war. That impact, as Hallin realized, is also intimately tied to the degree of consensus in society regarding the conflict. It also depends on the type of military mission American soldiers are called on to perform, with public opinion and media influence much more problematic for government officials in limited wars, a category of warfare whose conditions most closely resemble those characterizing peace operations. This chapter also reviews literature that provides strong evidence that news media—in particular, television—reports of American combat casualties per se do not lead to irresistible public demands for withdrawal from a conflict. These values have remained constant throughout the past century of journalistic coverage of Americans at war. Later chapters will show that the development of new media technology, including real-time television, has not fundamentally changed the conditions necessary for the media to have an impact on public opinion and policymaking. That impact will depend on whether leaders and the public share a consensus, on whether there is, in Clausewitzian terms, a binding trinity of the people, commander, and army in wartime.[1]

A second purpose of this chapter is to summarize the history of government/military restrictions on the news media in wartime and the struggle between journalists and soldiers for control of the information that was sent to the home front. This review sheds needed light on the current adjustment the news media and the military are making in their relations in the peace operations era, with the balance of power shifting, no doubt temporarily, to journalists. Throughout the history of this democratic society and to this day, public officials have practiced a balancing act during wartime, using the news media negatively through restrictions on access and content, and using them positively by offering journalists access and a measure of independence. In the Persian Gulf War, the emphasis was on the former, with severe limitations on the news media that, in retrospect, some military commanders believe were unnecessary and even counterproductive given the high level of public support with which President Bush went to war.[2] In 1994, President Clinton sought to remedy his lack of public support for sending troops to Haiti with a proactive policy toward the news media. Given the limited nature of the mission, the other option—a broad crackdown on press freedoms—was not open to him. Throughout this century, and especially toward its end, the media and the military have battled over what the terms of their relationship should have been in the previous conflict. Like the stereotypical general, they seemed to be preparing to fight the last war.

This survey begins at the turn of the century, with the Spanish-American War, for several reasons. First, newspapers—the predominant medium of the day—appeared to influence strongly the decision to go to war. Second, the emotional atmosphere of the period and the outrage over reports of war atrocities bear at least a passing resemblance to conditions in the present era, in which televised images of inhumanity and suffering are thought to provoke public demands for government to take action. I then examine the two World Wars, conflicts in which American reporters largely served to support the goals of the administration. In the first, reporters labored under severe censorship in the field, coupled with a suspension of liberties at home. In the second, the broad popular and journalistic support for the war led to a lessening (although by no means elimination) of formal press restrictions. Korea is a transition case, in which the news media (including the new medium of television) largely remained allied with the U.S. military, although public support ebbed as the conflict and its costs dragged on. I devote more space to an examination of Vietnam, because it was the first war to feature extensive television coverage of combat and was also a limited conflict. In a process that would be duplicated much more rapidly a generation later in Somalia, Congress and other opinion makers withdrew their support for the mission U.S. troops were carrying out, which was followed rapidly by a similar erosion of support in the news media. Finally, the U.S. failure in Vietnam and the news media's supposed role in it prompted the military's return to circumscription of reporters—in Grenada in 1983, Panama in 1989, and the Persian Gulf in 1990–91. This last conflict, so successful from the U.S. point of view, set a false precedent for future media-military relations by seeming to usher in a new era of military dominance over the media.

Distant Echo: The Spanish-American War

The case of the Spanish-American War illustrates how the news media, whether it is the "yellow press" of President McKinley's day or CNN almost a century later, can help create the framework for decisions about military intervention, giving the appearance of a *push* effect. Media influence and its prerequisites have not changed despite a century's worth of stunning advances in communications technology.

The impact of the powerful new communications tools on the polity of McKinley's day has been aptly compared with the power of present-day technologies. Comparable, too, was their focus on the emotional and the gut-wrenching, including Spain's real and imagined abuses of Cuban rebels, and the accompanying demand from the American public that their government officials "do something!" The mass circulation presses of William Randolph Hearst and Joseph Pulitzer, the telegraph, and the development of a more popular writing style aimed at the masses "created a situation similar to the change wrought by the advent of television and particularly by CNN-type coverage" a century later. "In both cases mass appeal was activated by a simplistic portrayal of events in emotive images."[3]

Certainly Hearst thought the war was his own work, writing later that year:

> The force of the newspaper is the greatest force in civilization. Under republican government, newspapers form and express public opinion. They suggest and control legislation. They declare wars....[4]

Hearst's sentiments are almost exactly those expressed by Kennan and Boutros-Ghali in the introduction. Hearst and his fellow press barons had reason to boast. The circulation wars of the "yellow press" were fueled by accounts of Spain's harsh rule in Cuba and the heroism of the Cuban rebels. Nothing was too lurid or sensational, and the truth was no barrier to a good story. The vivid stories and drawings helped spark rallies across the United States supporting the Cubans.[5] The explosion of the USS *Maine* under mysterious circumstances in Havana harbor provided new fuel for the press' paroxysms of outrage and demands for U.S. national honor to be upheld. "Remember the *Maine* and to hell with Spain!" Hearst's papers exclaimed. Although Madrid had made diplomatic concessions (short of Cuban demands for independence), McKinley on April 11 asked Congress for authority to use force.

The focus of the yellow press on Spanish atrocities and its demands for American action to stop them sound today like the news media's implicit or explicit demands for intervention in places like Haiti, Somalia, and Bosnia-Herzegovina. Yet Hearst and Pulitzer no more made the decision for intervention inevitable than did the television images from Somalia or

Bosnia. Like their successors, the media of the 1890s had an impact because they reinforced real policy considerations and, in this case and others, appeared in a vacuum of presidential communication, if not leadership.

The press—in a manner we will see repeated time and again with other media—dominated the debate because the executive's voice was absent. McKinley, trusting the will of the people, did not believe it was his role to shape or even lead that will. "In this case, the media was given a free hand in the market-place of ideas and, through its eventual influence upon the people, prevailed." Yet, if McKinley had "possessed a different conception of the presidency, he had tools to make a fight of the issue."[6] He was harmed by his own public silence on Cuba, which left definition of the issue—what today might be called "spin"—to others: "Had he defined his position publicly in 1897, and certainly in the great crises of 1898, he might have rallied some added public opinion to his side. He could not have prevented the war, but he could have clarified and justified his own record."[7]

Many other factors affected the decision to go to war:

> Newspaper pressure helped cause the war by keeping diplomacy unsettled in the face of mounting public opinion and ranting congressmen. Yet neither Cleveland or McKinley assigned it first place among their woes. It is not too much to say that, had all other forces except the sensational newspapers been active in 1898, war would have come without the yellow press.[8]

The Reporter as Warrior: The World Wars

The Spanish-American War marked the rise of the United States from a largely insular nation to a Great Power. For the first time, large numbers of U.S. soldiers would be sent far beyond the nation's borders to fight and die. Reporters would be there with them, and a second great battle—between the military and the media—would begin in earnest.

The two World Wars, like the later Persian Gulf War, were "total" wars. The nature of these wars gave U.S. leaders a far greater ability than they would have in later, limited conflicts to mobilize the nation and establish the "value" of the wars to justify their costs.[9] Once a rough social consensus emerged on the wars' purposes, a journalistic challenge became less likely. Another factor helped ensure journalistic support for the wars once American society was engaged. In World War I and the years that followed, the press and officialdom moved closer together. Mass urbanization created a market for large-circulation newspapers, making large profits possible and freeing publications from their political patrons. Even as government officials came to realize the power of the news media, reporters were coming into their own as members of the establishment—the Fourth Estate. The journalistic ethic of objectivity was on the rise, and reporters increased their credibility as nonpartisan deliverers of the news. As a result, government officials had to treat them with more care and caution. But objectivity also forced journalists to depend to an unprecedented degree on the government and its spokespersons. In a world where all views were considered equal, those of authoritative "officials" were more equal than others.[10] Both sides needed each other more than ever before. Finally, World Wars I and II are interesting in that both involved the press' identification with the goals of the war, but in quite different ways. The lack of consensus regarding America's entry into World War I led government officials to remedy this through severe restrictions on the media and on dissent at home. In World War II, consensus was deeper and the war more popular. Newspaper and radio correspondents responded to this consensus and more closely identified with U.S. troops and the war effort.

As was the case with McKinley and the Spanish-American War, President Woodrow Wilson took the United States into World War I against his instincts and despite his hopes otherwise. Again, the press helped shape the atmosphere surrounding the decision, but that was the extent of its push role. On March 1, 1917, American newspapers headlined the infamous Zimmerman note from the German foreign minister on a German-Mexican alliance against the United States. But the decisive blow came two weeks later, when German submarines sank four unarmed American merchant ships without warning. "Wilson still did not want hostilities, but the initiative was out of his hands. One Philadelphia newspaper hit the nail on the head when it remarked that 'the difference between war and what we have now is that now we aren't fighting back.'"[11] The final decision to go to war was Wilson's. Despite repeated insults from Germany, and even the attacks, the American public was badly divided. Like every chief executive, especially those recently elected on a platform of peace, Wilson had considerable opportunity to shape the debate and the nation's course.

World War I affected American society and the economy as no other war had. This "total" war at home and abroad occasioned a massive effort to manage public opinion, leading to what one scholar has called "America's first effort to create an official culture."[12] Not just the military, but the economy, the educational system, and the entertainment and information industries were put into service to support the war. On the home front, harsh measures, including the Espionage Act of 1917 and the Sedition Act of 1918, were used to ensure support. The atmosphere was not conducive to dissent.

Efforts at censoring press dispatches (and restricting access) during wartime had originated during the Civil War, chiefly in reaction to the invention of the telegraph, and continued during the Spanish-American War. But for the first time, these efforts were institutionalized during World War I, both in the war zone and at home. The precedent that would last for much of the rest of the century was established: correspondents were permitted access to the front; in return, they voluntarily submitted to review of their dispatches. Many correspondents simply chose to censor themselves. In a lament that would be echoed years later in the Persian Gulf, *New York Herald Tribune* correspondent Frederick Palmer wrote,

> There was not the freedom of the old days, but there never can be again for the correspondent. We lived in a mess with our conducting officers, paying for our quarters, food and automobiles. . . . Day after day we sallied forth from our chateau to different headquarters and billets for our grist, and having written our dispatches, turned them over to the officers for censorship. We rarely had our copy cut. We had learned too well where the line was drawn on military secrecy. The important items were those we left out; and these made us public liars.[13]

World War II was the high-water mark of wartime cooperation between the military and the media. This was true in part because the nation's division over whether to join the war (which was deeper than is often remembered) was sealed by Japan's attack on Pearl Harbor and Germany's declaration of war on the United States four days later. The tension between reporters and the military over what the public could be told did not disappear, but it was muffled by the broad consensus over the goals of the war, which did not come under challenge as they would in America's next two wars in Asia. This consensus allowed for restrictions on the news media that were, by World War I standards, relaxed. While censorship was imposed, the operating philosophy, as spelled out in an April 1944 memorandum from the Allied High Command, was that "the minimum amount of information will be withheld consistent with security." There were disputes, of course, over censoring what reporters considered politi-cally, rather than militarily, sensitive information. Also, terrain played a role in determining press restrictions, as it would in later conflicts, although this basic variable is rarely taken into account in discussions of the topic. Restrictions were tighter in the Pacific—where reporters could largely be controlled aboard Navy ships—than in the land wars of North Africa and Europe.[14] But overall, the atmosphere was one of camaraderie and mutual benefit. Journalists were integrated into combat units and did not see themselves as completely separate from them. General Dwight D. Eisen-hower believed strongly in the importance of the press in maintaining public support. "The commander in the field must never forget that it is his duty to cooperate with the heads of the government in the task of maintaining a civilian morale that will be equal to every purpose," he wrote after the war.[15]

What is important for the purpose of this study is not only the all-out nature of World War II, but how, given the rough consensus that existed over the war and its goals, setbacks and combat casualties were presented to the American people. World War II demonstrates that what matters for public opinion purposes is not the casualties themselves, or even whether they are reported by black-and-white photograph or real-time television, but the context in which they are received. One cynic has suggested that if the modern news media had covered the D-Day landing, they would have portrayed it as a debacle, focusing on the massive casualties and General Eisenhower's alleged affairs—"General with Roving Eye Loses 10,000 Troops in France."[16] While the mock headline is amusing, it ignores the role of context. President Roosevelt actually encouraged media coverage of stark conditions on the battlefield to take the sting from Americans' pri-vations at home. Press and radio *did* report the death and suffering of American boys in Normandy and elsewhere. The important thing, then as now, is *how*. "Violence and suffering were represented within a framework highly supportive of the overall war effort."[17]

Introduction to Limited War: Korea

There is no such thing as a limited war for those who must fight one, or for civilians who must suffer the consequences of battle. But the case of Korea provides further evidence of how the goals of a conflict, whether they aim for victory or merely containment, determine public support and the context in which challenges to that support—chiefly in the form of rising casualties—take place. In other words, the public withdraws its support for the leaders' pursuit of war aims when there no longer seems proper justification for loss of life or expenditure of national resources, or when the original justification offered by leaders changes or proves false. The justifications of government officials, especially in the initial stages of a mission, determine later news media impacts on public support when casualties occur, as will be seen with regard to Vietnam. Finally, Korea, when compared with the later conflict in Vietnam, further erodes the idea that the advance of technology has changed these basic variables. The public reacted quite similarly to the setbacks in Korea and Vietnam, although the first was not televised and the second was.

Public support was high—77 percent approved—when President Truman sent U.S. troops into combat in response to North Korea's invasion of the South. In July 1950, one month after the North's attack, most Americans were convinced the war would be short. China's massive counteroffensive in late November, and the huge casualties suffered by UN forces in short order, changed that view and altered public support. One-quarter of the population changed its mind, from agreeing that the United States had done the right thing in Korea to agreeing that it had been a mistake.[18] The costs of the conflict, and to some degree the mission, had changed. This initial shock of mass casualties and the prospect of a war extending beyond expectations were the prime movers of public opinion. Public opinion about the wisdom of the Korean venture did not change significantly in the next two and a half years, despite a slower but steady increase in casualties and events such as Truman's dismissal of Gen. Douglas MacArthur.[19] Nor did the increase in mission costs (in casualties and time) lead to irresistible public demands for withdrawal. After November 1950, support for withdrawal edged up only slightly over time.[20] There seems to have been somewhat greater support for escalation of the war and for bombing China, although it varied with time and the phrasing of poll questions. Overall, the public seems to have been reflecting its leaders' own divisions over these questions and exhibiting considerable frustration over what to do next.[21] This, in turn, suggests that the public was giving President Truman considerable policy leeway and that it would have supported whatever course he took, as long as it was a step away from stalemate.

As in World War II, context was important in determining the impact of the news Americans were receiving about the war. Increasingly, the costs of battle could not be presented as a step on the road to a defined goal. Truman was caught in a Cold War trap. The United States could not "win" the conflict without risking a wider war with China and the USSR. Nor could Truman and his aides afford to back away from Korea with the right wing and its idol, Gen. MacArthur, doing everything in their power to push for total victory, including wanting to use the atomic bomb. As a State Department official who closely followed public and private polls during the Korean conflict said years later, "Those polls showed that the country stood up well when we were winning … and when we were losing … but the country went to pieces when we were suffering casualties in an indecisive war. I see a parallel to that in Vietnam today."[22]

Until the end of 1950, the roughly three hundred print, radio, and newsreel correspondents in the Korean theater operated under voluntary censorship. But after the Chinese intervention and stories of the panicked retreat of UN forces, formal censorship was imposed, requiring all reports—including film—to be cleared by the Eighth Army headquarters. Although military officers in Korea complained that reporters had breached security by, among other things, reporting on troop movements, the military and the press largely maintained the same cordial relations they had enjoyed in World War II.[23]

The Consensus Shatters: Vietnam

It hardly needs to be said that America's experience in Vietnam was a watershed in the nation's experience with warfare and its coverage by the news media. No American conflict has been more studied, no media performance more critiqued. Despite attempts by recent presidents to overcome the Vietnam Syndrome, its influence remains profound. To understand what "Vietnam" means in the quite different world of the 1990s, fact must be separated from fiction, while remembering that the fictions and misunderstandings from that era may retain a powerful hold on the decision makers and public of today.

A newly predominant news media technology—television—came of age in reporting the Vietnam War, a conflict that has been described as America's first "living-room war." While TV had been around during the Korean conflict, in Vietnam (with the advent of communications satellites and the accelerating pace of air transport) it was possible for the first time to get the camera's daily "take" from the field to millions of television screens not long after the action occurred—although at a pace that would be considered snail-like today.

But journalists' coverage of Vietnam was defined as much by the nature of the conflict in Southeast Asia as by the technology available. In the mid-1960s, the U.S. military considered formal battlefield censorship of the media but decided it would be impractical. The principal reason was that Vietnam was a limited war, without censorship or controls on the home front.[24] As suggested at the beginning of the chapter, the more limited the conflict is in its objectives (excluding brief military assaults), the less likely the government can impose strict social controls, including curbs on the news media. The United States never made a formal declaration of war on North Vietnam or its proxies in the South. Correspondents were largely freed of the overt censorship that had prevailed in earlier wars. Reporters, editors, and producers decided, although not without significant unwritten government pressure and inducements, what would be seen and read about the conflict, helping to shape public understanding. The most trusted and beloved of them even helped define the beginning of the end. During that watershed within a watershed, the January–February 1968 Tet Offensive, CBS News anchorman Walter Cronkite, who, like most of his colleagues, had supported the war until then, traveled to Vietnam for a personal look. Upon his return, he told an estimated nine million viewers, "It seems now more certain than ever that the bloody experience of Vietnam is to end in a stalemate." When Cronkite made his assessment, according to President Johnson's press secretary, George Christian, "the shock waves rolled through the government."[25] During and shortly after Tet, there was a brief rise in public support for U.S. escalation in Vietnam. But by March 1968, a growing number of Americans identified themselves as "doves"—and wanted the country out of the war.[26]

But did Cronkite and his colleagues in television, newspapers, and magazines turn the country against the war? Did the nightly parade of bloodshed on TV poison public opinion and eviscerate America's ability to carry out the war? A closer look suggests a different chain of cause and effect and provides some important insights for a discussion about the news media's role in peace operations.

Television, Casualties, and Withdrawal

In the years since Vietnam, it has become almost an axiom for American political leaders (and foes abroad) that the American public has an inherently low tolerance for casualties and will press for withdrawal from a conflict as soon as casualties begin to mount.[27] Fear of just such a reaction has given pause to post-Vietnam presidents who face the decision of sending troops to battle. Television, because of its graphic and emotive portrayals of bloodshed, is said to exacerbate this phenomenon. Yet in Vietnam, both the role of television and the impact of casualties on public opinion were far more complex than popular and journalistic debate have suggested.

First, television. John E. Mueller's study of poll data on the Korean and Vietnam wars found nearly identical patterns in decreasing public support for the conflicts over time.[28] This drop occurred gradually and, as we saw in Korea, did not seem to be closely tied to specific military or diplomatic developments. Mueller concluded, "Many have seen Vietnam as a 'television war' and argue that the vivid and largely uncensored day-by-day television coverage of the war and its brutalities had a profound impression on public attitudes. The poll data . . . do not support such a conclusion. They clearly show that whatever impact television had, it was not enough to reduce support for the war below the levels attained by the Korean War, *when television was in its infancy,* until casualty levels had far surpassed those of the earlier war."[29] Edward Luttwak has noted that the Soviet public's disenchantment with the intervention in Afghanistan was nearly identical to the American experience with Vietnam—despite the fact that Moscow's state-controlled media printed and broadcast only what Soviet authorities directed them to.[30] Often overlooked are the simple facts that the American public endured years of warfare and thousands of U.S. casualties in Vietnam before the lack of public support became a serious problem for policymakers and that only 2 percent of television accounts of the war showed actual bloodshed.[31] Clearly, television alone did not cause the U.S. withdrawal from Vietnam.

The relationship between wartime casualties and the public's preferred course of action in a conflict is not as simple as it might seem. In both Korea and Vietnam, Mueller found a direct correlation between casualties and public support for war: public support dropped by about 15 percentage points every time American casualties increased by a factor of ten.[32]

This finding suggests that those whose support for a conflict is weak drop off as casualties begin to rise; the remaining supporters become inured to the costs of war and are shaken only when costs rise by an order of magnitude. Yet the polls on which these results were based asked a version of this question: Did the United States do the right thing or not in entering the conflict in the first place? While Americans clearly began to regret the decision to intervene in Korea and Vietnam as those conflicts dragged on, it does not necessarily follow that they demanded a summary withdrawal of U.S. combat troops. A more recent analysis of polls from the Korea and Vietnam eras found that even as approval sagged, a growing number of Americans wanted to *escalate* the war—to finish the job and get out. "As costs grew, the public's cry that grew loudest was the cry to escalate."[33] The point here is that Americans were unhappy with the status quo. American frustration with stalemated conflicts revealed itself as early as the Mexican-American War and as quickly as during the relatively brief prelude to the Persian Gulf War. One suggested explanation is this country's "can-do" mentality.[34] The public desire for a resolution to a standoff gives policymakers more room to maneuver than is indicated by the simple formula of rising casualties = irresistible demand for withdrawal. Public opinion puts pressure on leaders for action, and television, by reporting on both the course of the conflict and public attitudes, heightens time pressures on leaders, as will be discussed in the next chapter. But neither determines what the new policy, if any, should be.

While U.S. combat casualties are important in the public's determination of the costs of conflict and in affecting continuing public support, the cases of World War II and Korea suggest that the most important factor is the context within which deaths or other losses take place. The media, of course, help frame the context in which casualties are communicated to the public. But to a great degree, and especially at the beginning of a conflict, political leaders can shape context through their communications to the public, which in turn affect how the news media cover events. In his review of the Vietnam War, Col. Harry Summers contrasts the "price" of the war, as portrayed by the media, with its "value," which he says the government failed to establish.[35] As we will see later, the same gap opened in Somalia in October 1993. I now turn to those two competing sources of shaping perceptions, the news media and the government.

The Problem of Limited Warfare

Most, if not all, of President Johnson's problems with the news media and public opinion in Vietnam had to do with the fact that he wanted the war to remain limited. In 1965, when the first large-scale troop commitments were made, Johnson rejected a recommendation by the Joint Chiefs of Staff for a wartime mobilization of the country, fearing it would mean the end of his Great Society programs: "He chose to take the country to war ever so slowly, to slip in the needle an inch at a time so the patient would never jump. This came close to the nub of the American difficulty in a limited war: Johnson, the U.S. government and the bulk of the U.S. public wanted to win the war in Vietnam, but they did not want it all that much. . . . It was not an overriding goal, but one to pursue at limited cost and limited risk."[36]

Each critical decision that drew the United States deeper into the war was shielded as much as possible from public view and debate. The American public, and the press, at first accepted the view of the government and other opinion makers that Vietnam was a place where the United States could and should confront global communism; but they were given little information on the costs and time that might be involved, an issue on which some U.S. policymakers dissembled and others were badly mistaken. Johnson thus gave up much of his ability as president to rally the nation. The strategic stakes would differ greatly a quarter century later in Somalia, but in both places, the American people were not fully informed or prepared for the expanded missions and their costs.

In his survey of the *New York Times'* coverage of Vietnam from 1961 to 1965, Hallin highlights a February 12, 1962 story that illustrates the Kennedy administration's dilemma as it sought quietly to increase U.S. support for the government of South Vietnam:

> The reluctance of the United States government to divulge and explain publicly the extent and ramifications of its commitment in Southeast Asia is based on a possible enemy reaction.
>
> The heart of the problem, it is said, involves how to call attention to increased United States support for the South Vietnamese struggle against Soviet-supported Communist guerrillas without provoking the enemy into raising the ante.
>
> Tied to that problem is the fear that Americans are not ready to accept the idea of a long, drawn-out struggle. It is felt that they might insist on a quick, clean victory.

Also linked to the public relations problem, officials say, is the increase in casualties in a guerrilla war that is being fought 7,000 miles away.[37]

Read today, the story is breathtaking in its irony. It shows that concern over public reaction to casualties and a "long, drawn-out struggle" was integral to White House strategy as early as 1962, undoubtedly as a result of the earlier experience in Korea. This concern, then, predated the extensive television and other media coverage of the conflict in Vietnam that supposedly turned public opinion against the war. Both Kennedy and Johnson knew that a major escalation in Vietnam would very likely provoke a serious confrontation with China and the USSR. Johnson "repeatedly told his aides that what scared him most was what he called the 'great beast' of American public reaction that would demand a dangerous escalation of the conflict." As they tried to tread the fine line of a limited and undeclared war, President Johnson and his advisers feared those pressures as much as they feared the antiwar movement.

The Media Follow

Throughout the Vietnam War, the news media followed elite (and, to a lesser extent, mass) opinion, although it undoubtedly increased the currency of that opinion and played a crystallizing role, confirming and spreading a new consensus as it emerged. This was attributable to several related factors.

First, to an extent that is hard to grasp even half a decade after its end, the Cold War provided the framework for U.S. foreign affairs reporting for more than forty years. In all its myriad facets, the superpower competition *was* the story. This gave the president and his aides ample opportunity to ensure broad support from the news media and public opinion. To oversimplify somewhat, before Tet, presidents found their *tactics* (such as Kennedy's reliance on Ngo Dinh Diem) rather than their *policy* under challenge.

Second, prior to the latter stages of the Vietnam War and the Watergate scandal, journalists were far less distrustful of government officials than they are today. They empathized to a considerable extent with the policymakers they were assigned to cover. In *The Press and Foreign Policy*, Cohen described a symbiotic relationship between reporters and foreign policy officials. Almost by definition, foreign affairs correspondents were (and are) overwhelmingly internationalist in their outlook, a trait reflected in the press' support for postwar U.S. global leadership through initiatives such as the Marshall Plan and the Bretton Woods monetary system.[38] While this relationship has frayed somewhat, most officials interviewed for this study, including members of the military, agree that they and reporters cooperate to a far greater extent than is generally realized. This point is important to understanding the media's impact on foreign policy, including peace operations.

Finally, journalists, both in the Vietnam era and today, rely to a great extent on official sources for the news. This study does not warrant a full discussion of the journalistic credo of objectivity. But the rise of modern journalism as a profession has discouraged reporters from inserting their opinions into their work and has forced them to depend on others for information and analysis. By virtue of their position and access to information, those "others" are usually government officials.[39] My own experience covering the State Department and White House is filled with examples of how, for journalists, these rules or strictures can be a prison of their own making. My colleagues and I perform our adversary role, of course, challenging official statements during press briefings and challenging them even more harshly in later conversations among ourselves. But the actual reports we file usually reflect only in pale form the private doubts of highly knowledgeable and experienced correspondents. For competing accounts of reality, we must again rely on others: credible opposition figures such as members of Congress or their aides, interest groups, or public policy experts. We know when we are being used, and we resent it. But our limits are set by the rules of the game. In a much broader sense, one only has to pick up a newspaper or view a television clip from ten, twenty, or thirty years ago to be reminded of the extent to which the news media reflect the values and mores of the time—whether on foreign affairs or racial and sexual issues—more than they challenge them. Issues considered outside the mainstream—homosexuality, for example—remain there unless and until a new national consensus begins to emerge.[40]

Hallin conceived a useful model to understand journalism's interrelationship with society. He divides the reporter's world into three concentric circles: the sphere of consensus, containing issues that are beyond challenge or debate; the sphere of legitimate controversy (the arena of acceptable political debate, where most of the journalist's activity takes place);

and the sphere of deviance, in which views and individuals deemed unworthy of serious attention reside. Hallin noted that whether journalists follow a "balanced" or "adversary" role "depends on the political climate in the country as a whole" and on the journalist's medium.[41] To take the concept one step further, when government policy is absent or in flux, or when societal consensus breaks down, the sphere of legitimate controversy on a particular issue expands, giving the news media more room to roam and more opportunities to perform as adversary. This concept of the news media's role in American society is vital to understanding its influence on public support for the war in Vietnam and on public attitudes toward the peace operations that are the focus of this study.

It is a simplification to say that the news media were a mere tool of government in leading the nation into the Vietnam War. Yet in that crucial period, when policies coming out of the White House would ultimately engulf the United States in a protracted war that rent its social fabric, few journalists questioned the wisdom of a war against communism in Southeast Asia.

There can be little doubt that the abrupt change of heart among important media figures in 1967 and 1968, such as Cronkite and Time Inc. editor-in-chief Hedley Donovan, influenced their readers and viewers, playing some role in national disillusionment with the war. Yet their pessimistic reports were based on interviews with midlevel officials in Vietnam, many of whom had themselves soured on the war. (That pessimism in the field had provided the basis for earlier, gloomy reports by Vietnam-based correspondents that clashed with Washington's official optimism and, at times, were watered down or killed at the home office.) Equally important was the fact that the transformation of many in the media from ardent war supporters to advocates of de-escalation was based on their sense of the country's shifting mood. As Max Frankel, then a *New York Times* correspondent in Washington, recalled,

> We were part of the change. As protest moved from left groups, antiwar groups, into the pulpits, into the Senate—with [Senators J. William] Fulbright, [Ernest] Gruening, and others—as it became a majority opinion, it naturally picked up coverage. And then naturally the tone of the coverage changed. Because we're an Establishment institution, and whenever your natural community changes its opinion, then naturally you will too.[42]

And, according to another journalist,

One reason the press was not "on the team" was because the country was not "on the team." To a substantial degree, the newsmen represented and reflected American society, and like the rest, they had no deep commitment to or enthusiasm for the war. As reporters learned more about Vietnam, they became more pessimistic, with inevitable impact on the public. The view of the public, in turn, influenced the mood of the press.[43]

In Hallin's construct, the sphere of legitimate controversy had expanded, and the very purposes of the Vietnam War were now ripe for public and journalistic debate.

Now I return to the main question raised at the beginning of this section: Did the media's portrayal of the war—especially the Tet Offensive—shatter public support for the effort in Vietnam (or worse, mislead Americans about which way the conflict was turning) and thus cripple Johnson's policy? Many Americans were deeply troubled by dramatic reports of the Viet Cong's attack on the U.S. embassy compound in Saigon; Eddie Adams's Pulitzer Prize–winning photograph of South Vietnam's police chief summarily executing a Viet Cong prisoner; and the sometimes over-hyped coverage of the fate of besieged Khe Sanh. But the pictures, the film footage, the headlines, and the stories about the war did not appear in a vacuum. Like similar news media reports examined in the discussion of present-day peace operations, their effect depended on many other factors:

- They seemed to run directly counter to what Americans had been told in general about the course of the war, and were particularly at odds with the "Success Offensive" the Johnson administration had launched months before.

- Like the pictures from Somalia decades later, they came at a time when support for the war was decreasing anyway. Opposition to U.S. involvement in Vietnam had been increasing steadily throughout 1967, as the costs in lives and money escalated. The first time the Gallup polling organization found more Americans responding that it had been a mistake to intervene in Vietnam than those who said it had not (46 percent versus 44 percent) was in October 1967, shortly after Johnson proposed a tax increase to pay for the war.[44]

- The Johnson administration, perhaps in shock over Tet and the public response, did not forcefully respond with its own message.[45]

- The administration was divided by now. Defense Secretary Robert McNamara, who had made the journey from hawk to dove, was on his way out when Tet occurred. The new defense secretary, Clark Clifford, had been an ardent supporter of the war. But as he surveyed the post-Tet landscape, he could find no acceptable military solution to the conflict.

The role of the news media in the Vietnam War highlights two critical phenomena that arise time and again. First, *the news media's ability to influence policy is inversely related to the degree of consensus in the government and society.* This should not be surprising, given the news media's reflection of prevailing norms, as well as a definition of "news" that elevates conflict and tension. Second, *the news media enhance and accelerate shifts in policy or national sentiment that are already under way.* The news media alone do not—cannot—turn a society 180 degrees, nor can they create policies on their own. The news media's effect on the policymaking process is entirely dependent on other policy actors. This phenomenon is seen in the governmental and public responses to crises in Bosnia, Somalia, Rwanda, and Haiti between 1992 and 1995, further demonstrating how the march of technology has not changed the prerequisites for government officials to maintain public support of military operations.

Hell Hath No Fury Like a Reporter Wronged

Despite their institutional and personal frailties, most journalists most of the time are devoted to the search for truth as defined by the profession's conventions. Their words and pictures are the sum total of their efforts. The short delay between gathering news and transmitting the product to an audience of thousands or millions creates a unique connection between reporter and story that is different, say, from that between author and book. The price for being wrong can be severe—loss of credibility and retribution from sources, colleagues, and superiors. When a journalist has reported opinions, statements, and statistics from official sources as fact, only to find out that the information is false or incomplete, the natural, even understandable, tendency is to turn on the source. Military officers felt similarly wronged after Vietnam. Having expected the media to be part of the war effort, they began to think of them instead as an unnecessary battlefield complication at best and an enemy at worst. As veteran NBC News anchor John Chancellor put it, "Relations between the press and the

American military deteriorated when the United States began to engage in undeclared wars of uncertain popularity."[46]

What happened between the media and military and political leaders because of the Vietnam experience stretched (but by no means severed) the bonds between reporter and official. The lessons that each institution drew from the crucible of Southeast Asia were incomplete. The news media could have studied their failure to investigate and report in depth on Vietnamese culture and history, a failure that only reinforced senior U.S. officials' own gross ignorance on this subject. Reporters might have pondered why they asked too few questions early on about the importance of Vietnam to U.S. interests and the potential costs of involvement. From the errors in reporting on Tet, they might have learned to be more cautious in future real-time reporting from within the fog of war and crisis. They did not.

However, the military *did* learn, at a heavy price, to fear engagement of its troops without a clear goal, public support, and use of overwhelming force at the outset. An uninterrupted cautionary line runs from Vietnam through the nonintervention of the late 1970s, the Weinberger Doctrine of 1984, the "Powell doctrine" of the early 1990s, and, later, the Clinton administration's May 1994 policy on peace operations.[47]

After Vietnam, the U.S. military, especially the Army, became almost obsessed with the subject of battlefield news reporting. It began to study the media as never before. Courses on the topic became standard in advanced training for officers. The military learned enough that by 1994, when the ground rules were being set for news media coverage of the U.S. intervention in Haiti, the military was more informed about the media's workings than were civilian officials—and more willing to be open.[48] But more often, while politicians paid lip service to the need for public and congressional support for U.S. military engagements abroad, civilian and military officials' emphasis was not on explanation but on controlling the message and keeping the media at bay.

Return to News Management: Grenada, Panama, and the Persian Gulf War

Defense Secretary Richard Cheney's remark that begins this chapter neatly sums up the Pentagon's view of the Persian Gulf War and, by extension, the role of the news media in it: the White House and the Pentagon were not about to let the news media "screw up" the war effort. In reaction to the media's perceived sins in Vietnam, the military already had reestablished some measure of control over reporters in two previous major U.S. interventions: Grenada in 1983 and Panama in 1989. These three deployments span the period during which real-time reporting—particularly by CNN—began to assert itself. The next chapter will examine in more detail how these developments, and the end of the Cold War, affect policymakers' daily lives. The discussion below is concerned primarily with the impact of the media and officials' public communications on public opinion.

When U.S. troops invaded Grenada on October 25, 1983, no reporters accompanied them. The Reagan administration delegated control of information policy to the military, which would not allow reporters onto the island until the operation was almost over.[49] This new kind of censorship, by physical exclusion as opposed to traditional censorship in the field, was partly a reaction to the increasingly sophisticated technologies employed by the news media. "Rather than attempt to control media content, a very difficult task given those innovations, civilian and military censorship planners opted during the Grenada campaign for a total ban on press access to the war zone."[50] President Ronald Reagan was also following the precedent established the year before by his close ally, Prime Minister Margaret Thatcher of Britain, who had kept the British press at a distance during the Falklands War. As Reagan undoubtedly noted, the war was overwhelmingly popular in Britain.[51] The Grenada invasion also was popular, with between 66 and 71 percent of Americans agreeing with President Reagan's action (despite embarrassing revelations afterward that two-thirds of U.S. casualties were caused by "friendly fire" or by accident).[52] "The American people had finally been given a clear-cut old-fashioned victory, not much of one, but the first since MacArthur's triumph at Inchon thirty-three years before."[53]

Bitter mutual recriminations over coverage of Grenada led to meetings between media executives and the military "about how to arrange coverage of the smaller combat operations that were now predicted in a world no longer dominated by East-West tensions."[54] A panel, chaired by Army Maj. Gen. Winant Sidle, released its recommendations on August 23, 1984. The most important recommendation was the formation of press pools, small groups of reporters who would accompany troops into combat and share what they gathered with the rest of the news media. The Sidle Panel envisioned a limited role for the press pool, recommending that it be used if it "provides the only feasible means of furnishing the media with early access to an operation." The pool would be as large as possible and disbanded as quickly as practicable in favor of wider access for reporters. That access would be based on the old system of voluntary media compliance with security and other guidelines laid down by the military.[55] The pool system received a brief test during the 1987 U.S. Navy escort of Kuwaiti oil tankers through the Persian Gulf. Then came Panama.

When the first waves of Operation Just Cause struck at 1 a.m. on December 20, 1989, the media pool was not with the invasion force. The first journalists arrived in Panama four hours later, but they and subsequent groups were prevented from leaving Howard Air Force Base and other U.S. military installations in the country unescorted until Saturday, more than three days after the invasion occurred.[56] The first Pentagon pool to arrive was escorted to a room, where its members watched the invasion unfold on CNN! (The network had reporters stationed in Panama City.[57]) They also were treated to a diplomat's dissertation on the history of the Panama Canal Zone. Much of the combat and its consequences for Panamanian civilians went uncovered. The story of the invasion was largely that told by the U.S. Southern Command in Panama and senior Bush administration spokespersons in Washington, who emphasized military successes, downplayed civilian casualties, and detailed the corruption and bizarre behavior (later found to have been exaggerated) of Panamanian dictator Manuel Noriega. In a situation that would become familiar in the peace operations era, reporters who were already in Panama City, and thus less restricted by the U.S. military, fared better, although only slightly. Many were unable to leave the Marriott Hotel, which was controlled by the Panamanian Defense Forces until the second day of the operation. Virtually all commentators agree that in Panama the pool system did not work as the Sidle Panel had intended. Pentagon spokesman Pete Williams acknowledged later that "it took too long to get reporters to the scene of the action."[58] Like Grenada before it, the Panama episode prompted a round of soul-searching among members of the U.S. news media. But the precedents of pool coverage and prior military review of stories were by now well established:

A new, unlovely, and largely unremarked phenomenon came to American journalism: a willingness by the media to accept government regulation. Important journalistic organizations accepted the unprecedented official requirement to register, to be "responsible" in their coverage, and to countenance sanctions (loss of pool accreditation) for breaking the rules. Indeed, they accepted the very requirements that, when presented in a foreign country, journalists properly denounce as the abridgments of a totalitarian or Third World order.[59]

Why was the military able to place such restrictions on the news media in Panama and Grenada but unable to do the same in peace operations just a few years later? First, in both Panama and Grenada, the White House could make the case that a national interest was at stake—the lives of American citizens. Second, as it had in World War II and would in the Persian Gulf, terrain played a role in journalists' mobility, especially in their inability to get to the island of Grenada. Finally, the brevity of the two actions was a determining factor. "At least in the short term, the press is easily led. It has a strong tendency to cover an event initially from the perspective of those who have orchestrated it."[60]

Grenada and Panama reinforced the post-Vietnam model of military operations: use overwhelming force, do the job quickly, keep casualties to a minimum (nineteen servicemen were killed in Grenada, twenty-three in Panama), and attempt to control what the public sees. Once under way, the Panama invasion was overwhelmingly popular with the American public and caused few divisions between Congress and the Bush administration. With opposition muted, the media had few openings to challenge or criticize the military operation without being seen as unpatriotic or sniping.

Unlike any war in history, the Persian Gulf War began on live television. On the night (along the east coast of the United States) of January 16, 1991, millions of viewers watched, electrified, as CNN reporters Bernard Shaw, John Holliman, and Peter Arnett described the opening stages of the allied bombing and cruise missile assault on Baghdad from their room in the Iraqi capital's al-Rashid Hotel. This truly seemed like a moment when the global village had come to pass: millions of people around the world were watching the same historic event as it happened. Among the viewers were a U.S. president and his aides seeing a war that they had just ordered unfold, on schedule and on television. Bush's national security adviser, retired Lt. Gen. Brent Scowcroft, knew to the minute when and where the bombs were supposed to fall. Turning on CNN and watching the attack occur as planned was "one of the eeriest moments of my life," he recalled.[61] CNN viewership shattered all previous records that week, with an estimated thirty-two million households watching at some point during January 16–17 and millions more seeing CNN footage carried on their local network affiliates.[62] That first night set the tone for the news media's subsequent coverage of the war and CNN's domination of it.

For this study of the news media and peace operations, three salient features of the Persian Gulf War stand out. First, the Bush administration and senior military officers had absorbed the lessons of Vietnam regarding the necessity of public support and the difficulties of limited warfare. Second, the presence of real-time television was both a potential hazard and a potential tool of great power for administration policymakers, depending on how it was used and on the events themselves. Third, the administration effectively used that tool to frame the crisis, explain its actions, and enlist public support. Having successfully done this, the White House transformed the news media from a potential threat into a partner in the war effort.

A "Lesson" Learned Well

Addressing the nation from the Oval Office at 9:01 p.m. on January 16, President Bush declared, "[T]his will not be another Vietnam. . . . Our troops will have the best possible support in the entire world, and they will not be asked to fight with one hand tied behind their back."[63] The legacy of Vietnam was never far from the minds of White House and Pentagon officials as they prepared and executed operations against Iraq. It affected how the administration would fight the war, what it would tell the public, how it would handle the subject of casualties, and how it would deal with Congress and the news media. This would not be a limited war.

Hoping to shape the way the war would be seen at home, the Pentagon reinstituted the media pool system that originally had been intended to apply to smaller-scale operations. New restrictions were added on what could be reported. Unlike Vietnam, there would be no correspondents roaming the battlefield, interviewing soldiers and the country's populace almost at will. The culture and landscape of Saudi Arabia was an added obstacle for journalists. The restrictions, announced by Pentagon spokesman Pete Williams on January 7, 1991 (nine days before the air campaign

began) and revised on January 14, began with standard wartime prohibi-
tions: there could be no reporting on numbers of U.S. troops, weapons
and their movements, future plans, intelligence gathering and special operations, operational tactics and rules of engagement, or the effectiveness of
camouflage and deception. But additional restrictions signaled a return to
pre-Vietnam censorship policies. Press pool reports were to be reviewed
for sensitive information by the military's Joint Information Bureau (JIB)
in Dhahran, Saudi Arabia, before being released. While in theory the final
decision to publish or broadcast in the event of a disagreement remained
with the media, in practice the time consumed by appeals often rendered
disputed information worthless as news. Finally, media pools, escorted by
military public affairs officers, would be the only method of combat coverage. Williams's superiors rejected his earlier proposal to do away with the
pools as soon as independent combat coverage became feasible, as the
Sidle Panel had recommended in 1984.[64] The media largely accepted these
arrangements. Indeed, competitive news organizations fell to fighting
among themselves for coveted pool slots, of which there were 192 for
roughly 1,400 news media personnel in the Gulf region.[65] A few correspondents, labeled "unilaterals," sought to circumvent the Pentagon restrictions and report independently from the field.

A major goal of the military's press relations, if not the major goal, was
to keep allied casualties off American television screens, in the belief that
televising casualties would erode public support. The news media were
barred from Delaware's Dover Air Force Base when U.S. war dead were
returned from the Persian Gulf, something that had not been done during
the Grenada and Panama operations. There were restrictions on news coverage of wounded soldiers in field hospitals.[66] When the U.S.-led ground
campaign into Kuwait and Iraq began on February 23 and the risk of
heavy casualties was at its highest, Cheney announced a virtual news
blackout, including a suspension of pool reports and news briefings at the
JIB. The policy was relaxed when it became clear how quickly the allied
forces were overwhelming the Iraqi military.[67] Although the media were
restricted from covering casualties, Bush and his commanders had also
drawn a proactive lesson from Vietnam about the costs of conflict and
public support. Unlike the Kennedy administration's policy in Vietnam,
described in the February 1962 *New York Times* article, the Bush administration did not try to shield the public from the potential costs before a

commitment was made in the Gulf. In Vietnam, U.S. commanders constantly predicted imminent success and gave out optimistic estimates of the enemy's dead and wounded; in the Persian Gulf, the public was inoculated with the knowledge that there might be severe casualties. While U.S. intelligence on Iraqi capabilities was incomplete, the tendency was to prepare the public for the worst, including the possibility of chemical warfare.

The news media, and others, protested the restrictions on information. But, as will be shown, it was the military, not the media, that was in synch with the public. During the war, an Army colonel wrote privately,

> It is interesting to me and surprising to most that in this war the generals are fighting the right war—right weapons, right tactics, right training, and the right troops. In comparison, the press, the protest movement, and our politicians—and even Saddam—are trying to refight Vietnam. Shame. The reasons for our success may be because, of these groups, only the military lost status, power, or political capital in the post-Vietnam era. The others were ascendant. Remember, power and status corrupt.[68]

The U.S. military had learned its lesson well.

Television

The primary medium through which the Gulf War passed for Bush, for Saddam Hussein, for audiences around the world, was television, often real-time television. The combat, and the diplomacy that preceded it, were played out on TV screens around the world. CNN was dominant. Bush, Saddam, and other leaders used CNN as a tool to send near-instantaneous messages to one another and to various (mostly elite) audiences, fulfilling a function once reserved for embassies and foreign ministries. After years of doubt (and sometimes ridicule), Ted Turner's Atlanta-based network finally came into its own. Polls consistently found the public giving CNN far higher grades than the other networks. As many as 61 percent thought it did the best job among TV networks.[69] The images of the war that endure are CNN's: the first night's air attack, as seen from the Iraqi capital; correspondents donning gas masks as Iraqi Scuds fell on Tel Aviv; near-constant live briefings from the Pentagon and the JIB; Peter Arnett's controversial reports from Baghdad.

Continuing a trend that began with U.S. presidential campaigns, the chief events of the war were staged for, and on, television. More than a decade of resentment among print reporters, who had seen their privileged place at the officials' table steadily eroding, came to a head. Some news-papers took their cue from CNN; the better ones shifted more and more to background and analysis of the breaking news their readers had seen on CNN the night (or even the morning) before. For newspapers, news-magazines, and especially for television, the expense of covering the six-month crisis and its aftermath was huge, although increased sales and viewership helped defray the costs. The numbers affected news organiza-tions' financial outlooks and temperaments in the ensuing years.

The level of television coverage overall was staggering. Between Decem-ber 1990 and February 1991, ABC, CBS, and NBC devoted 2,658 minutes of airtime to the crisis. The next most-covered event during that period, Soviet Foreign Minister Eduard Shevardnadze's resignation, received fifty-six minutes of airtime; the Soviet crackdown in the Baltics, thirty-eight.[70] The Persian Gulf was truly The Big Story, pushing all others aside.

What was the effect of all this television coverage? Of images such as the dazzling video of U.S. Patriot missiles streaking upward through the night and seemingly knocking out Iraqi Scuds? Of the Pentagon-supplied foot-age of smart weapons following electronically superimposed crosshairs down to destroy an Iraqi building? Evidence indicates that this intense tele-vision coverage, much of it involving real-time images, did affect public opinion. It may have caused a suspension of public reservations about the war and a decrease in tolerance for dissent.[71] Yet television failed to explore or convey the war's broader context. The longer people watched TV, the less they knew about many facts that might have complicated the Bush administration's explanation of the crisis. These facts included U.S. policy toward Iraq before its invasion of Kuwait; the monarchical rule of Kuwait's government; and Israel's occupation of the West Bank, which Saddam was attempting to bring into the discussions over Kuwait. There was a dis-turbing negative correlation between television, factual knowledge, and public support for the war:

> Despite all the coverage, people in the United States knew remarkably little about many critical aspects of the background and the context of the war. The more people knew, the less likely they were to support the war; the less they knew, the more strongly they supported the war. People who generally watched a lot of television showed dramatically lower levels of knowledge and were substantially more likely to support the use of military force against Iraq.[72]

The news media's, particularly television's, failure to provide greater context "made it far easier for President Bush to legitimate the war in moral and absolute terms."[73] And he did so with astounding success. While much has been written about the negative impact of CNN on policymakers generally, in the case of the Persian Gulf War, the very nature of instantaneous television helped the U.S. leadership shape how the public perceived the standoff with Iraq as it unfolded. Journalists rely overwhelmingly on official sources for reporting the news, and this reliance is even greater with regard to national security matters.[74] As a major source of news during the Gulf War, CNN followed this pattern, giving large amounts of airtime to policymakers (often via live, lengthy daily briefings in Washington or Saudi Arabia) and to experts, usually retired officers or former government officials who shared the policymakers' worldview. It also has been suggested that live or near-live coverage gives journalists less time to evaluate the information they broadcast, turning over to the viewer not only the words and images but the responsibility for interpreting them.[75]

Up to this point, this analysis of television's impact during the Persian Gulf War would suggest that the medium largely ensured public support for the war and, by implication, Bush administration policy as well. But it ignores two other factors that indicate a major role for policymakers. First, Bush and his aides had to exploit the opening created by this largely nonthreatening coverage. Second, *they helped create such an opening* by communicating their policies and building support in such a way that there were few dissonant voices among the elite that the news media could latch onto for a story.

Because of its temporal effect, real-time television forces policymakers to closely monitor the results of their policies and engage in constant communication or pay the consequences:

> If the lack of knowledge extant among the American people represented an opportunity for effective image management in the Gulf Conflict, it was the pressure of this instantaniety that provided the motive. For only by gaining control of the pace and direction of learning could political leaders hope to buy for themselves the chance to get in front of events and to establish and maintain control of their own policies. The options were clear: either one exercised spin control or one watched events spin out of control.[76]

Secretary of State Baker confirmed the eat-or-be-eaten nature of real-time television, which carries with it the implication that news media reports do not determine policy per se but shape the milieu (and a rather stark one at that) in which governing takes place. Baker recalled the beginning of the Persian Gulf crisis, when there was strong congressional opposition to fighting a war with Iraq. "You [can] fall behind the power curve very quickly," he said. "If we hadn't been out in front of that power curve, we might not have successfully built public support for that war."[77] In other military interventions captured on real-time television—such as Somalia—political leaders have found themselves "behind the power curve" rather than in front of it when explaining their policies.

Much of what has been written about the news media and the Persian Gulf War has focused on the Bush administration's attempts to control what was broadcast on television and the fact that TV coverage was largely devoid of images of the war's human and physical costs. The implication is that such media control was sufficient to ensure a supportive public. It is curious that both the U.S. military and its critics on the left seem to share the belief that more open news coverage, especially of American casualties, would have eroded support for the war. Yet as Vietnam demonstrated, televised casualties alone do not diminish support for wars. In World War II, graphic images of casualties were reported in a framework of overall support. Another possibility must be considered: that the favorable news coverage of the Persian Gulf War was as much a result of the supportive mood at home as it was a cause of that mood. Had President Bush failed to frame the crisis in his terms, communicate his policies, and ensure congressional and public support, media control alone could not have kept a lid on antiwar sentiment.

Framed

The news media in the United States, both print and television, failed to give the American people a coherent view of U.S. policy toward Iraq prior to Saddam's invasion of Kuwait. The media also failed to raise many questions about the Reagan and Bush administrations' previous support for Saddam.[78] Yet if this failure on the media's part left a vacuum, Bush still had to use it, to frame the confrontation in the way he believed it should be seen. He and the top officials around him did a masterful job of communicating their policies and the reasons for them at virtually every stage of the crisis—a point that frequently is lost amid the criticism of the media's performance during the Gulf War. Had they not done so, political opponents and the news media would have framed events quite differently.

The device that Bush turned to again and again was the demonization of Iraq's ruler, whom Bush repeatedly compared to Adolph Hitler. Bush first used the analogy on August 8, when he announced the initial wave of U.S. combat deployments to the Persian Gulf. The comparison appeared in the *Washington Post* and *New York Times* 228 times between early August and January 15, many of the comparisons occasioned by the president himself.[79] The rhetorical device fit Bush's purposes neatly: It simplified the Middle East's complex history and politics into a good-versus-evil contest; it provided historical reference (although of debatable value); it left no doubt as to how Saddam should be dealt with; and it separated Saddam from the Iraqi people, with whom Bush said he had no *casus belli.*

The White House effort to gather public and media backing for its policies in the Gulf was never trouble free. The media and members of Congress questioned whether Washington had indicated to Saddam prior to the Iraqi invasion that there would be little if any price to pay if he solved his decades-old border dispute with Kuwait by force—a controversy that got dumped on the shoulders of U.S. ambassador April Glaspie. As the situation stagnated in September and October 1990, public support for Bush's handling of the crisis dipped. The president seemed to have trouble telling the American people what the confrontation was about. Pressed by reporters at one point in mid-November, Secretary of State Baker provided an easy (and insulting) explanation: "to bring it *down* to the level of the average American—jobs."[80] Bush's chief pollster, Robert Teeter, "thought the administration had too many messages flying around. There was a lack of focus." He suggested that the president return to his emphasis on fighting aggression and protecting the lives of Americans held hostage in Kuwait. Baker worried that the plight of Kuwait, the principle of stopping aggression, and the need for secure supplies of oil were not selling the American public on the war effort.[81] There was a near-crisis later in November, when Bush announced that he was doubling the number of U.S. troops in Saudi Arabia, moving from merely protecting the kingdom to readying the capability to eject Saddam's forces from Kuwait. The administration badly mishandled the process of informing Congress of this crucial decision.[82] A White House statement said that U.S. allies had been consulted. But the most important among them, Saudi Arabia, had not.

"We didn't do enough to lay the groundwork with the Congress and the public," an official recalled. "The administration came to realize that its public relations strategy was either lacking or nonexistent."[83]

Bush's framing of the crisis was bolstered by groups such as the Citizens for a Free Kuwait, an entity funded by the exiled Kuwaiti monarchy, which contracted with the public relations firm Hill and Knowlton. The firm's focus groups found that the American public reacted most intensely to one theme: Saddam Hussein. Consequently, the firm downgraded its attempts to portray Kuwait as a progressive, pro-American ally in favor of emphasizing Saddam's brutality and the victimization of Kuwait.[84]

The Bush administration's use of the Hitler analogy and its highlighting of Iraqi atrocities conveyed a clear, but unspoken, message about Saddam: Here is a ruthless dictator who must not be appeased and who is outside the realm of diplomacy. Other options, such as continuing with the policy of economic sanctions, never were debated fully. Bush's framing of news about the Gulf crisis "led people to think more clearly about war than about other solutions to the problem."[85] The poll-tested communication strategies of the Bush administration and the Kuwaitis helped create a favorable climate for the actions Bush proposed to take. As early as August 1990, the month of the Iraqi invasion, 61 percent of respondents to a poll agreed with the Hitler-Saddam analogy. The public rejected parallels between the Persian Gulf and Vietnam by a 52 percent to 42 percent margin.[86] Bush had already told the American public—and would continue to tell it—that this would not be another Vietnam. Saddam's intransigence, his holding of Western hostages, and the atrocities his forces committed in Kuwait helped Bush make his case.

The Bush administration's framing of the crisis no doubt helped win popular support. But Bush also took concrete steps, at some risk, to secure that support. In November 1990, the UN Security Council voted to authorize the use of force if Iraqi forces did not leave Kuwait by January 15, 1991. In early January, Congress debated and ultimately approved Bush's policy in the crisis. This congressional support and the multilateral action authorized by the Security Council significantly strengthened public support.[87]

Home Front

Not only did the U.S. news media portray the Persian Gulf conflict in the way the Bush administration framed it, at times they seemed to become part of the war effort itself, in a fashion that recalled World War II. The broadcast networks showed "video postcards" of troops in the desert saying "Hi, Mom!" to the cameras. Newspapers passed out "We Support Our Troops" bumper stickers (often advertising the newspaper's name, too). Journalists began to use the pronoun "we" when they talked about the war effort and even when they asked questions of officials. "Those pathetic Iraqi soldiers who, waving white flags, actually surrendered to unarmed journalists unwittingly caught the essence—that, to most intents and purposes, the press was on the official side."[88] One pool reporter went further, actually firing artillery rounds toward Iraqi positions at the invitation of the troops he was accompanying.[89]

Why did the news media, filled with skeptics who had been through Vietnam and Watergate, suddenly seem to relax their objectivity? The answer goes beyond the Bush administration's official control of the news media in the Persian Gulf. Of course, reporters in Washington, rather than in the Gulf region, were under no formal or legal restrictions that crimped the way they reported the war. The answer seems to lie in the fact that Bush, for better or worse, forged a consensus with Congress and the American people on the justification of going to war against Iraq. In a manner repeatedly seen before—for example, after the United States entered World War II or when divisions among opinion makers over Vietnam became apparent—the news media were keenly attuned to social consensus, or lack of it:

> As soon as it became clear that the country was very strongly behind [the Gulf War], television became very wary of being caught on the wrong side of that consensus. It pushed television away from treating the war as a political policy and toward treating it as a kind of national celebration—like a moon shot or something.[90]

Hallin's observation emphasizes how television is especially unwilling to go against the grain of its mass audience. The print media also were attuned to the debate, although they paid more attention to elite opinion. A study of editorials in five major U.S. daily newspapers found that they were generally supportive of the president, and more: "At virtually every stage of the conflict, these papers' editorials refused to wander beyond the parameters of the discussion as it unfolded in Washington; while they differed in tone and degree, they displayed considerable consensus in their views of the Middle East, its people, and the interests of the United States in the region."[91]

On the rare occasion when debate and division surfaced, the media did join the fray. Before combat began in the Persian Gulf, there were two periods of relative media activism: Bush's November decision to double troop strength and the January 10–12, 1991 congressional debate and vote to give Bush authority to use military force against Iraq. The political conflict in both cases led the *New York Times* to devote more of its coverage to congressional and popular opposition to using military force in the Persian Gulf. Yet it came relatively late in the crisis and, in January, was swept aside by the supportive congressional vote and the beginning of the war:

> Faced with little sustained elite debate, few government power pegs on which to hang an opposition story, and a public that eventually supported government censorship of the news, the press never developed an independent grip on the story. Investigating the dynamic of press-government relations at almost any point from the August invasion through the war itself, finds a press that generally reported the official administration policy line in an uncritical fashion.[92]

Having suffered two decades of blame for the loss in Vietnam, members of the news media were eager not to be caught out of step with public sentiment:

> Ever since the Vietnam War (and Watergate), the press has been determined to prove not only that it did not lose the war but that it is also composed of the "right stuff," the stuff of red-white-and-blue-blooded, pork-rinds-eating, beer-drinking, flag-waving Americanism, hardly the sort of press that would undermine a war effort by raising embarrassing questions about an administration's earlier dealings with Saddam Hussein or about its involvement in the Iran/Contra affair. No one wanted another Watergate.[93]

The news media's room for maneuver was limited even more because the American public consistently supported the Pentagon's restrictions on reporters. Several polls detected this support, portraying a public that felt satisfied with the information it was getting from the media.[94] The live briefings gave most members of the public their first in-depth look at the messy process by which journalists attempt to extract news from government officials. The public's reaction was typified in a skit on the television comedy show *Saturday Night Live*, in which reporters at Gen. Norman Schwarzkopf's briefings in Saudi Arabia were portrayed as nosy, arrogant boobs, oblivious to the military's security needs. Paradoxically, perhaps, the public gave the media high marks for their reporting from August 1990 to March 1991. In a pair of NBC/*Wall Street Journal* surveys in late January and late February, 40 percent of respondents said they had gained respect for the news media since the war had begun.[95] As Pentagon spokesman Williams put it, the media gave the United States "the best war coverage we've ever had."[96]

In such an atmosphere, dissent, whether from the public or the media, became downright dangerous. CNN's Peter Arnett, the lone American reporter in Baghdad in late January and early February 1991, reluctantly complied with Iraqi demands to censor his stories before he went on the air. For this, Arnett was labeled a traitor by right-wing groups and Republican members of Congress, most notably Senator Alan Simpson of Wyoming. Representative Lawrence Coughlin of Pennsylvania, taking the Hitler analogy a step further, called Arnett "the Joseph Goebbels of Saddam Hussein's Hitler-like regime." CNN refused calls for Arnett's removal, but felt enough pressure to bring in a retired Air Force general who frequently differed with Arnett on the air. The network also read on the air viewers' letters criticizing the correspondent's reporting from Baghdad.[97]

By the time the Persian Gulf War began that January night, President Bush had built a consensus in favor of his actions, one that the news media helped construct and dared not challenge. As it turned out, the war was even briefer and less costly than the U.S. government and American public had expected, so much so that any grander conclusions about the Persian Gulf War should be treated with caution. This survey of the media and U.S. military intervention has begun to refute the notion that casualties, because they have been displayed on television or in other news media, automatically result in a drop in support for the further use of force. The Persian Gulf War offers no additional evidence about public tolerance for televised casualties, although it was a conflict in which the American people clearly believed national interests were at stake.[98] Nor can we know how far the public would have persevered with Bush had there been escalating costs, battlefield setbacks, or major changes in the mission. The president opted not to test the limits of his public mandate. While public support was strong and a majority wanted to continue the war until Saddam was toppled,[99] Bush decided to halt offensive ground operations short of that objective.

Aftermath

A combination of effective presidential communication and framing of the issues, supportive public opinion, and both formal restrictions and social conformity made it difficult, if not impossible, for the U.S. news media to approach the Gulf War more critically. Later, once the national victory celebration subsided, the media began to focus more clearly on the Bush administration's prior dealings with Iraq. A congressional investigation of Iraqgate (rather than media initiative) provided the framework for hundreds of critical stories, which were primarily the province of the print media, not of television. A host of other factors intruded to dim the war's afterglow: Saddam's survival in power and his brutal repression of domestic opponents; the flight of hundreds of thousands of Kurdish refugees toward Turkey and Iran; and, at home, the economic recession. In a perverse sense, the war was almost too easy: For most Americans, there was little sense of sacrifice or having overcome long odds, thanks in part to the Bush administration and the media. Football analogies are overused, but perhaps one is appropriate here: When the final score is 70–3, the victory celebration does not last very long. This is what the U.S. military's low-casualty, viewer-friendly style of warfare had produced.[100] It set a standard that future interventions would find hard to meet.

On many sides, the Persian Gulf War was considered a portent of how public opinion would be managed in future military endeavors. For the political left, in particular, the war seemed to be a realization of its worst nightmare: the use of the most modern communications technology by political elites to propagandize an unwitting public and a compliant media, all in the service of a national security state.[101] Reporters feared that the military's successful control of them had provided a textbook model for the future.[102] Many military officers thought they had at last regained mastery over the news media. As noted in the quotation which began this chapter, Secretary of State Baker had a longer-term, lighter-hearted, and—as it turned out—more accurate view. The news media would "bounce back."

In many ways, the Persian Gulf War was a false harbinger of the future international system and the news media's role in it. President Bush's New World Order, with its implications of global stability and like-minded communities of states working through the United Nations, lasted not much longer than the victory celebrations. The Persian Gulf War confirmed the technological revolution in media communications but it seemed to say more about the past than it did about the future of U.S. military engagements and media-military relations. The media-military fight over the last war would continue. But journalists, military officers, and foreign-policy makers, who had struggled in the arena of public opinion with increasing intensity as the Cold War wore on, would soon enter a new arena—one that was not framed by the Cold War consensus.

Summary

This opening chapter has introduced two themes that will be critical to the examination of the media's impact on foreign policy in the post–Cold War era and, ultimately, their impact on the conduct of contemporary peace operations.

First, it has surveyed the struggle between the news media and military and political leaders as America debated the use of military forces abroad. While the advantage in the struggle tipped back and forth throughout the past century, control rested largely in the hands of government officials. At times, journalists expanded the bounds of their freedom to report conflict from the field, but in the end they depended on the military for access and information. Chapter 3 will show how much this state of affairs has changed in the 1990s. In Somalia, Haiti, and elsewhere, *the military has often depended on the media for information and intelligence.* The traditional military doctrine of controlling the news media has come into question and, in some instances, has largely been abandoned for now. In the Persian Gulf War, the media's awesome new communications technologies served as a fresh motive for the military's restrictions on news gathering and reporting. But it was the nature of the conflict, and the climate of domestic opinion, that provided the means. For the traditional news media, little changed technologically between the Gulf War and Somalia. Instead, the media's newfound freedoms reflect the changed nature of military operations in the post–Cold War era. Peace operations do not involve vital national interests, as traditionally defined, and they do not require the emotional investment of the entire nation. As will be examined in chapter 3, there are salient explanations other than technology for the media's relative independence in contemporary peace operations: the shifting or nonexistent battlefield, the difficulty in identifying the enemy, the often-ambiguous outcomes of these missions, and humanitarian activities that military and civilian officials are eager to publicize.

The second theme of this chapter is that the impact of the news media on policymakers and public opinion, and the prerequisites for that impact, have not changed significantly. Throughout this study, I will show that Clausewitz's dictum for the successful prosecution of a conflict—a trinity of the people, military commander, and government—remains true in the era of peace operations and that the conditions for the news media to influence military engagements and related foreign policy decisions remain the same as before. This, in turn, raises questions about whether the advance of communications technology has fundamentally changed the conduct of warfare and foreign-policy making, as George Kennan and many others believe. In short, it raises questions about the *independent* power of the CNN effect.

Three of this chapter's findings are important in this regard. First, as we saw with the yellow journalism of the Spanish-American War, older technologies can have an impact roughly equal to that of modern-day television. To be sure, television has its own special characteristics, but if the impact of provocative drawings in Hearst's papers on American policymakers and public opinion in the late nineteenth century is similar to that of television today, clearly technological advances alone do not explain the media-policy relationship. Something more structural must be at work.

Second, we saw that American combat casualties did not reduce the level of U.S. public support for military operations or cause instant demands for withdrawal because they were portrayed in the news media. In World War II, casualties and suffering were presented in a framework that was highly supportive of the war effort. Indeed, President Roosevelt encouraged reporting on privations at the front to steel Americans at home for the war effort. In Korea and Vietnam, there were similar correlations between rising casualties and declining public approval of the military operations, although the Korean conflict was not televised to any significant degree. Even this declining level of support did not lead to a clear policy directive from the public: it wanted change, but might have supported escalation in Korea and even in Vietnam if leaders could have offered convincing explanations about how they would finish the conflicts. The Soviet government suffered a drop in public confidence (although without the political turmoil that a democracy would encounter) at home because of rising casualties in Afghanistan, despite its control over the state-run media. The lesson here is that the public pays attention to the costs of a conflict—the casualties—and weighs them against the interests it judges to be at stake. In this process, television, and the media generally, are the communicators of bad news, not the creators of it.

The third finding is the most important. In the Spanish-American War, Vietnam, and the Persian Gulf War, the size and scope of the news media's impact depended on whether there was strong and credible communication of policy from the president and whether there was a social consensus on the goals and costs of the conflict. When those conditions were met, Hallin's sphere of legitimate controversy shrank. The news media cannot oppose much of anything themselves; they need a source, whether it be a disgruntled field commander, a divided Congress, or an eloquent (or violent) opposition group. Lacking such "pegs," the media follow. When there is a vacuum created by weak leadership or a lack of domestic consensus, the media's impact on policy increases.

Of course, the argument here is not that the media have no impact on foreign or national security policy. Their potential impact is enormous and has grown with the new reach and speed of communications technology. The next chapter will examine some of these effects, including the temporal effect mentioned in the introduction. Rather, the argument is that the media do not independently determine foreign-policy making, which depends on much else. Notwithstanding Kennan's concerns, most of the determining factors remain, for better or worse, in the hands of government policymakers.

2

Driving Fast
without a Road Map

The News Media and Foreign Policy Today

"We will do the worst thing to you—
we will deprive you of your enemy."
—*Georgi Arbatov*

"Foreign policy without the Cold War
is a little like baseball without
the World Series."
—*Madeleine K. Albright*

For journalists, the Cold War was perhaps the greatest story of them all. It had, on a grand scale, all the elements that Journalism 101 professors tell their students are the components of news. It had tension and conflict. It had immediacy in every locale—the fear of nuclear Armageddon. It had good, hard facts, like defense budget numbers, Soviet weapons specifications, the MIRVs and ABMs of superpower arms control. It played out in new ways nearly every day, from summit meetings to proxy wars in Afghanistan or El Salvador. It, and its impact on the role of U.S. journalism, lasted for more than forty years.

By its very nature, the Cold War had powerful effects on the relationship between U.S. foreign-policy makers, Congress, the news media, and the American public. For reasons of national security, these institutions largely deferred to the president in setting their agendas on foreign and domestic affairs. Thus, in 1966, in an era when presidential power was on the rise, *New York Times* correspondent James Reston could write:

> We may report the news, but he makes it. . . . [T]he President almost always has the initiative over both the press and the Congress if he chooses to use the instruments at his command. . . . [F]or the present, nobody need worry much about the press overwhelming a President who has all the miracles of modern electronics and transportation at his disposal.[1]

This statement is a far cry from modern-day claims of profound media influence on policymakers. As much as any other factor examined in this study, the passing of the prolonged national emergency that was the Cold War accounts for the seemingly enhanced power of the news media relative to the presidency. In times of crisis today, the occupant of the Oval Office still has tremendous tools to rally the nation around him. But in the mid-1990s, the institution of the presidency seems less powerful when compared with Congress or with its own past. President George Bush and his successor, Bill Clinton, the first true post–Cold War president, faced a much more complex and demanding challenge in communicating their foreign and national security policies. No longer could they point to a common enemy to rally an unruly Congress or uncertain public opinion. As Clinton began to make the case for deployment of twenty thousand American troops to monitor the Dayton peace accords in the former Yugoslavia, his White House was told by the television networks that, in essence, he had one shot. He could not count on repeated access to the airwaves for live addresses to the nation. In the past, such requests would have been granted routinely.[2]

During the Cold War, the government's foreign policy agenda drove the media's decisions about what was news more than it does today. Bernard Gwertzman, the foreign editor of the *Times*, told his staff in a December 1992 memo:

> When one looks back, it is remarkable but not astonishing how much of newspaper coverage since World War II was devoted to foreign affairs, and how much hinged on the Cold War and East-West rivalries. This competition consciously and subconsciously dominated government policies, affecting newspaper coverage as well.[3]

This is not to say that from 1945 to 1991, the American news media reported what U.S. government officials wanted them to, only that they reported a great deal about the issues that U.S. foreign policy officials saw as important. As we saw in miniature in pre-Tet Vietnam, criticism tended to be over tactics, not goals. Gwertzman went on to say what every foreign affairs reporter knew was—but is no longer—true: the Cold War created a huge market for foreign affairs news, because virtually any development overseas could be tied to the East-West, life-or-death conflict.[4] In the pecking order of journalists, the foreign affairs beat—whether in Washington or in foreign capitals—was considered one of the most, if not the most, prestigious. U.S. news organizations spent huge sums of money to maintain bureaus and correspondents in capitals central to the East-West conflict. This investment, in turn, influenced what the U.S. public would think about and how it would view the world beyond its shores. To take but one example, for reasons of both geopolitics and journalists' access, the entire Soviet Union (and most of the rest of the East Bloc) was seen through Moscow.[5] Ethnic tensions in the outlying Soviet republics, which simmered beneath the surface, went almost uncovered. Many other stories went unnoticed, underreported, or relayed to readers and viewers only through a Cold War lens.

This view, presumably, is what the American public wanted to see, hear, and read about regarding foreign affairs. In the 1990s, that changed, too, dramatically affecting what (and how much) international news newspapers would print. Television was affected even more.

The absence of this old bipolar agenda alone fundamentally altered the way the U.S. news media reported on foreign affairs and their impact on those charged with making foreign policy. But those changes were magnified a few years before the end of the Cold War by the appearance of new technologies that have transformed how news is gathered and reported to publics around the globe. Broadcast journalism graduated from the film bag[6] of the 1960s and 1970s to the era of the compact, portable Minicam and lightweight satellite communication devices. Now, the videocamera can be taken anywhere—not just by reporters, but by average citizens, soldiers, and guerrillas as well. Its digitized images can be sent live from virtually anywhere around the world via satellite and broadcast nearly instantly to virtually any spot on the globe. Reporters' communication with home base is accomplished with a satellite telephone, a laptop computer, and perhaps a portable printer and fax machine as well. These technological revolutions have profoundly changed how television reporters do their job. But many veterans of the profession do not think the change is for the better.

Most of all, these developments virtually obliterated the factor of time from diplomacy and foreign affairs. Television correspondents now are expected to report the latest developments (or just report in) constantly. For policymakers, global television news services such as CNN and its growing number of competitors are a double-edged sword. The president can make his policy more rapidly known to leaders around the world and to the American public. But opponents and allies can respond just as quickly, attempting to reach not just the president but his electorate as well. Officials feel pressure to react to televised images far more quickly than they would like. The public can vicariously experience war, diplomacy, and even the death of a famine victim as they happen.

Almost simultaneously, the earth has shifted twice under the media-official relationship: once because of geopolitics, once because of technology. The subsequent impact on the American body politic perhaps can be best assessed with a metaphor: If officials, journalists, and the public are riding in a vehicle, technological advances are driving them faster than ever before—and no one seems to have a road map that goes beyond the familiar path of Cold War rivalry with the Soviet Union.

Reporters and Officials: The Struggle for the Agenda

The end of the Cold War has freed the U.S. news media to a significant extent from the agenda of the White House and the State Department, allowing reporters, editors, and producers to pursue stories more unambiguously based on what the audience is thought to be interested in. For television, especially, this pursuit has led to a reassertion of its own agenda and time-honored notions of what is news. War, conflict, and human tragedy, all of which make good pictures and can be found abundantly in the 1990s, have come to dominate the televised picture of the world that most Americans receive.[7]

The latent (and at times overt) message in these reports was that the United States (or more broadly, the West) should intervene to right whatever wrong was being portrayed on the television screen—at least until late 1993, when the costs of such remedial action were made plain in Somalia. This mode of reporting, which recalls the days of William Randolph

Hearst, reflects the Wilsonian, reformist bent of many reporters, an impulse that might be a prerequisite for the job.[8] It reinforces the idealistic strain in American foreign policy best typified by President Woodrow Wilson himself.[9] This, in turn, helps explain the angst regarding television's power expressed by senior members of the realist school of U.S. foreign policy such as George Kennan and Henry Kissinger.[10]

While there were an estimated twenty-five crises around the globe in 1993, cameras were not following each one, of course. But, increasingly, where the camera is and what it captures determines whether the crisis is on officials' agenda and among the public's collective foreign policy concerns.[11] Other conflicts and other tragedies, no less costly in human life, are ignored. It takes a major effort of political will and communication by officials to put these events before the public eye, one that is rarely undertaken since officials are not anxious to highlight new problems to solve. This paradox is captured in the quip that the Sudan's brutal civil war is "Somalia without CNN." (Like so many statements regarding the media's influence, this one is both handy and simplistic. In fact, according to CNN's executive vice president, the network's Nairobi bureau chief did visit Sudan several times, but was refused a permit to work there. Likewise, he left Rwanda with a gun at his head. However dangerous, Somalia was open by comparison.[12] Sudan also had a functioning government.) A reporter for another American network put it this way: If sixty-eight people are killed when a mortar shell explodes in a Sarajevo marketplace (as they were in February 1994), it gets attention because cameras were there to record it. But if a thousand people are killed off-camera in Huambo, Angola the same day, it "has absolutely no impact on anybody's thought processes whatever."[13]

Television's newly powerful agenda-setting ability accounts for a large portion of the complaints by foreign ministers and other senior government officials about the impact of today's news media. The intensity of coverage that television devotes to a particular country or crisis may bear little or no relation to its importance to the national interest, at least as seen by officials. Official priorities may receive far less coverage, particularly if they cannot live up to television's picture-driven, story-telling needs. And it is the foreign-policy makers who traditionally have seen themselves as setting the nation's agenda overseas, rather than having the agenda set for them.

These developments, taken together, seem to point to new leverage on the part of the news media over policymakers and public opinion. But three caveats are in order. First, journalists' agenda-setting power is hardly new. The press "may not be successful much of the time in telling people what to think," Bernard Cohen wrote in *The Press and Foreign Policy* in 1963, "but it is stunningly successful in telling its readers what to think *about*."[14] The daily press briefing at the State Department illustrates how the news media for decades have helped set the agenda and force foreign policy decisions. Throughout the morning hours of almost every working day, public affairs representatives in each of the department's bureaus develop "press guidance," approved statements of policy to be used by the spokesperson at the briefing, based on anticipated questions from reporters. These policy statements often are drafted in response to events worldwide. But just as often they are reactions to stories in the morning newspapers or the network newscasts the night before. Thus, agenda and actions are influenced, and sometimes policy is made in the process. On particularly sensitive issues, the secretary of state's senior staff or the secretary personally oversees the preparation of press guidance. The process works in the negative, too: if reporters pepper the spokesperson with questions that he or she is not prepared for, that issue rapidly makes it onto the department's agenda—particularly if the spokesperson has easy access to the secretary of state and other senior officials. What has changed since Cohen's study is television's ability to bring these foreign policy problems to the attention of senior policymakers much more rapidly and graphically. This, in turn, begins a snowball effect, as editors and reporters from other major and minor news outlets drop what they are doing and latch on to the new story, pushing it higher on the agenda for all concerned. TV can thus reinforce the type of pack journalism that has long been criticized inside and outside the field. And, as many print journalists lament, television has an impact in a way that they never can. Printed stories of atrocities, casualties, and so forth can almost always be denied, disputed, or downplayed; video cannot be so easily dismissed, even if it lacks the context and background of a newspaper report.

Second, one has to clearly distinguish between the power to set an agenda and the power to make policy decisions. Granted, as any corporate executive or committee chairperson will attest, whoever sets the agenda and decides what is and is not a priority has won much of the battle. Yet this is not the same as deciding what action to take on a particular problem or actually taking that action. These are things that the news media—for all their intrinsic power to say "Do something!"—cannot do. As many senior Western diplomats complain, the print and broadcast media can urge action without being responsible for the consequences. Inevitably, the details and execution (and consequences) are left up to policymakers, diplomats, and military planners.

Third, the president, the secretary of state, and other foreign policy officials retain formidable agenda-setting powers of their own. When the president chooses to highlight a foreign policy problem or makes a decision on relations with another state, the news media are compelled to report it—the print media almost always, television less so. The problem is that, given the current state of U.S. foreign policy, such actions now often seem without context. The superpower conflict helped presidents explain their policies through the news media and helped the news media in turn report them to the public. As of this writing, neither the Clinton administration nor the foreign policy establishment, by their own admission, has come up with a satisfactory replacement for the doctrine of containment as a guiding principle for U.S. foreign policy. New rules for American military intervention are still being fleshed out. This is not meant as a political criticism, but as a description of the facts of life in the post–Cold War era. Here, the phenomenon that was noted in the previous chapter comes into play—*the influence of the news media expands to fill a vacuum left by lack of societal consensus and strong presidential leadership and communication.* This fundamental principle operates at both the macro level, regarding America's approach to the world, and the micro level, regarding how to respond to a specific crisis, such as Bosnia. As Ted Koppel, the veteran ABC correspondent and *Nightline* anchor, told Congress:

> Outside factors tend to influence the formation of foreign policy, to a greater or lesser degree, in almost direct proportion to the amount of credible information and policy direction that a government otherwise makes available.
>
> To the degree, in other words, that U.S. foreign policy in a given region has been clearly stated and adequate, accurate information has been provided, the influence of television coverage diminishes proportionately.
>
> To state that premise in reverse, television's influence increases in regions where an administration has (a) failed to enunciate a clear policy and/or (b) has done little or nothing to inform the American public on the dangers of intervention or failing to intervene.[15]

The end of the bipolar world has opened up a huge vacuum in the larger sense. As we will see later, within that larger vacuum Western governments largely failed to communicate a coherent view of the first major post–Cold War crisis, Bosnia, especially in the early years of the conflict. Having failed to do so, it is hardly surprising that the news media defined the stakes according to their own professional criteria. What has changed is not so much the media's behavior as their opportunities for pursuing their own agenda. The lack of an overarching guide to foreign policy and the availability of new technologies have granted TV and the rest of the news media an independence from officialdom that they have not enjoyed since Hearst's time.

The preceding argument emphasizes officials' communication strategies as a way to mute the media's agenda-setting influence. It must be said, nonetheless, that officials' communication strategies have their limits, no matter how coherent or well thought out. Koppel's observations fail to take into account the effects of television's focus on images, or even of network budget cuts, which sharply limit what makes the evening news. No matter how hard they try, government officials will have difficulty persuading the networks to cover the Middle East peace process, trade, or nonproliferation policy absent a dramatic crisis. Images define. By early 1995, President Clinton's foreign policy had come to be negatively defined by images from Bosnia and Somalia. The news media can thus not only profoundly affect the government's foreign policy agenda, but also, in the view of officials, distort the public's perception of that agenda.[16]

Other social and technological developments also raise questions about the ability of government officials to influence public opinion in the way that they had come to expect. The *mass* media came into being along with other elements of the industrial revolution, notably mass production, mass labor, and bureaucracy in government and corporate life. Through large-circulation journals, radio, and then television, American leaders (and advertisers) were able to reach large sections of the populace at once. Now, American society may be fragmenting into any number of smaller groups, with much narrower, distinct patterns of information consumption, each of which has to be addressed separately.[17] The vehicle by which leaders address society, the media, also has fragmented. Network television remains a powerful communication tool, of course—its audience dwarfs that of virtually any other medium. This includes CNN, whose audience is relatively minuscule unless there is a crisis or other galvanizing event, such as the O. J. Simpson trial. But the nightly news broadcasts of CBS, NBC, and ABC are no longer as dominant as they once were as Americans' principal sources of information. In 1995, 48 percent of Americans polled said they regularly watch a network evening news broadcast, down from 71 percent in 1987.[18] And, increasingly, network television and mass-circulation newspapers compete with hundreds of cable channels, thousands of special-interest magazines, colorful talk-radio hosts, and the explosive force of the Internet and other computer information services, which give individual users a custom selection of games, news, video, sound, and electronic mail. The most banal and yet the most powerful development affecting official communication strategies may be a television set's remote control, which an estimated 80 percent of American TV watchers wield as they channel-surf, flitting from image to image.[19] Officials must engage in more complex and sophisticated communication strategies involving a variety of media to reach these different audiences.

Not only do these developments reduce the power of government to communicate its foreign policy agenda, but they also reduce the power televised images have over the public. Both statistical and anecdotal evidence indicate the growth of the fatigue factor, in which the viewing public, over the years, becomes desensitized to images of suffering or horror that they feel powerless to do anything about and that do not directly touch them (this excludes vivid images of American soldiers or civilians suffering or dying). Viewers simply tune out. The intense television coverage of the Bosnian conflict produced this effect by the summer of 1993.[20] Television coverage of the former Yugoslavia was down 28 percent in 1994 compared with the year before.[21]

Together, the remote control and the fatigue factor make a powerful combination. An audience researcher for NBC was told by one respondent: "If I ever see a child with flies swarming around it one more time, I'm not going to watch that show again."[22]

The News Media and the Public: The Domestic Context

In a process that began long before and accelerated after the fall of the Berlin Wall, American network television and newspapers, with few exceptions, have cut back on coverage of foreign news. They also have altered what they do cover. Television networks focus on fewer stories but cover those few as intensely as, or more intensely than, they did before. The result is a profound change in the picture of the world relayed to the American public.[23]

Without the Cold War's immediacy, editors and producers, who are responsible for news gathering and presentation, have a much harder time defending foreign coverage to those primarily interested in the financial bottom line. And without the Cold War context, explaining conflicts and crises abroad typically requires much more elaborate and involved treatment. Different media and different news organizations have reacted in different ways.

The *New York Times* maintains a serious commitment to foreign news coverage, but space for such news was down significantly in 1992, according to Gwertzman.[24] In late 1994, Gwertzman said the reduced "news hole" for foreign news "is a problem for me." On an average day at the *Times*, when there is no "cataclysmic" news event, foreign news is assigned 15 columns of space at 800 words per column, for a total of roughly 12,000 words. Many of the stories are shorter than before.

What the newspaper chooses to report has changed even more. Political developments that in the past would have merited attention because of the East-West conflict are now less compelling. "Now a coup in an African country is still a coup in an African country," Gwertzman said. "As a news story, it's marginal. . . . [D]o you need to report it?" In that sense, he said, "We're no longer a paper of record." The ability of CNN to report worldwide developments long before the morning papers arrive on doorsteps has presented newspaper reporters and editors with dilemmas that they have not yet resolved: How much to focus on those breaking or "spot" stories that must be reported but which readers already know about from TV? How much to focus on supplying analysis and background? According to Gwertzman, "We do have more analysis, in the sense that we know that if there's a major story, they're going to hear about it first on radio or TV." Yet, he said, "We still write our stories as if they were not reported anywhere else first."[25]

The *New York Times* and other newspapers have put more emphasis on social and economic developments in foreign lands, especially those that strike a chord with readers at home. These include other countries' strategies for dealing with problems the United States is facing, such as violent crime, health care, and budget deficits. The *Dallas Morning News* won the Pulitzer Prize in 1994 for a series of articles on violence against women around the world. Newspapers in some major U.S. cities have closed bureaus in Europe but opened or enlarged them in Asia and Latin America, parts of the world that have growing economic impact on the papers' home cities or regions. The Associated Press (AP) maintains its extensive network of bureaus around the world but now sees those bureaus less as vehicles to report a single nation's politics and more as bases to cover stories with worldwide or regional import, such as the environment, poverty, or Islamic radicalism. More and more correspondents are on the move, aided by technology, of course.[26] Louis D. Boccardi, AP's president, describes why reporters need to reorient themselves:

> We may feel on more solid ground reporting politics. But in today's world, how much does it matter? No present head of state has the personal authority of a Churchill, a Stalin, or even a Margaret Thatcher in her heyday. Rare is the contemporary leader who can set policy on the basis of personal conviction and expect it to roll forward unimpeded. Modern leaders, far from setting the agenda, seem themselves to be increasingly buffeted by economic forces, environmental worries, religious movements and the like. . . .
>
>   More than before, the news is in fact the broader trend, the analysis we bring to the events. It is less what some participant "said today."[27]

This reduced emphasis on *policy*, including U.S. foreign policy, reduces officials' ability to influence what is printed or broadcast. The State Department is no longer the center of the journalistic universe that it was in previous decades. The networks and many major regional newspapers no longer assign a reporter to accompany the secretary of state on every mission overseas. During the Cold War, especially during the late 1980s and early 1990s, these trips were major news events, with second- and third-tier news organizations vying for seats on the secretary's airplane. The confining "bubble" of that Air Force jet and the entourage on the ground brings reporters and officials closer together, giving the secretary and the secretary's top advisers and spokespersons powerful tools for influencing both the topic and the substance of news reports. More and more reporters now cover such trips independently—perhaps they are based in the region the secretary is visiting—giving them wider access to additional sources of information.

The changes in coverage by the nation's most prestigious newspapers and their number one wire service pale when compared to those undertaken at ABC, CBS, and NBC. Network news, once considered a loss leader—that is, a public obligation undertaken at a financial loss—is now expected to make a profit. All three networks have closed foreign bureaus over the past decade and are deploying fewer foreign correspondents than they once did.[28] In fact, the very notion of a foreign correspondent, a journalist based in a defined bureau in a foreign capital but free to wander the countryside in search of a story, is fast becoming an anachronism in broadcasting. Economics have doomed this way of life. Satellite communications links are enormously expensive (the excess baggage costs for air transport of the equipment alone can be staggering) and must be accompanied by large crews of technicians and producers.[29] The expensive package of equipment, network anchor or well-known correspondent, and crew is deployed only for the biggest of stories. This phenomenon—in which television journalists literally descend on a crisis, report until the drama has evaporated, and then leave—has come to be known as "parachute journalism." In 1994, NBC, like the other networks, had no full-time correspondent covering events in Bosnia but, rather, relied for coverage on a camera crew stationed there.[30] The same can be said for other places, such as Haiti, where peace operations are in progress. On-air correspondents arrive when the story gets hot—American troops land or leave, fighting intensifies, atrocities are committed.

For reasons of both economy and sheer physical danger, broadcast and cable networks are relying more on foreign sources for the raw material of their newscasts, including the use of freelance "stringers" (who are frequently non-American) and video purchased directly from foreign media organizations.[31] Sometimes, different networks buy the same video from the same foreign supplier and then add their own correspondents' voice-overs. This practice further contributes to a lessening of diversity on the screen and, it can be argued, a sense among channel-surfing viewers that their television is relaying *all that has occurred*, rather than just a particular slice of it. Marvin Kalb, a former network foreign correspondent, said: "One of the ironies of today's foreign coverage is that as the technology has grown more sophisticated, the end product has grown more skimpy."[32] U.S. networks have signed news-sharing agreements with their foreign counterparts, such as those between ABC and the British Broadcasting Corporation (BBC), or

NBC and Britain's Independent Television News (ITN) and Germany's ZDF. A greater globalization of the news seems to be the clear trend.

While many stringers are talented and intrepid, they do not have the same loyalties to a news organization that a full-time correspondent has, nor does that organization exert the same control.[33] In Somalia in October 1993, footage of a dead U.S. soldier being dragged through the streets of Mogadishu was taken for CNN by a Somali stringer. The British news agency Reuters had given a videocamera to its own Somali stringer when it pulled its full-time staffers out after three of its journalists were killed in a single incident. While there is no evidence the stringers were trying to influence American public opinion for their own or someone else's motives, the chances of such incidents increase as activists and guerrillas gain access to portable videocameras.[34] During the Persian Gulf War, the networks used dramatic footage of Kuwaiti resistance fighters inside Iraqi-occupied Kuwait. The footage had been distributed as part of the exiled Kuwaiti government's propaganda effort, for which it paid the public relations firm Hill and Knowlton more than a million dollars.[35]

In the midst of these changes, the airtime that the networks have devoted to stories from overseas has dropped precipitously, from a peak of 4,032 minutes in 1989 to 2,763 in 1994, a decrease of almost one-third.[36] There are fewer foreign stories on the evening news, and those that make the cut tend to be the big stories to which network executives have decided to devote expensive news-gathering teams. Deploying these teams has its own inexorable logic: given the expense, the odds are that correspondents will file voluminous amounts of material and that the broadcasts will use it. As one observer notes, "To a certain extent logistical considerations, not journalistic ones, dictate what gets covered and how."[37]

What is the effect of these forces on the end product of news gathering seen by the American television viewer? Andrew Tyndall, who monitors the three major broadcast networks' newscasts each night, finds that major stories, such as the war in Bosnia, the Israeli-Palestinian conflict, and the election of Nelson Mandela as the first black president of South Africa, get as much coverage as ever or even more. It is what he calls the "midlevel" stories that have been chopped back. The result? "You're not getting as rounded a picture of international affairs," Tyndall concludes.[38] Sir Brian Urquhart, one of the grey eminences of the United Nations, says of modern television: "It gives an impression of mayhem which is absolutely, completely misleading, in a way that print journalism doesn't. . . . Television doesn't report the 99.9 percent normality of life. It reports the .001 percent of abnormality. . . . I think it's a problem."[39]

It can be argued, of course, that CNN and the many other international news broadcasts now available on the cable-equipped American television set, such as Britain's ITN and even Russian television, fill the gap left by the networks. Indeed, CNN marshaled seventy reporters, producers, and other staff to cover the South African election and maintained a bureau in Sarajevo longer than the other networks. But, as already noted, the audience share of even CNN, let alone the other cable venues, is relatively small in noncrisis periods. In the arena of foreign news, CNN's audience jumps dramatically only when U.S. lives or interests are at stake. Even historic events, like those in Beijing's Tiananmen Square or at the Berlin Wall, do not significantly raise viewership.[40]

In sum, for reasons of economy and technology, the picture of the world beyond America's shores as presented by television is an increasingly cramped and frenzied one, a world of formless, detached events that seem to come from nowhere and then disappear as suddenly as they arrived. There is an understandable, but distorting, focus on the lives of U.S. soldiers and citizens. For this book's purposes, what is important is that these trends pose particular problems for staging peace operations. Three out of the four cases I examined (Somalia, Rwanda, and Haiti) involved military operations with defined entry and exit points that bracketed an amorphous and relatively uneventful middle phase, punctuated only by something dramatic (and usually negative) that occurred to reawaken media interest.

This characteristic of the media was noted by Walter Lippmann in an age when "the press" still meant newspapers: "The press is no substitute for institutions. It is like the beam of a searchlight that moves restlessly about, bringing one episode and then another out of darkness into vision. Men cannot do the work of the world by this light alone."[41] And later by Bernard Cohen:

> The correspondents are not only drawn to the "big story," but their predilection is to make the arenas of conflict and controversy the subject of these big stories. But quite apart from the particular news values in any particular conflict—quite apart even from the substantive content of the big stories—*the very process of focusing attention on one problem area after another, seriatim, makes for discontinuities in the points of information that*

compose one's picture of the foreign policy world. It is like a very slow radar scanner, or one that does not keep scanning the same area; the information it yields comes in so slowly and in such unregulated segments that a sense of the whole cannot be gleaned.[42]

This effect of the media is not new, but thanks to CNN and other developments in gathering and presenting international news, Cohen's "radar scanner" is no longer a slow one.

A final question for this section: are television executives giving Americans what they want by de-emphasizing reporting on foreign affairs and developments abroad? Events from President Clinton's 1992 election on a promise to "focus like a laser beam on the economy" to the 1994 midterm elections, in which control of Congress switched hands with the help of numerous freshmen who were unsupportive of an activist foreign policy, have raised questions about whether the United States is returning to a pre–World War II isolationism. Public opinion surveys reveal a more complex picture. Public interest in foreign news and U.S. relations with other countries dropped only slightly between 1990 and 1994.[43] One major poll found that Americans support continued U.S. involvement in world affairs, but the general public does not want the United States to be the "world's policeman."[44] The public, like candidate Bill Clinton in 1992, sees foreign policy essentially as an extension of domestic concerns; its top five foreign policy priorities were stopping international drug trafficking, strengthening the economy, stopping the flood of illegal aliens, protecting the global environment, and ousting Saddam Hussein as leader of Iraq.[45]

These findings resonate in the belief, held as gospel among senior network news personnel and the editors of all but the prestige newspapers, that, absent the Cold War, the American people are not interested in foreign news unless it touches their lives in some way. "Everyone is grappling with what are the new realities, what are U.S. interests? We tend to report on U.S. interests," said NBC News vice president Bill Wheatley. The networks have made attempts to adjust their coverage, for example, focusing more attention on international economic stories, such as the North American Free Trade Agreement and global trade generally. But these are difficult to explain to viewers in a minute or two.

In 1994, crime (including the O. J. Simpson case and other high-profile events such as the Tonya Harding–Nancy Kerrigan melodrama) was far and away the most prevalent topic on the ABC, CBS, and NBC evening newscasts, accounting for nearly two thousand stories. Health issues and the economy took second and third places, respectively; international events were far behind, holding the lower rankings.[46] In 1995, CNN's ratings (and thus income) soared thanks to its live, nonstop coverage of the O. J. Simpson trial.[47] Little wonder that programming executives gave the audience plenty of O. J.

This focus elsewhere does not mean that international events, such as the conflict in Bosnia, do not get significant television coverage. But broadcast executives understand there is a limit to the public's appetite for such news absent direct U.S. involvement. According to Koppel, every time he devotes an evening of *Nightline* to Bosnia, Somalia, or the like, "ratings go in the tank." These shows can be supported only by frequent coverage of events like the Simpson trial, which attract much larger audiences.[48] Speaking of Bosnia before President Clinton's decision to deploy U.S. troops there, Wheatley said: "My fear . . . is the public is not very interested to begin with. And even if interested, have a great difficulty understanding it. Once again, the American interest there is quite difficult to define."[49]

The U.S. news media always have reported primarily on U.S. interests, of course. But during the Cold War, those interests were broader and, to some extent, clearer.

The Television Reporter: Technology and Time

It's 1964. Bernard Kalb is Asia correspondent for CBS News and stuck in Laos, one of the continent's remotest corners. Word comes over his short-wave radio that Jawaharlal Nehru, the architect of India's independence, is dead. Kalb is aching to be in New Delhi to cover the story, but there are no instructions from CBS News headquarters in New York. "In a burst of Machiavellian inspiration," he unzips his typewriter and types a cable to the foreign desk: he will leave for New Delhi unless he hears to the contrary "WITHIN NEXT THREE REPEAT THREE HOURS." Kalb hops in the local version of a rickshaw, trundles down to Vientiane's PTT (Post-Telephone-Telegraph) station, and hands the cable over for transmission. Kalb knows Laotian culture, and so he knows that there is not a chance the cable will make it to New York before he is gone. He charters a small plane, and he and his cameraman fly to Bangkok, en route to New Delhi. "The foreign desk never had a chance," Kalb recalls with an almost visible smirk.[50]

Kalb, who later became a State Department spokesman, goes on to recall a time not so long ago when foreign correspondents immersed themselves in the regions where they were stationed, lived there, and raised families there. They covered the big events, the Cold War stories, of course, but also had the time and freedom from the home desk to "look at life behind the headlines," to cover life itself, like soccer matches in Djakarta or Benny Goodman and the king of Thailand blowing jazz in the royal palace.

> I remember when the change began: in Saigon, from the mid-'60s on, with technological innovations that, like executioners, one after the other did away with distance and time. . . .
>
> Now New York is everywhere, with the power to dial, call, summon, dispatch, edit. You're in the middle of nowhere, and New York has still got you locked into its electronic crosshairs, trapped, triangulated, at the end of its global yo-yo string. . . . True, spot news and backgrounders still come in, but there's an ache for more time to flesh out your piece, more details, more context. But it's "bird" [satellite] time, and off goes the piece, you're on the air, sometimes so fast, much to your own surprise.[51]

Barrie Dunsmore, an ABC News veteran who retired at the end of 1994, said that in "those good old days," the reporter spent a lot of time "in places where there was no indoor plumbing." He, too, describes the change:

> Now you still go to the same places. . . . There is still no indoor plumbing. . . . But New York can contact you on the satellite phone while you are sitting in one of those places without that plumbing. It has happened to me in eastern Turkey and northern Iraq.[52]

These two news veterans' musings about wars past are colorful and nostalgic, but they reveal much more—how technology and time have altered forever the job of the television foreign correspondent, and with it the very fiber of broadcast news. Too often now, television correspondents are less *reporters* in the traditional sense of the word and more human adjuncts of the electronic news-gathering packages deployed by headquarters. Which stories get covered, and sometimes even the scripts, are determined more and more by editorial committees in New York or Atlanta rather than by the enterprising, digging reporter.[53]

Technology has wondrous advantages, to be sure. Handheld videocameras and all the rest of the equipment make it possible for journalists to bring the outside world closer, eliminating delays that in the past meant viewers and readers would be served yesterday's or last week's news. A

British newspaper correspondent roaming across Africa can file stories instantly from even the most technologically bereft locations by simply plugging hand-held equipment into a car's cigarette lighter and transmitting to London via the INMARSAT satellite system.[54] The American public and millions of others around the world were able to witness on television, as events unfolded, the massacre of Chinese students in Tiananmen Square, the 1991 coup attempt against Soviet leader Mikhail Gorbachev, the December 1992 landing of U.S. special forces in Somalia, the October 1993 storming of the Russian White House, and many other historic events. During the Persian Gulf War, CNN conveyed different viewpoints and a sense of the interconnectedness of events, switching instantly among reporters at the Pentagon, the White House, Saudi Arabia, Iraq, Jordan, Israel, and elsewhere. Technology, combined with a proliferation of cable television outlets, offers the potential of a far greater opportunity for those interested in public policy to learn about the day's events in a way that would have been impossible fifteen years ago.[55]

If this is the potential, what is the reality? As we have seen, the public's interest in foreign affairs news is narrow and specific to begin with. What about at the other end of the communications link? What is the effect of real-time technology on the work and product of the television reporter?

Simply put, the capacity to "go live" rarely means improved journalism; it often means the reverse. The essence of a reporter's work, after all, is reporting and analysis. The demands of logistics and the drumbeat of constant deadlines mean that in many, although certainly not all, instances there is less time to do both. When television moved from the era of film to electronic news gathering, broadcast journalists lost "the twenty or so minutes think time" they used to have while the film was being processed.[56] Now, editing begins as soon as the video is shot. Live television—in which correspondents talk as events unfold around them—eliminates this think time altogether. As Dunsmore puts it, "In live situations, too often information can come into a television correspondent's ear . . . and out the mouth . . . without ever touching the brain."[57] The issue here is more about missing context than making factual mistakes, although these do occur: the issue is that reporters now have relatively less time to analyze and put into perspective what they have just seen and heard. (Unless the subject of the report is an official event, such as a Pentagon news briefing, which gives officials the ability to speak directly to viewers, journalists may gain an advantage, however. At least until subsequent reports, real-time television means officials have less opportunity to spin the reporter toward their policy view.) In a bit of pointed exaggeration, the shift toward live coverage during the Gulf War has been called the "end of journalism," as journalists, more than ever before, become part of the events they are witnessing.[58] A CNN correspondent dons a gas mask in front of the cameras as Iraqi Scud missiles, erroneously thought to carry chemical warheads, streak toward Tel Aviv. In the previous chapter, we saw some of the effects of this kind of reporting on the viewer and policymaker during that war.

Time, of course, always has been in short supply for journalists. But rather than a single deadline for the evening news, TV reporters covering a breaking news story for, say, ABC now are expected to feed the overnight news program, *Good Morning America*, television newsmagazines, and *Nightline*. These demands often mean there is less time to sift through the facts, assess the value of conflicting accounts, and search for more information—in essence, the art of reporting.[59] "Going live," rather than improving this situation, worsens it. In many instances, reporters can ill afford to stray far from the satellite dish that provides the link to a headquarters that might need their services at any moment. This phenomenon has been called "palm-tree journalism," a reference to the palm-lined hotel pool near which the satellite dish might be stationed. An illustrative story concerns a BBC correspondent who unexpectedly ran into an American counterpart away from the hotel, upcountry in Nicaragua, and asked what he was doing there: "'I'm on my day off,' came the reply. No longer chained to the satellite dish the reporter could actually go and attempt to see something of the events he had been reporting on 'live' for the previous week."[60]

The near-universal cry from veteran reporters is that, far too often, their superiors want to use technology simply because it is there—not to serve some journalistic purpose. One result is the increasing use of "two-ways," live dialogues between reporter and anchor, often after the report has just aired. Rarely do these dialogues reveal new information. More often, they generate a false sense of momentum, relaying more urgency and action than is actually the case.[61] But the expense of today's equipment means it will be used whenever possible once deployed. These two-ways also steal from the reporter's time. One senior CNN correspondent "has issued a standing threat to answer the on-air question 'What's happening, Richard?' with the reply 'I have no idea what's happening because I've been standing on this hotel balcony for two hours waiting for you to ask me that question.'"[62]

Thirty years ago, James Reston wrote of the press: "Most of the time ... we rush from crisis to crisis, like firemen, and then leave when the blaze goes out."[63] He urged a new kind of reporting, one that involved "more attention to the *causes* rather than merely the *effects* of international strife."[64] But clearly little has changed for the better, and perhaps much for the worse, since *The Artillery of the Press* was published in 1966.

There remains much in television news to admire, of course. When the reporting is thorough, the analysis cogent, and the pictures telling, television has no equal in bringing home events and the costs of leaders' policies, particularly the human costs. Many "long-form" news broadcasts, such as *Nightline* or some of CNN's magazine-style programs, ably flesh out the skeleton of the news. The Public Broadcasting System's (PBS) *News-Hour with Jim Lehrer* (formerly *The MacNeil/Lehrer NewsHour*)—which commands a large, if largely elite, audience—in particular eschews sound-bite journalism. The program gave coverage to Somalia throughout the U.S. deployment there, not just when U.S. troops arrived and when they later began to engage in combat.[65] But technology and economics too often force television coverage toward the superficial, the incoherent, and the live for the sake of live. There is an unfortunate mesh between these trends and the very characteristics of modern peace operations. The media's potential effect on American foreign policy is magnified. And policymakers, of course, are not immune to the illusion that television shows more of events than it actually does. To quote Koppel once more:

> Coverage, in other words (as in the recent cases of Haiti, Rwanda, Somalia, and to a lesser degree, Bosnia), . . . tends to be intense, but relatively short-lived. And to the degree that administrations here in Washington are reactive to public pressure, the intense focus on particular crises is developing an unfortunate tendency to reflect that sporadic coverage.[66]

Officials: Time, Tele-Diplomacy, and CNN

Before examining how CNN and other news media affect U.S. government policy decisions in the arena of peace operations, we should take a look at the *structural* effects of CNN, or how the advent of an around-the-clock television news service with real-time, global capability affects the day-to-day lives of senior government policymakers. By structural, I mean how government officials receive information, make foreign policy decisions, and communicate those decisions to other policy actors and the public. Part of this study's central argument is that these structural effects, while less commonly discussed, are more profound than policy effects. U.S. government officials alluded to these structural effects time and again in interviews. They concluded that rarely, if ever, did television determine the precise content of the policy response. This was self-evident in some cases. However, such comments must be viewed critically: policymakers may be understandably reluctant to admit that their powers have been usurped or diminished by the news media.[67]

As stated earlier, "real-time" television is defined as video images beamed back by satellite from the field, either live or with a delay of no more than an hour or two.[68] *From the perspective of the policymaker (although not of the journalist!), there seems to be little, if any, functional difference between video that is live and video that is a few hours old.* This is the definition of "real-time" used by Nik Gowing, diplomatic editor of Britain's ITN, in his 1994 study of real-time television's impact on foreign policy. Gowing's study focused on the conflict in Bosnia and was based on more than one hundred interviews with senior government officials and politicians, primarily in the United States and the United Kingdom.[69]

Gowing asked an obvious, but often overlooked, question: how much television do senior foreign policy officials watch? He concluded that it was less than might be supposed.[70] While Gowing is correct in many respects, his findings in this area need refining. In the American context, at least, he gives insufficient weight to the distinction between senior policymakers and their staffs, between noncrisis and crisis situations, and between the State Department and the White House.

It is true that senior policymakers are simply too busy with meetings, paperwork, preparations for public appearances, and other duties to watch television regularly during the course of the business day. J. Brian Atwood, administrator of the U.S. Agency for International Development (AID), which is on the front lines of the U.S. response to international humanitarian crises, said he rarely watches the television in a corner of his spacious fifth-floor office in the State Department building. "My day is too busy," Atwood said in an interview, during which the television set was off. Atwood said he will flick on the television when he "hears about something."[71] But senior officials do not have to watch television all day to be aware of it. They have public affairs aides who monitor television closely throughout the working day. When there is a crisis and television is broadcasting images that have the potential to impact U.S. policy, those charged with making that policy usually hear about it first from "public affairs."[72] Atwood's director of press relations at the time, Jay Byrne, had a bank of four TV monitors in the hallway outside his office, one floor down from Atwood's. When I visited, two monitors were tuned to CNN, one to CNN's Headline News Service, and one to C-SPAN (the Cable Satellite Public Affairs Network). Televisions in the White House press office are constantly tuned to CNN or C-SPAN, while White House press secretary Michael McCurry has a bank of televisions, with four networks going simultaneously, in his personal office. Much the same is true in the office of the defense secretary's spokesperson.

CNN is now an integral part of the operations centers and situation rooms found throughout the national security and foreign policy agencies of the U.S. government. Often, CNN provides "intelligence" about real or potential crises before the traditional intelligence channels—the U.S. intelligence community and American embassies—report in. In the White House Situation Room, there is a mahogany cabinet with banks of screens to monitor cable traffic and other intelligence. Sitting on top of the cabinet is a small portable television that seems to have been added years later. "Especially in a crisis, that's the one that everyone's watching," said Jeremy Rosner, a National Security Council aide during 1993–94.[73]

Moreover, senior officials can now watch CNN without having to turn the television on at all in the traditional sense. Thanks to new computer technology, some officials have CNN (or another channel) running in a small window in a corner of their computer screen throughout the day, allowing them to glance at it even as they carry out other duties and turn to it rapidly if necessary.

And while most top government officials not directly involved in public affairs do not watch television throughout the day, they will watch it in times of crisis or drama—even the president will take time out to view. In October 1995, President Clinton stepped away from his desk in the Oval Office for a few moments to watch the verdict being read in the O. J. Simpson trial. Two years earlier, in October 1993, when U.S. Army Rangers became bogged down in a firefight in Mogadishu that claimed eighteen lives and helped precipitate the U.S. withdrawal from Somalia, television sets were on in nearly every corner of the White House, tuned to CNN.[74] On Saturday, February 5, 1994, U.S. ambassador to the United Nations Madeleine Albright was in a meeting with her staff in New York when the telephone rang. She was informed that a mortar shell had landed in a busy Sarajevo marketplace. "I did what anyone would do," she said. "I turned on CNN. For the rest of the day, I sat in my living room, watching television, telephone in hand."[75]

There seems to be a difference between the use of television at the White House and at the State Department. As mentioned earlier, in the White House, where there is arguably more concern with the political ramifications of events, television is followed closely. Career State Department officials, by contrast, seem highly skeptical and sometimes outright dismissive of the news media, including television. The State Department attitude may be a legacy of centuries during which diplomacy was the province of a secret priesthood, carried out far from the public eye, and of the very nature of diplomacy and negotiations themselves.[76] While covering the State Department on a daily basis from 1989 to 1994, I rarely interviewed senior officials (at the assistant secretary of state level or higher) who had a television in their office that was on when I entered the room. But the State Department's spokespersons—who, like all other spokespersons, are by job definition closer to the press and public opinion—may alert their principals to television reports and thus add to the pressure for a policy response to those reports, particularly if they have immediate access to their principals. Margaret Tutwiler, Secretary of State James A. Baker III's spokeswoman and top political aide, was renowned for assuming such a role at key points.[77] Tutwiler's role often put her at odds with the State Department bureaucracy.

Much has changed in a generation. Years after the 1962 Cuban Missile Crisis, Defense Secretary Robert McNamara almost nonchalantly admitted that he did not turn on a television set during the entire two weeks that the crisis was at its peak.[78]

So much for use of television by senior policymakers. What are its effects on them? While I and others have spoken of a CNN effect, it probably is more accurate to speak of CNN *effects*, for there seem to be many.

There is little doubt that real-time television images of dramatic foreign policy developments greatly increase temporal pressures on senior officials to come up with a response, either in word or in deed, to the events portrayed. That pressure is not irresistible, but it is resisted at the risk of media and political criticism and, ultimately, even one's own political health. "One of the downsides of that kind of instant coverage, it does put a lot of pressure on decision makers. . . . It forces decision makers to move more quickly than is prudent," according to former White House spokeswoman Dee Dee Myers. During the Somalia crisis in October 1993, "every single day we were forced" to respond to developments and do so within the same news cycle, she said.[79] According to retired Gen. Brent Scowcroft, President Bush's national security adviser, CNN "routinely became the first way we found out about crises," long before the U.S. embassy or the CIA had reported in. "Five minutes after that, the press would want to have a U.S. policy response on it." While it was possible to resist the pressure, "you could only do that for so long" before the news media began to accuse the administration of being caught flat-footed, Scowcroft said.[80] Former secretary of state Baker, recalling his experience as a political campaign manager, said that in the old days a rule of thumb was that a candidate had to respond to an opponent's charges within the same news cycle. "We no longer have a news cycle, in my opinion, in the way you used to." CNN, he said, "makes everything instant." Baker also noted that media organizations now have communication facilities "that are every bit as advanced as government." And CNN's reports from Moscow, for example, don't have to go through a "policy scrub" as the U.S. embassy's do, Baker said, meaning that they reach policymakers first. "You have to respond to media reports a lot quicker."[81]

The concern here is that the highest levels of the U.S. government will respond to instant television images that later turn out to be inaccurate, incomplete, or otherwise distorted. The official's nightmare is that a war will be started, relations with another country ruined, or the U.S. government embarrassed because of policy responses to dramatic television reports that later turn out to have told only half the story.

During the Cuban Missile Crisis, President Kennedy, Secretary of Defense McNamara, and the rest of the president's top advisers (the "Ex Comm") were able to take six days in October 1962 to decide, in private and virtually free of worries about the news media, how to respond to the Soviet Union's emplacement of missiles in Cuba. They were able to consider a wide range of policy alternatives in a complex and dangerous crisis before going public with their policy. They were free of demands for instant action and response. Reflecting years later, McNamara asked rhetorically:

> Would the actions in the Cuban Missile Crisis have been different had there not been time to consider this thoughtfully in secret? Well, I think probably they would have been different. . . . I fear that some of our initial judgments [in favor of an air strike], later changed, would have had greater influence.[82]

We now know, of course, that a U.S. air strike on the missile sites in Cuba, advocated by some of Kennedy's military advisers, would have provoked a harsh Soviet-Cuban response, possibly even triggering a nuclear exchange.

A former senior official with experience in several administrations pointed out two other instances where reaction to events portrayed on television was too swift and the response less thoughtful than it should have been: the Soviet invasion of Afghanistan and the Soviet shooting down of Korean Air Lines Flight 007. However, instances like this don't always turn out for the worse. In the early 1980s, when the Israeli Defense Forces were shelling Beirut, President Reagan saw an image of a child whose arms had been torn off by an explosion. Reagan called Israeli prime minister Menachem Begin and prevailed on him to cease the shelling. It later turned out that the image had been faked. But "[i]t did . . . help bring peace to Beirut."[83] Scowcroft often cited a dictum to colleagues while in the White House: "First reports are almost always wrong." The very real danger, he said, is that policymakers will feel pressured to act before all the facts are in, responding to a television image "that may be, by its very nature, very distorted."[84]

But other officials said that the dangers of false response are overstated or at least that the time pressures inherent in real-time television can be managed. "American public opinion is not looking for an instantaneous reaction. What they're looking for is a wise reaction," said a former senior official. A model of restraint under pressure, this official said, was how Adm. William Crowe, then chairman of the Joint Chiefs of Staff, dealt with the accidental shooting down of an Iranian airliner by the USS *Vincennes* on July 3, 1988. Adm. Crowe "was much more careful in the early hours," when it was unclear what had happened. "That's the way to do it."[85] Former State Department spokesman Richard Boucher said that television reports do speed up the process of making decisions. However, in direct contrast with

McNamara, he said, "But they're probably the same decisions we otherwise would have made." He added: "As often as not, we buy ourselves time when things happen. If we think we need the time to decide, we take the time to decide." Boucher recalled that during the Persian Gulf crisis, an Iraqi spokesman would appear on CNN every day at around 11 a.m.—just before the State Department noon briefing—with Baghdad's latest challenge or parry. "We always faced sort of intense pressure to respond at 12:30 or 1 o'clock. It seems to me, we managed not to," Boucher said. The Bush administration did not do anything different or change policy because of CNN's immediacy. Rather, for rhetorical purposes, "we found something to say."[86] This tendency to respond to media pressures with rhetoric rather than true policy change will be seen more clearly in chapter 4. So, too, will Boucher's statement that policy that is thought out and planned prior to the arrival of the latest image on CNN allows for a more measured response. By presenting a challenge to policymakers and their policy, real-time television puts a premium on leadership and consensus within an administration, both of which help officials resist public pressure and take the time for a more considered reflection.

Defense Department spokesman Kenneth Bacon was perhaps the most adamant in saying that the time pressures associated with real-time television are exaggerated or at least are decreasing as officials gain experience with CNN and the like. "Policymakers are becoming more adept at dealing with the CNN factor," he said. "We do not have a big problem with saying, 'Yeah, this looks really awful, it is awful, but let's find out what the facts really are.'"[87]

So far, this discussion has addressed real-time television as if it were a one-way phenomenon. But CNN and its brethren are less like a blunt instrument than like a double-edged sword. CNN's effects are not all negative from the policymakers' viewpoint. In fact, CNN can be an immense boon to them—and, significantly, to other actors—if they know how to use it. Real-time television allows these actors to disseminate their policies and positions almost immediately; to send signals to adversaries and allies alike; and to view the results, correcting where necessary. And CNN, because of its real-time nature, is probably less judgmental than the print news media and more akin to news wires, which typically distribute the first written, factual accounts of news events. Numerous officials and journalists referred to CNN as a "video news wire." This side of CNN was perhaps best summed up by Bacon, who said: "Everyone talks about the CNN factor as being bad. But in fact, a lot of it is good."

One way CNN and modern communications technologies help senior government officials is that they allow them to make their positions known quickly to a large audience mostly made up of other elites, both in the United States and around the world. "In a way, it's easier," Bacon noted. Bacon also mentioned an unglamorous use of technology, the Federal News Service, a nongovernmental firm that provides journalists, policy-makers, and others with an electronic transcript of press conferences, speeches, and similar events soon after they occur. Bacon was interviewed one afternoon as he was preparing to escort a senior Defense Department official to the Pentagon briefing room, where the official would provide reporters with a background briefing on U.S. policy toward Bosnia at a critical juncture in the conflict. The official's every word would soon be in the hands of those the department was trying to reach, Bacon noted. "This is something you couldn't do five years ago. This is a huge leap, a powerful and useful tool," he said. CNN, the Federal News Service, C-SPAN, and the like are "a powerful extension of the briefing podium," he said.[88] Margaret Tutwiler, the former State Department spokeswoman, similarly spoke of television as an extension of the traditional briefer's podium. When Tutwiler conducted the daily State Department briefing, she often directed her comments not to the reporters in the briefing room, but to the bank of TV cameras behind them. She knew she had "a much larger audience than the men or women in the room." She also knew that if the reporters were giving her a particularly tough grilling, "TV-land was basically going to be on my side."[89] This is another instance of the effect noted in chapter 1 regarding the Persian Gulf War, where audiences, getting a live peek at the messy interaction between journalists and officials, seem to instinctively side with the officials.

Bacon mentioned another positive asset of real-time television: officials' ability to correct, or at least attempt to correct, what they see as inaccurate or distorted reporting. Bacon said he and Defense Secretary William Perry had a high regard for CNN Pentagon correspondent Jamie McIntyre. But if they felt that one of McIntyre's reports was in error or incomplete, Perry could and would call him and try to "spin" the story a different way. With ABC, CBS, or NBC, "you get one shot—the evening news," Bacon said. With CNN, "You get twelve, sometimes twenty-four times a day to make the changes."[90] A senior White House official was less enamored of this aspect of CNN, noting that it is errors spawned by CNN in the first place that officials usually find themselves trying to correct.[91]

Taken together, in a time of crisis, these attributes of CNN add up to what has been called *tele-diplomacy*, the conduct of diplomacy in near real time through the use of CNN or some other medium. Of course, the use of the news media to conduct diplomacy in public predates the creation of CNN. But in previous crises, such methods were haphazard, slow, and not assured of success. During the Cuban Missile Crisis, Fidel Castro jammed Voice of America (VOA) broadcasts to the island. President Kennedy and his aides, wanting to ensure that his October 22 television address to the U.S. public was received on the island, resorted to patching the VOA signal into seven commercial radio stations that could reach Cuba.[92] Communications between Washington and Moscow were so primitive—it took six to eight hours for a classified message to be transmitted—that Soviet leader Nikita Khrushchev was forced to send messages to Kennedy via Radio Moscow. "In the modern atmosphere, a television anchor might well have provided the useful forum for American and Soviet officials to communicate instantaneously."[93]

Today, world leaders can be confident that a diplomatic signal sent via CNN will be received in time, although they cannot know whether the message will be interpreted correctly by the intended recipient. During the Persian Gulf crisis, White House officials were told by CBS correspondent Diane Sawyer that Iraqi president Saddam Hussein constantly watched CNN. Scowcroft said that he and other officials were worried about the impression antiwar demonstrations in the United States were making on Saddam; they used CNN in an attempt to signal their resolve (as well as to counter propaganda on Iraqi radio, which had a powerful transmitter).[94] CNN was often the best way to converse with Baghdad, according to Baker. He cited President Bush's Rose Garden statement vowing that Iraq's invasion of Kuwait "will not stand" and his own address to U.S. airmen in a hangar near Ta'if, Saudi Arabia, on the eve of the UN Security Council's deadline for Iraq to pull its military forces out of Kuwait. Baker's stern warning that the deadline was firm and that U.S. military strikes would begin soon thereafter was intended more for Saddam than for the Air Force pilots and crew present in the hangar. These were "all examples of us trying to use the media to send a signal," Baker said.[95] CNN's instantaneity and global reach often result in what correspondent Ralph Begleiter calls a "diplomatic ping-pong match," with adversaries and allies rapidly serving and returning messages through the network.

One significant aspect of CNN and modern television in general is that it allows nonstate actors—guerrilla leaders, freelance diplomats, dissidents —a potentially much greater role in communicating to publics around the world and thus attempting to influence public opinion. Former president Jimmy Carter is a prime example of a figure who has realized CNN's potential and used it to further his diplomacy from North Korea to Somalia. With U.S. peacekeeping troops bogged down in a bloody campaign to capture Somali warlord Mohamed Farah Aidid, Carter deliberately used an interview with CNN's Judy Woodruff to attempt to defuse the situation and send a signal to Aidid. He knew that the Somali leader watched CNN.[96] We will see in later chapters how all sides attempted to use real-time television to send messages or advance their positions during peace operations, especially those in Haiti and Somalia.

There is some evidence, then, that real-time television can erode government officials' primacy in crisis management and communication, boosting the impact of "lesser" actors. One should be cautious in drawing larger conclusions, however—there is an equal amount of evidence that journalists continue to give added weight and time to officials' statements, as Hallin found during Vietnam.

Several CNN correspondents said they knew they were being used at times by officials and others to send signals, although they quickly added that they always applied journalistic skepticism and news judgment to what they were being told, and by whom.[97]

Another aspect of global, real-time television that reveals its double-edged nature for officials is the way it can instantly inform publics of foreign crises that raise questions of U.S. action or even intervention. The ensuing public pressures on officials often are unwanted—but not always. Television images can help build a public constituency for U.S. involvement abroad. Foreign policy officials, it must be remembered, favor an activist U.S. foreign policy almost by job definition. Several officials suggested that CNN might be one of the last lines of defense against an isolationist U.S. public. "Somehow, it relieves us of the need to make the case," Boucher said. Thinking back to the flood of Iraqi Kurdish refugees into Turkey and Iran after the Persian Gulf War, he said that news media images "make the case of the need to be involved sometimes more than we can." At times, presidents will actively use such images and remind the public of them to build the case for American involvement. President Bush did so in 1992 as he explained why the United States should send troops to Somalia to stop mass starvation, Boucher recalled. "The media provided the basis for policy decisions that we then didn't have to spend as much time postulating an argument for," he said.[98] When, in November 1995, President Clinton had to convince Congress and the American public to support the deployment of twenty thousand American troops on a peace operation in Bosnia, he frequently referred to previous images of horror from the former Yugoslav republic as a basis for building support.[99]

Baker, while believing that television focuses much too heavily on dramatic crises, also sees some benefits. "You no longer have to educate the public on horrible things that are happening in a far-off place," he said. "It makes the general public a heck of a lot more attentive to issues they would have paid scant attention to before the communications revolution."[100] Officials much farther down the policymaking ladder also noted how television can bring crises to the attention of the president and other top leaders in dramatic fashion. As we shall see, some of these officials, who favored humanitarian intervention in a particular crisis, used television to send a signal to, or put pressure on, their superiors.

Television coverage generally, and real-time television coverage in particular, of foreign crises brings pressure on top government officials to respond. Sometimes the pressure is unwelcome, sometimes it is beneficial. And both forms can occur during the same crisis—depending on the administration's policy stance. As we will see in chapter 4, the images of horror from Bosnia in 1992 complicated the life of top Bush administration officials. But by February 1994, when the Clinton administration was ready to pursue a more activist policy, the real-time reports of the bloody mortar attack on a Sarajevo marketplace opened a window that made the task of building public support immeasurably easier.

One last structural effect of real-time television worth examining is the way it seems to push written communications—both the media's and government's—into a more analytical style. With CNN quickly reporting the "facts" of an event, newspaper reporters, U.S. diplomats, and intelligence officers are freed up to analyze, rather than merely report. Indeed, their survival may depend on their doing so. As mentioned earlier in this chapter and in the previous chapter regarding the Persian Gulf crisis, real-time television has had significant effects on the print news media by virtue of its ability to report breaking news much faster. More and more, reporters find that their editors are asking them to answer not only "What happened?" but also "Why? What does it mean? Whom does it help or hurt?" In short, many newspapers have adopted a more analytical style as real-time and near real-time television reporting has spread. Many officials of both the United States and the United Nations, officials who use the *New York Times* as their principal source of news and a standard by which to judge other media, volunteered that they felt the *Times* was becoming less objective. By this they seemed to mean that the newspaper's reporters were less willing to simply report what they were told by the responsible officials but, rather, injected their own analysis of an event into the story. A senior White House official said he felt that in this way, newspapers were not serving their readers well. While reporters increasingly write their stories assuming the reader has been watching CNN all day, the official pointed out that this is not necessarily true.[101] As we have seen, the network's audience is quite small in noncrisis periods.

This same evolution from objective reporting to deeper analysis can be found among U.S. diplomats posted abroad. The rise of CNN, and especially its daily use to send high-level diplomatic signals during the Persian Gulf War, led to speculation that diplomats stationed in foreign capitals would soon become anachronisms. Recall H. Ross Perot's assertion that instantaneous worldwide communications have made embassies and their inhabitants "relics of the days of sailing ships." But diplomats have not become relics. Rather, they have adapted to real-time television in ways that are strikingly similar to the ways newspaper reporters have. CNN and other real-time television services "fill a role that, interestingly, we don't have to do anymore," Boucher said. "In the State Department . . . people are realizing we can't be a wire service." Many a State Department cable from a political officer overseas will now begin with the phrases "You will have seen . . ." or "The crisis as seen on TV . . . ," Boucher said. Rather than report the news, foreign service officers will add their interpretation of it and recommendations for action, he said. But CNN, he said, represents information, not diplomacy as practiced by diplomats on the ground. As for diplomacy, he said, "CNN has no way of getting involved in these things."[102] Even in the closeted world at the top of the U.S. intelligence community, real-time technology has fostered significant changes. The CIA and other intelligence agencies now have their own in-house versions of CNN, distributing time-sensitive intelligence information on television screens. According to a senior U.S. intelligence official, military and political "customers" who use U.S. intelligence products increasingly want them delivered not in written form but on their computer or television screens, or via videoconferences. In the near future, this official said, these customers will use a classified computer network similar to the Internet, where, rather than being passive recipients of intelligence data, they can search and choose among the reports that have been "posted" on the network.[103]

Summary

This chapter has analyzed how two major developments of the past decade have affected the relationships among journalists, government officials, and the public. The first was the end of the Cold War, a geopolitical phenomenon that served as a kind of road map that guided the exchanges between the government, the public, and the media. The second was the rise of global, real-time television, which ensured that all three groups would be "driving" faster than ever before, with the attendant consequences.

The chapter sets the stage for the following examination of how the news media affect specific peace operations in terms of political-military management and public support. After looking at how reporters, the military, and other actors deal with news coverage of peace operations in chapter 3, the themes here—especially those in the final section of this chapter—will be examined in greater depth in chapters 4 and 5, with a more intensive focus on the policy process in specific cases.

While it is impossible to precisely apportion responsibility between technology and geopolitics for the seemingly enhanced powers displayed by the news media, this chapter and chapter 1 have shown that much more is at work than technological advances, no matter how awesome they may be. The factors that determine the relationships among U.S. political leaders, the news media, and the public remain fairly constant despite advances in technology. The contours of the relationship are affected more by the events themselves than by the media through which they are communicated. In the case of the Cold War, national security threats, both real and imagined, permitted officialdom great sway over determining the issues of the day and, to a lesser extent, how they were seen by the public. When the Cold War ended, the initiative passed, at least temporarily, to the news media, which were armed with powerful new communications devices. It is worth pondering—and history will show—whether the period between the late 1980s and the mid-1990s represented a unique moment in the history of media-government relations, when the dissolution of the old order, coupled with technologies being widely introduced for the first time, allowed journalists a brief opening to break free of official imperatives. Some of this newfound power already shows signs of losing its luster, as the public tires of outrage after outrage illuminating its television screens and the news media follows by reporting less of it. As we will see later, the costs of the U.S. intervention in Somalia proved to be a corrective to whatever power the images of humanitarian suffering have to move American foreign policy. By late 1995, President Clinton faced a situation much different than President Bush had when he decided to send U.S. troops to Somalia. Rather than responding to public pressures to act generated by news media images, Clinton was attempting, with great difficulty, to use the news media to persuade a wary Congress and public to support a peace operation in Bosnia. Surely, this is a reversion to earlier patterns of officials' leadership before the first years that CNN came on the scene.

There is no doubt that real-time television puts intense pressure on officials to respond rapidly, increasing the difficulty of policymaking and, in theory, increasing the margin for error. In short, real-time television has literally changed officials' lives. AID administrator J. Brian Atwood was asked what had changed during the twelve years he was out of government between serving in the Carter and Clinton administrations. "CNN," he said.[104]

This pressure is not necessarily a disadvantage for a democracy: it is now simply harder for officials to make policy in a vacuum, ensuring at least a modicum of transparency and pluralism in the governmental decision-making process. But real-time television also provides the means —a new and more powerful means—for U.S. foreign policy officials to inform, persuade, and cajole the electorate. CNN affects the *process* of policymaking more than it affects *policy itself.* To those who do not understand, or misunderstand, the media's power, to those who only fear it or do not have well thought-out policies or cannot communicate those policies no matter how sound they may be, the communications technologies associated with the letters "CNN" are indeed a negative force. To those officials (and other actors) who understand how to use real-time television, it can be a powerful, if uncertain, tool in their favor. Kenneth Bacon, Richard Boucher, and others who deal with the news media every day believe that government officials increasingly understand how to use this tool to their benefit, or at least understand how to operate in a policy world where CNN and the like are a permanent part of the landscape.

Real-time television, like the preceding era of news media studied by Cohen and others, can rapidly put an issue on the government's agenda. It can cause policymakers to have to change gears quickly, to address an issue that they would rather ignore, to make decisions more quickly than they would like, to simply respond in some fashion. But this chapter, and those that follow, confirm Gowing's conclusion that the connection between instant images and policy is not nearly as linear as is often assumed. What happens when an image appears on the screen that cries out for action or when other actors challenge Washington via word or deed captured on camera is, to a great extent, a function of leadership. Whether officials can resist the televised images, if those images suggest policy choices different from their own, depends to a great extent on how firm that policy is; how well it has been communicated; how internally unified an administration is; how willing officials are to take political risks for the policy; and, finally, how well they can utilize the new medium themselves. This view was suggested by Boucher, Koppel, and many others on both sides of the camera.

Real-time television and other modern news media are like the weather, a phenomenon that wiser officials learn to stop complaining about and become acclimated to, taking the good with the bad. They are, in Margaret Tutwiler's words, "part and parcel of governing."[105]

3

Reporting the New Story

The News Media and Peace Operations

> "We need the pictures, always the pictures."
> —*Official of the UN High Commissioner
> for Refugees*

> "You have to have the pictures."
> —*Roy Gutman, Pulitzer Prize-
> winning reporter for* Newsday

When U.S. troops are deployed for a peace operation, the news media, the military, and the nation's political leaders find themselves in an environment that is different in virtually every important respect from traditional combat. While the Persian Gulf War is still a recent memory and dominates much of the debate about media-military relations and about conflict and public opinion, that war offers little guidance for the missions in Bosnia, Somalia, Rwanda, and Haiti. This chapter analyzes the unique aspects, both physical and political, of modern peace operations and their effect on the way the missions are reported and characterized by the news media.[1] It describes the interactions between reporters and the numerous actors, familiar and unfamiliar, who are typically on the scene, regardless of who is leading the endeavor. For journalists, it is the value of news, of the marketplace, and to some extent even of entertainment, rather than any political, much less geostrategic, considerations that determine story selection and presentation. How does a peace operation present itself as a story to the news media? For the journalist, how does it compare, as a story and as an assignment, with other forms of conflict and conflict resolution? What, if anything, is unique to the relationship of the media and peace operations? Does the relationship between the media and other actors differ according to the type of peace operation?

Lights On, Lights Off: Two Vignettes

Just after midnight on Wednesday, December 9, 1992, U.S. troops in the vanguard of Operation Restore Hope landed on the beach off Mogadishu, Somalia. There, Navy SEALs and Marines were met by a potentially hostile force, but not the one they had prepared for. Toting rifles, their faces smeared with camouflage greasepaint, the soldiers stepped onto the beach and into the glare of TV lights. The journalists, hundreds of them from around the world, had gotten there first. When the lights went on, they temporarily blinded some of the soldiers who were wearing night-vision equipment designed to magnify what little ambient light had been expected. Had there been any snipers, the soldiers coming ashore would have been lit-up targets. It was the military commander's worst nightmare—an intrusive, irresponsible media made the mission more difficult and potentially put his troops at risk. The soldiers had been prepared, as they always are, to expect armed resistance.

This now-famous incident prompted much criticism of the media's performance by the military, the public, and even some within the media. The whole encounter had a made-for-Hollywood feel about it. In a classic example of parachute journalism, the American networks had sent their stars to cover the story of American-troops-as-saviors: Ted Koppel of ABC, Tom Brokaw of NBC, Dan Rather of CBS. Some of the criticism undoubtedly was warranted. CNN vice president for news Ed Turner acknowledged that "it was wrong to turn on those portable lights" and that the hundreds of viewers who called CNN to complain "were properly angry."[2]

But the story does not end there. The media were not the only moving force behind the incident. Civilian and military officials of the U.S. Defense Department wanted favorable news media coverage of the landing just as much as the media wanted to be there. While Pentagon officials may have been surprised at the size of the news media contingent, and even more surprised by the TV lights, they could not have been surprised that the media were there in the first place. Pentagon and State Department officials had invited coverage, telling reporters with some specificity where and when the landing would take place. "In effect, it was a photo op," CBS News vice president Joe Peyronnin said the next day.[3] In Washington, Navy officials gave details on the landing to inquiring reporters. In Mogadishu, reporters were encouraged to cover the event. Keith Richburg, who had been in and out of Somalia for the *Washington Post* since January 1992, said that at a prelanding news briefing in the Somali capital, U.S. Marine Brig. Gen. Frank Libutti told reporters: "I recommend all of you go down to the beach if you want a good show tonight."[4]

At a Pentagon press briefing at midday on Tuesday (Washington time), Pentagon spokesman Pete Williams did not ask television camera crews not to use lights. Williams did not begin asking the networks to move their cameras until later that afternoon in Washington, minutes before the first reconnaissance teams came ashore in Somalia. After the first live pictures were beamed back, he asked the networks to tell their crews to turn off their television lights.[5] According to one account, Defense Department public affairs officials had failed to tell those responsible for conducting the landings that the news media had been informed of the timetables.[6] From this vantage point, the entire incident looks more like a mixture of media frenzy and poor public affairs planning. As always in the push-and-pull struggle between the military and the media, history would not be repeated in precisely the same way.

The issue of lights would resurface less than two years later, in September 1994, when the United States was preparing to invade Haiti to remove the ruling junta and restore President Jean-Bertrand Aristide to office. Many of the nearly one thousand journalists who would cover the deployment of American troops and its aftermath were already in Haiti, waiting for an invasion. With the memory of Somalia in mind, the U.S. government asked the television networks not to shine klieg lights from the rooftop of the Hotel Montana (the journalists' headquarters in Port-au-Prince) on paratroopers descending from the skies or on the planes that brought them. The request and other proposed guidelines for coverage were relayed to TV networks in Washington by David Gergen and other senior Clinton administration officials and from the Defense Department to the U.S. embassy in Haiti. The networks also were not eager for a repeat of the Somalia spectacle and instructed their personnel to behave responsibly. The television networks agreed with the U.S. military to use night-vision devices instead of bright lights and to delay broadcasting video of the invasion until after U.S. troops were safely on the ground.[7] The issue became moot when, on September 18, de facto Haitian leader Lt. Gen. Raoul Cédras agreed to step aside. U.S. troops entered Haiti without resistance the next day—in daylight.

Freedom

The requests to television networks to refrain from using powerful lights and to delay video transmission were not the only restrictions the U.S. government contemplated for the news media in the Haiti operation. As the U.S. military intervention approached, Pentagon officials called the U.S. embassy in Port-au-Prince and asked what to expect from the news media: "Can we just tell them to stay in their hotels for the first twelve hours?" The reply: "I don't think you can do that."

By that late date, some television networks had surreptitiously placed microwave dishes at key points around the Haitian capital, such as the Defense Ministry, where fighting was expected. Other dishes had been set up, in an apparent first, on the top of the U.S. Information Service (USIS) building next to the embassy. The dishes were there to transmit video to the Hotel Montana headquarters and, through it, to the world. Network representatives took turns spending nights in the USIS building in case the invasion came. There *was* one way the media could have been thoroughly controlled: by dropping a platoon of U.S. soldiers to block the narrow, winding road that was journalists' only way to get from their hotel in the hills overlooking Port-au-Prince to the city itself. Said one official: "It was muttered about once and never seriously considered."[8]

These anecdotes illustrate several salient characteristics of a newly empowered international news media operating in an open environment that is not quite peace, yet not quite war. In Haiti and Somalia, U.S. civilian and military officials had to treat the news media as increasingly independent actors. Many of the media were there before the troops arrived. In contrast to the Persian Gulf War, most media personnel operated independently of military units. Richburg, for example, expressed irritation at U.S. military officials' attempts to channel his reporting once they had landed in Somalia. "They thought we were there to cover them," he said. His attitude was, *I was here before you guys.*[9]

In peace operations, the news media are largely free of the traditional restrictions on correspondents covering a conventional wartime deployment, have access to information independent of U.S. and UN channels, and have a smorgasbord of diverse sources on which to draw. In Haiti, "[t]here was no need to do some of the things that were done in Desert Storm [to control the media]. . . . This is part of the peace operations environment," said Army Col. Barry E. Willey, the chief military spokesman in Port-au-Prince. "They knew much more than we did about what was going on out there. They knew more than the commanders did."[10] Contrasting the Haiti experience with the Persian Gulf War, which was conducted out of full view of the media, and also with Vietnam, where by today's standards there were few reporters, Willey said that in Port-au-Prince there were reporters and camera crews "literally on every corner, wherever you turned."[11] This almost fatalistic view of the news media's role in peace operations, delivered without detectable rancor, was shared by Col. Steven F. Rausch, who was chief military spokesman during the last phase of American military involvement in Somalia, from mid-October 1993 to March 1994: "It's kind of like the Super Bowl, and the media's down on the playing field while you're trying to run a play. But if you know that going in, you can accommodate them."[12]

In peace operations, the military rationale for restricting information and access is largely absent. Rather, political leaders' need to attract and maintain public support, and the absence of a "vital interest" argument on which they can draw, may call for the maximum possible openness (which helps explain what happened on the beach in Somalia in December 1992). In Somalia, Rwanda, and Bosnia, nongovernmental organizations (NGOs) also encouraged and expedited the news media's presence, hoping to move governments to act by drawing international attention to mass human tragedy.

In the case of Desert Storm, essentially the same technologies were available to the news media as appeared later in Somalia. In both cases, the United States led an international coalition of military forces. Yet the news media's freedom to report from the field—and the ability of military and political leaders to restrict them—differed dramatically in the two cases. It would seem from this evidence that the nature of the military mission (as well as simple facts of geography), rather than technology per se, is the predominant factor that determines the media's independence from officials and potential impact on their policies.

Sometimes officials' attempts to encourage media coverage take unexpected turns, as they did in Somalia, making officials more wary of possible subsequent interventions and the media's role in them. If nothing else, the seemingly trivial issue of bright lights in Somalia and Haiti shows that government officials and the news media can learn from the past and adapt accordingly—probably more quickly than they could have in the calcified Cold War environment.

A Multiplicity of Institutions

Another facet of the freedom that peace operations present to journalists stems from the nature of the policy actors involved and their relationship with the reporter. Previous studies have defined one model of interaction between the media and government officials: that of the beat reporter who covers only, or primarily, a single agency. Such reporters balance the role of adversary, critic, and investigator with that of confidant, colleague, and adviser to those officials they cover and converse with on a daily or near-daily basis. Regardless of which role beat reporters emphasize, they become intimately familiar with "their" department or agency and sympathetic to its history and bureaucratic needs; in some sense, they even become a part of it.[13] A parallel, but even closer, relationship may develop in times of war, as was seen during the Persian Gulf War and as was widely agreed to be the case in World War II. Most studies of wartime reporting have found that when a nation was at war, journalists tended to cover the conflict from the perspective of their "side" and their nation's soldiers, producing accounts that were patriotic at best, and nationalistic at worst.[14]

Peace operations present a different model of coverage. The traditional arguments of national security and vital national interest are largely absent. As the very word "multilateralism" indicates, the mission may extend far beyond the purview of a single nation or military. And the military itself is only one dimension of a story that also includes not only powerful humanitarian elements, but strong political components at home and abroad.

Certainly, characteristics of the traditional bonds between reporter and soldier are retained in some cases at some points, particularly when a large U.S. military deployment is involved. One example is Somalia, where more than twenty journalists accompanied the Marines as they prepared for and conducted the beach landing.[15] But these reporters cover only one piece of a larger story and, over time, are likely to peel away from the protective embrace of the military and its public affairs structure. For the vast majority of journalists covering a peace operation, the bonds break down even further. There is no "beat" to be covered, but a multiplicity of institutions, none of which may dominate the reporter's attention at all times. These additional actors may include diplomats and other political representatives, a variety of nation-states, the United Nations and its representatives, other international organizations, NGOs, the parties to a conflict, and victimized civilians. Each may have sharply differing views of the conflict and what actions the international community should take.

As humanitarian operations have grown in number and complexity, the U.S. military and NGOs, institutions with radically different operating styles and little understanding of each other, have found themselves operating side by side for the first time. There were 109 private and UN-affiliated relief organizations at work in Kigali, Rwanda in September 1994. To coordinate and centralize relief efforts during Operation Support Hope, civil-military operations centers (CMOCs) were established in Uganda, Rwanda, and Zaire.[16] These efforts, as well as exercises, symposia, and informal coordination away from the field, have helped ease each side's unfamiliarity with the other. But in the Rwandan case, differences in policy, tactics, and styles persisted. U.S. and international relief officials complained about what they saw as the U.S. military's limited commitment, its rush to pull out in order to minimize the potential human and financial costs of its mission, and its emphasis on military security.[17] These tensions inevitably surfaced in news media reports, given the open environment of peace operations and journalists' ability to travel freely.

From the journalist's viewpoint, this is an optimal situation. Good journalists want access to as many sources of information as possible, both to cross-check their analysis of a situation and to report more than a single side of the story. (Being restricted primarily to a single source of information, U.S. military spokespersons, was the basic complaint of American journalists covering the Persian Gulf War.) Several of the reporters interviewed told of seeking information from another institution when the first one proved barren, or using a piece of information gleaned from one source to pry information from a second, and so forth. The conflicts among civilian, military, and relief organizations supposedly working toward the same goal are themselves newsworthy. Thus, in at least some peace operations, the reporter's task looks less like covering a war and more like covering a policy debate in Washington, where the sound and fury of different government agencies, political parties, and interest groups can be heard and felt. Following the Rwandan experience, U.S. military officials proposed to relief groups that in the future, they participate in the military's centralized operation for dealing with the news media: the JIB. It remains to be seen whether this proposal is feasible and, if so, what effect it would have on media relations.[18]

The case of the U.S. military and relief groups in Rwanda is, of course, just a small piece of the problem. Policy differences between the United Nations and the United States in Somalia or between NATO and the United Nations in Bosnia have more than just direct effects on the mission. When picked up and communicated by the modern news media's technological tools, these differences can affect how the mission is viewed at home and by potential or actual parties to a conflict in the field. For military and relief officials conducting a peace operation, the cacophony can make it more difficult to communicate coherently, whether it involves telling the local populace the purpose of a mission and rules for use of force by peacekeepers, or informing political leaders and citizens at home.

The weakening of reporter-official ties raises a more fundamental issue, much debated during and after Desert Storm: to whom do the news media "belong"? News organizations traditionally have had a national character that government officials could appeal to if need be. The technology- and economics-driven globalization of news may be weakening such connections.[19] CNN views itself as a global news organization, and its personnel are prohibited from using the word "foreign" on the air, the reason being that what's foreign in Washington might not be foreign in Wellington.[20] In the Falklands conflict, a British admiral called the venerable British news agency Reuters to ask that it withhold information on British shipping movements. He was told by a German who answered the phone that Reuters was an international agency and could not be answerable to a particular national interest.[21]

The Media and the United Nations

In Bosnia, yet another form of journalistic freedom appeared, one that is intimately related to the effects of the end of the Cold War and the lack of a defining focus for U.S. and Western foreign policy, which was discussed in the preceding chapter. The wars in the former Yugoslavia began in 1991 and continued for four years without the public's receiving any clear guidance from the NATO governments on the nature of the conflict, guidance those governments surely would have given if the superpower competition had been a going concern. The Clinton administration described the Bosnian conflict at times as a war of aggression and a threat to U.S. values, and at times as a three-sided civil war.[22] This vacuum gave the U.S. news media freedom to define the conflict in their own way.[23] This, and the freedoms noted above, put the media and the United Nations in conflict.

The UN Protection Force (UNPROFOR), the peacekeeping operation in the former Yugoslavia, was mandated by the Security Council under Chapter VI of the UN Charter, which has been the basis of neutral UN peacekeeping for four decades. Beginning with Canadian Brig. Gen. Lewis MacKenzie, a veteran of seven traditional UN peacekeeping missions, UN commanders in Sarajevo, with few exceptions, interpreted their mandate as one of strict neutrality among the Bosnian government, Bosnian Serb forces, and Bosnian Croats. As UN officials pointed out, they were given neither the imprimatur nor the resources for a more forceful mission beyond ensuring the delivery of humanitarian-relief supplies. Most important, UN officials and international mediators representing the United Nations and the European Union tended to blame all three parties equally for the conflict.

The *New York Times*, *Newsday*, CNN, ABC, National Public Radio (NPR), and other major news-gathering organizations, in varying degrees over time, reported a quite different war. Their reports characterized the Bosnian conflict as a one-sided and deliberately brutal war of aggression by the Bosnian Serbs against the Muslim-led Bosnian government in Sarajevo. This coverage included many award-winning reports, including the 1993 Pulitzer Prize awarded jointly to Roy Gutman of *Newsday* and Jonathan F. Burns of the *New York Times*.[24] UN forces in Bosnia "have, by and large, a different analysis of the war than the press has," said Tom Gjelten, who covered the wars in the former Yugoslavia for NPR.[25]

The intent here is not to determine which analysis is more nearly correct but to point out the perceptual gulf that separated the United Nations from much of the international media in Bosnia. UN officials and reporters from the United States described the gap between them as particularly wide—in part, perhaps, because the United States did not commit troops to Bosnia during this phase of the conflict. The resulting tensions and distrust were severe at times.

"The media's coverage of it influenced policy for the worse," said a senior UN official who served in Bosnia and dealt with the news media.[26] He argued that U.S. news reports in particular lacked any historical understanding of the Balkans and simplistically dredged up memories of Nazi concentration camps, reducing the war to a one-dimensional struggle of good (Muslim) versus bad (Serb). These reports, coupled with graphic TV images of mass suffering and demands for action from columnists such as the *Times*' Anthony Lewis, had a profound impact on the Clinton administration's policy, the official said.[27] In his view, they pressured the U.S. government into withholding support for UN efforts at reaching a peaceful settlement short of the Bosnian government's demands, thus scuttling the diplomacy of special envoys Cyrus Vance and David Owen.

> That seemed to be the judgment of the *New York Times* and *Washington Post* editorial boards and the news pages. That was reflected in calls for arming the [Bosnian] government, intervening militarily, pushing the Serbs back physically and trying them for war crimes. . . . The media was conditioned to respond morally to the awful things that they saw. And that was an understandable first response. . . . When there was no option, no likelihood of military intervention, they kept hammering away for the impossible, and in so doing, totally disparaged the peace efforts. They, in fact, became spoilers of the peace process.[28]

On the other hand, many U.S. journalists accuse the United Nations, in its quest for neutrality, of covering up Serb wrongdoing and inflating atrocities supposedly committed by Bosnian government forces, thereby attempting to mislead the news media. When a mortar killed at least seventeen people waiting in a bread line on Vasa Maskin Street in Sarajevo on May 27, 1992, Gen. MacKenzie told reporters and others that the explosion was the result of an "own hit"—a Bosnian Army mine deliberately placed in order to win international sympathy.[29] Gjelten said that MacKenzie, despite the lack of evidence for his charge, was eager to portray all sides in the conflict as equally complicit. "MacKenzie was desperate for the Bosnian government to do something bad," said Gjelten. "It's a little bit unfair to automatically assume that UN officials have no ax of their own to grind."[30]

UN officials blocked journalists' access to some areas of operations in Bosnia in an effort not to jeopardize the mission's neutrality. "We have a gentleman's agreement with the Serbs. We promised not to show things that might embarrass them to journalists," one UNPROFOR officer said after UN troops denied reporters access to Serb-controlled eastern Bosnia. The United Nations also refused to release a videotape of Bosnian Croats blowing up an ancient bridge in Mostar.[31] During the crisis over Gorazde in spring 1994, one of MacKenzie's successors, British Lt. Gen. Sir Michael Rose, accused reporters and the Bosnian Muslim government of over-stating the extent of casualties in the Serb-besieged town. But when one suggested that he allow reporters aboard UN helicopters to see for them-selves, Rose refused, saying that to do so would "irritate the Serbs" and jeopardize UN access to Gorazde.[32]

To some extent, this phase of the Bosnia conflict may have been unique in relations between the news media and the United Nations, given the lack of direct military involvement by the major powers, the nature of the conflict, and UNPROFOR's tenuous position throughout most of its exis-tence. Yet diplomats, Pentagon officials, and reporters were virtually unan-imous in giving the world body low marks for its dealings with the news media, not just in Bosnia, but in Somalia and elsewhere. They cite a num-ber of factors, including a closed bureaucratic culture that has not adjusted to changing conditions and a lack of high-level attention to press relations and communications generally. Roy Gutman recounted his attempts to get information from the United Nations after he had determined, through interviews with fifteen Muslim and Serb witnesses, that UN peacekeepers had taken sexual advantage of Muslim and Croat women who had been forced into prostitution in Serb-held Bosnia. Sonja's, the restaurant–boarding house where the mistreatment took place, was 150 feet from a well-known Serb-run detention camp that UN officials never bothered to investigate. MacKenzie, along with commanders of the UN Military Observer (UNMO) mission, denied responsibility and referred Gutman to UNPROFOR's press center in Zagreb. He said he contacted spokeswoman Shannon Boyd half a dozen times and eventually sent a letter by fax, requesting to see logs of UNMO movements. He never got a reply. Just before publishing the story, a desperate Gutman called Fred Eckhard, a spokesman for UN Secretary General Boutros Boutros-Ghali in New York. Eckhard told him to call Boyd. Gutman said UN investigators ran into their own roadblocks, finding that the movement logs had been destroyed. However, the investigators privately told him they had determined that UNMO personnel had been at Sonja's and urged him to continue his own investigation. In 1994, Yasushi Akashi, Boutros-Ghali's special envoy in Bosnia, announced the results of the UN investigation, saying it disproved the charges in Gutman's articles. However, the investigators' report was never made public, despite Gutman's attempts to prod the United Nations into releasing it. Reflecting on these and other experiences, Gutman, now in Washington, said:

> I would like to see the UN deal with us in a more professional way. As much as I despise so much of what passes for government relations here with the State Department, it's regularized, it's channeled. . . . It's time for the UN and representatives of the press to sit down and discuss overall press relations.[33]

The United Nations gradually seems to be coming around to the idea of more open dealings with the news media, although its ability to get its message out to the media and others in the area of operations is hampered by member states' unwillingness to fund what they see as public relations activities.[34] In December 1994, two and a half years after the Bosnian war began, UN undersecretary general for peacekeeping operations Kofi Annan announced that journalists would be allowed aboard UN flights in Bosnia. Echoing the conclusion many U.S. military officers had already reached, he said: "Peacekeeping operations in particular depend for their support on widespread public awareness of the conflicts, and we are committed to doing everything we can to facilitate the work of the media."[35]

Objectivity

In mid-November 1994, a small group of journalists gathered at UN headquarters in New York to discuss the news media's coverage of the war in Bosnia. The usually hushed rooms of the UN Correspondents Association on the third floor of the UN building rang out with accusations and counteraccusations between the panelists and the audience. The panel, which included David Binder of the *New York Times*, Alexander Cockburn of *The Nation*, and *Harper's Magazine* publisher John R. MacArthur, leveled charges that, to reporters, are as serious as any can be. The U.S. news media, they said, have focused almost exclusively on the plight of Sarajevo and the Bosnian government, ignoring the atrocities on all sides; have been taken in by the clever propaganda of the Bosnian and Croatian governments; have ignored the historical roots of the Balkan conflict; have distorted coverage of the war by focusing intensely on the plight of Sarajevo, where reporters and satellite dishes congregated; and have been guilty of a "herd mentality" that discourages reports going against the grain. "Our press coverage . . . is Wilsonian in its simple-mindedness," MacArthur said. These and other comments—which closely parallel the views expressed by many UN officials—not surprisingly brought a harsh reaction from many correspondents in the audience.

What was going on here? Why were journalists fighting so bitterly among themselves over what constitutes fair and accurate coverage? Why did this occur with respect to Bosnia?

Within the journalistic community, the war in Bosnia opened deep fissures over the most sensitive of issues for a reporter—objectivity. Reporters' professional ethos of objectivity, and the roles they sometimes take that are at odds with that self-view, were articulated by Bernard Cohen in his study of the press and foreign policy.[36] Virtually all the journalists I spoke to who were involved in covering Bosnia acknowledged that the savagery of the fighting there and the outside world's competing views of the conflict forced a sometimes painful examination of their own role and conduct. This sentiment is crucial to an examination of the news media and peace operations because horrific ethnic fighting, atrocities, and even genocide form the backdrop for many peace operations, and this is very likely to continue to be true in the future. The debate over Bosnia was repeated, albeit in a far more muted form, in another case I examine in this study —Rwanda. The key issue here is that of *atrocities*. While news media portrayals of atrocities do not automatically cause a significant change in U.S. foreign policy, the charge that the news media have misportrayed the conflict in Bosnia to policymakers and the public is a serious one.

Tom Gjelten won several awards for his reporting from the former Yugoslavia. He and most other reporters I spoke to said the reporting of the Bosnian war has been accurate, if a little oversimplified at times. Roy Gutman would add that the international news media were slow to realize what the Serbs were doing when they began their campaign of "ethnic cleansing." But both reporters acknowledged that values played a role in the conflict and their coverage of it. "I, as an American journalist, do not operate in a value-free environment," Gjelten said. In his book *Sarajevo Daily*, Gjelten chronicles the wartime struggles of the Sarajevo newspaper *Oslobodenje* to maintain its editorial independence and multiethnic character, values he says he believes in. "Values are unquestionably at stake in this conflict," he said. When Gutman discovered that Bosnian Serbs were torturing, raping, and murdering Muslims at camps in northern Bosnia, he consciously tried to move policy. He contacted the U.S. consulate in Zagreb, Croatia, the White House, and congressional committees to find out what they knew and more: "I did everything I could to ring the alarm bell."[37]

In a way, too, so did much of the rest of the Western news media. As David Rieff writes:

> Surely one more picture, or one more story, or one more correspondent's "stand-up" taped in front of a shelled building would bring people around, would force them to stop shrugging their shoulders or blaming the victims. ... In truth, the international press corps has sympathized with Sarajevo to a degree that is altogether out of character for this group of professional skeptics. In a world where the diplomats and politicians who could have done something to save Bosnia have seemed determined to watch as it is destroyed ... journalists found that they believed in "Western values" even as the Western political elite continued to betray them.[38]

Gjelten made a distinction between *objectivity* and *neutrality*, suggesting that accurate reporting includes determining responsibility. Any news reporting of Bosnia that ascribes equal guilt to all sides

> is quite simply incorrect. . . . Objectivity in this sense does not mean a kind of even-handedness, giving one paragraph to the atrocities of one side, one paragraph to atrocities of the other side, one paragraph to atrocities of the third side. . . . There is, I think, a tendency in media to balance competing political forces or competing political pressures.[39]

Richburg of the *Washington Post*, who reported on the massacres of an estimated half-million ethnic Tutsis in Rwanda, is more blunt when speaking about the Hutus who were responsible for the killings: "The Hutus were evil."[40]

In both Bosnia and Rwanda, the news media have been accused, with some cause, of oversimplifying the ethnic warfare and the circumstances that led up to it.[41] The *New York Times'* Binder, for example, said that World War II and the Cold War conditioned "many, if not all, journalists to see the world in terms of good guys and bad guys, them and us." This outdated worldview, he suggested, was carried over to Bosnia. Yet the crux of this argument is that the U.S. news media missed or ignored atrocities committed by the Muslims and the Croats against each other and against the Bosnian Serbs, as alleged by Binder at the November meeting and by another individual on this side of the journalistic debate, Peter Brock, in the quarterly journal *Foreign Policy*.[42] The argument falls apart in the face of the evidence, including a 1995 CIA report that the Bosnian Serbs were responsible for 90 percent of the atrocities in Bosnia and that they were the only one of the parties to engage in systematic ethnic cleansing.[43] That is the story Gutman, Gjelten, and many others have reported.

The character of modern warfare and the lack of cues from top government officials created a dispute over the nature of the ethnic conflicts in Bosnia and Rwanda, and over the journalist's proper role in reporting on them. News media reports have often shown the idealistic, emotional, and humanitarian emphases discussed in previous chapters. Television, in particular, has had difficulty portraying the complexities and histories of conflicts such as those in Bosnia and Rwanda. However, within these limitations, reporting has been accurate on the whole.

The Media and Relief Organizations

If the United Nations and the U.S. news media often find themselves in conflict, that same news media and humanitarian-relief agencies are more likely to have similar goals in peace operations and the crises that precede them. They depend on and use each other more than either would probably admit.

Long before the troops arrive, or if they never do, relief organizations are toiling at the scenes of conflict that give rise to peace operations. These organizations include international bodies such as the UNHCR, national agencies such as AID, and a broad array of NGOs and other private groups known collectively as private voluntary organizations (PVOs). These groups see the news media as crucial, yet erratic and frustrating, allies in gaining first the attention and then the resources of national governments. Television, with its presumed power to move the masses, is their tool of choice. As one UNHCR official put it: "We need the pictures, always the pictures."[44]

This official saw a direct correlation between dramatic television images of suffering—especially of children—and calls to the official's headquarters from concerned American citizens, who asked: "What are you doing about it?" "What are governments doing?" "What can I do?"

Relief agencies work through the news media in a variety of ways. Often, they will facilitate journalists' travel to affected regions to attract worldwide attention. In this role, they and the news media work together, generating pressures on governments to act (although journalists may not have this as a conscious goal—and certainly would not describe it that way). It was for these reasons that the American Red Cross took reporters from CNN, the *Washington Post*, and AP to Somalia in April 1992. The UNHCR also took journalists to Somalia prior to President Bush's November 1992 decision to dispatch troops there. Sometimes, aid agencies face a dilemma: should they bump relief cargo or their own personnel to make room on the airplane for TV cameras and crews that provide much-needed publicity?[45]

At other times, members of relief organizations will simply state their case to the news media, a practice that is prevalent. Prior to President Bush's decision to launch Operation Restore Hope, CNN gave as much time to appearances by representatives of humanitarian-relief groups advocating action as it did to actual video footage of Somalia.[46] Often, spoken or unspoken alliances are formed between relief agencies and government officials, with both groups hoping to mobilize public opinion in a way that compels senior policymakers to act on a brewing crisis. In such situations, the path of cause and effect, action and impact, looks circular. A news story becomes a "super interoffice memo."[47] In late November 1992, Inter-Action, a coalition of 160 U.S.-based relief groups, sent President Bush a letter outlining the security problems for NGOs working in Somalia. The letter, while not specifically requesting U.S. troops, asked for the United States to aid the United Nations in enhancing security for relief operations. Andrew Natsios, the strong-willed and bureaucratically savvy director of AID's Office of Foreign Disaster Assistance (OFDA), received a copy of the letter and took it to Walter Kansteiner, who oversaw African issues on the National Security Council staff. "You guys need to read this," Natsios recalled saying. Kansteiner, in turn, brought the letter to a meeting of the subcabinet Deputies Committee. "That certainly influenced the process," Natsios said. Bush referred obliquely to the letter in a December 4 Oval Office address to the nation in which he announced Operation Restore Hope. An InterAction official said later: "We almost don't know our own power. . . . We have to be careful how we use it."[48] Natsios said he frequently used the news media to educate the public about what his office was doing and to set the agenda, but also "to drive the policy."[49]

The same InterAction official recalled a 1995 meeting between NGO representatives and a senior State Department official on the subject of Zaire. The State Department official asked, "Where's Zaire? How come you guys aren't pushing for Zaire?" The InterAction official said of the meeting: "It's almost like a reversal of roles, where they are saying, 'We can't move forward until you push the right [public] buttons.' . . . They can't move forward until PVOs move forward."[50]

Relief officials are most interested in generating media attention early on in crises, when the costs of action are presumed to be low and the chances for averting tragedy are high. At this point, however, the news media's interest in the story may be minimal. This is especially true of television, which relies on "good" visuals—starving masses, long lines of refugees, bodies. Several NGO representatives said their agencies tried to interest the news media when ethnic massacres broke out in Burundi and Rwanda in 1993, but to no avail. The media did not arrive en masse until the violence in Rwanda reached genocidal proportions the next summer.

To members of the media, relief organizations can be a highly credible source of information. Often, relief workers have labored in a country for months or years before the country's situation becomes major international news. They are on the front lines, delivering aid and assisting development projects. They thus offer reporters an accurate read on the background of a conflict and current conditions. Moreover, organizations such as the International Committee of the Red Cross (ICRC) or Médecins sans Frontières (Doctors without Borders), to name just two out of hundreds, are by definition attempting to "do good," largely unsullied by the political motivations suspected of other actors. In Rwanda, "I think that relief agencies were overwhelmed, but they were doing a tremendous job, sort of saints on earth," said John Stack, foreign news director of NBC News. "They have to act as PR [public relations] directors to try to impress journalists to cover their particular activity. That's what they have to do, but the world would be a better place if they stayed with their real roles."[51] *New York Times* Africa correspondent Donatella Lorch said that while the ICRC and Médecins sans Frontières "were only putting a Band-Aid on the problem" in Rwanda, "[t]heir presence . . . kept the issue in world headlines.

Young Rwandan refugees fleeing the mass slaughter in their country plead with Zairian soldiers on August 20, 1994 to cross the border the soldiers had just closed. Wrenching photographs such as these contributed to U.S. officials' decision to send a peace mission to Rwanda to handle the two countries' refugee crisis. (AP/Wide World Photos.)

The body of a U.S. Army Ranger killed in an October 3–4, 1993 firefight during the hunt for Somali warlord Mohamed Farah Aidid is dragged through the streets of Mogadishu. The video and photo of the scene eliminated what little support remained for the U.S. mission in Somalia. (Photo by Paul Watson/Sygma.)

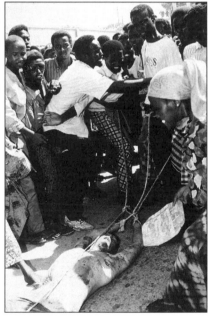

CNN correspondent Peter Arnett, whose face personified real-time television coverage of Operation Desert Storm, reporting from Iraq. (Photo courtesy of CNN.)

A U.S. Special Forces soldier scurries past the media's cameras following a "stealth" beach landing of U.S. forces near Mogadishu's main airport in the early morning hours of December 9, 1992. Unbeknownst to the landing forces, CNN and other news organizations had arrived beforehand to cover the beginning of Operation Restore Hope live. (AP/Wide World Photos.)

Bosnian soldiers carry a casualty from a mortar attack on Sarajevo's main market-place on February 5, 1994. At least sixty-six people were killed and dozens more wounded in the attack, which prompted NATO to threaten to retaliate against Bosnian Serb forces surrounding the city. (AP/Wide World Photos.)

[The ICRC team] worked under incredibly grueling circumstances. They were virtually all stranded, but really stuck to their guns."[52] Asked if he felt he had been used by NGOs, Richburg of the *Washington Post* said, "You're always being used by everybody, to some degree." This is not bad, he said, "if your agenda tracks with their agenda. . . . I wouldn't gratuitously quote some aid group. . . . I give credit where credit is due."[53] In Bosnia, *Newsday*'s Roy Gutman said that while the United Nations and national governments—including the Bosnian government—were unhelpful, he made heavy use of international relief organizations such as the ICRC and the UNHCR. "I would tend to go to them. That's my secret," he said. "When they are really most useful is when you have something, you go to them. . . . I did that with my key stories." The ICRC, in particular, has changed its operations and become "much more open to the press."[54]

As dealings between the news media and relief organizations move from the relatively new and unfamiliar to the routine, and as reporters become more sophisticated in their coverage of relief activities, it is likely that the media will focus more on the relief groups themselves. The news media should then be better able to tell which programs are working, which represent waste, and which are undertaken merely for the camera's benefit. "The PVO community always gets good press, because we're doing God's work," the officer of InterAction said. "If we want better coverage, we've got to be prepared for more thorough coverage of our operations."[55]

The Media and the U.S. Military

On the eve of the U.S. intervention in Haiti in mid-September 1994, David Wood, a seasoned national security correspondent for Newhouse News Service, was handed a highly classified copy of the invasion plan, right down to the detailed operational orders. Such transfers are the stuff of legends about leaks and military commanders' fears that operational security—the element of surprise—will be blown. But this was no leak. The documents had Wood's name on them, and he carried them around openly in a loose-leaf notebook stamped "Top Secret." Wood and other members of the Pentagon's national media pool were given a detailed briefing on the plan and received a visit from Army Lt. Gen. Hugh Shelton, commander of the Haiti task force. He told them: "If you are not happy with what you're doing, please let us know and we will make every effort to accommodate your needs."

Wood, a veteran who has covered conflict since the 1977 war in the Ogaden Desert, hoped to be on what he calls the "tip of the spear," reporting with the very first waves of U.S. troops that entered Haiti. This strategy was vital, in his view, because hundreds of reporters were waiting in Haiti to cover the invasion from the "outside." Wood was assigned to ride in the command-and-control aircraft that would oversee all airborne aspects of the planned invasion—the first time a journalist would be allowed to fly on this top-secret aircraft. But it was not to be. The aircraft waited on the runway at Pope Air Force Base in North Carolina but never took off. The last-minute diplomatic mission by former president Jimmy Carter, former chairman of the Joint Chiefs of Staff Colin Powell, and Sen. Sam Nunn negotiated away the need for a forced entry into Haiti. The Pentagon's media pool plans fell apart. Those reporters who were supposed to go in with the first waves never made it to Haiti. Other pool members who were supposed to come in with reinforcing troops on Day 2 or Day 3 ended up going first. Still others were stuck on an island in the Caribbean. Some pool reporters scrambled to get to Haiti on their own, aided by the Pentagon. Wood writes: "As far as I know, only two written pool reports were ever filed, and they were not distributed to other pool members."[56]

While to some degree the beginning of the Haiti operation may be a unique case given the last-minute change of plans, it is this very mixture of political and military objectives, as well as the rapidly changing environment *off* the battlefield, that distinguishes peace operations.[57] In such situations, the basic compact between the military and the media—the pool system—is of limited relevance. Journalists in Haiti were where they wanted to be. The day before the invasion, CBS anchorman Dan Rather interviewed Lt. Gen. Raoul Cédras, the man the troops were coming to oust. When the first U.S. troops landed by helicopter at Port-au-Prince airport and dropped to their bellies, guns pointed ahead, photographers stood inches in front of them, "shooting" back. Reporters and cameras followed U.S. troops on foot patrols through the streets of Port-au-Prince, capturing their reactions as they stood by while the Haitian police clubbed Aristide supporters. On a later visit to Haiti, Wood said he found the military spokesman's office, the JIB, unhelpful. Rather than wait the three to four days it would take to secure approval for a visit to the field, he simply drove to where he wanted to go—and was warmly welcomed by U.S. troops. "I think the whole Vietnam thing has gone away, out in the field," he said. "More often than not my problem out in the field is, How do you shut these guys up?"[58]

The common perception of relations between the news media and the U.S. military is one of unremitting tension, fueled by the experiences in (and sometimes clouded recollections of) Vietnam, Grenada, and the Persian Gulf. Yet this perception is rapidly becoming dated, at least regarding news media coverage of peace operations. Of course, the media's skepticism toward the military remains, and reporters' unfamiliarity with military life grows, as a generation has passed since the all-volunteer force was instituted. This complaint was nearly unanimous from officers who deal with the press, as well as the older generation of combat correspondents. The military's desire to control all elements on the battlefield will endure as well. But interviews with military and civilian officials and a close reading of recent military writings on the subject lead to the conclusion that the U.S. military is taking a far more activist approach toward media relations than is generally realized. The new and growing view, more pronounced in some of the uniformed services than in others, is that media relations are an important part of "winning the war" and should be understood at all levels, from the strategic to the tactical commander. (According to military officers, this puts new burdens on commanders, who must assume additional roles that they have not traditionally been called upon to play. When Gen. Shelton stepped out of a helicopter and onto Haitian soil, the first thing he did was hold a press conference.) The focus is on telling the military's side of the story, using the same new communications technology the news media employs.[59] This focus has been accompanied by growing attention to military-media relations in the senior service schools and by the conduct of training exercises for peace operations in which "reporters" (sometimes played by real correspondents) are part of the "battlefield." Planning for the news media has become an integral part of doctrine and training for peace operations.

The underpinning for this change is a realization that past conflicts in which the news media were successfully controlled, such as the Falklands, Grenada, and the Persian Gulf, are poor guides for the present and future.[60] As noted at the beginning of this chapter, the U.S. and international news media will have a near-pervasive presence on the scene of most peace operations, whether the military likes it or not. Col. Willey, the military spokesman in Haiti, expressed this fact succinctly, saying: "We didn't have anything to hide. We couldn't hide anything."[61]

Willey contrasted the media planning for the Haiti operation with Grenada eleven years earlier, when he was public affairs officer for the Eighty-Second Airborne Division and had to deal with a seething press corps that was kept away from the action. In Grenada, he said, no thought was given to the news media ahead of time. In Haiti, by contrast, the plans were extensive and elaborate, although they had to be altered significantly when circumstances changed. Before the Haiti intervention, Willey said, he spent a month discussing press contingencies with operational commanders and was briefed on one plan, under which U.S. forces would enter Haiti without using force (later, he was briefed on the top-secret invasion orders). The bottom line for him, he said, was "to get in as early as possible," before the troops landed. "The first day was really the key one as far as we were concerned. Getting the message back that everything was going OK." He would link up with Gen. Shelton "and get him on CNN." (Because air traffic in and out of Port-au-Prince was blocked, Willey at one point was ready to go to the neighboring Dominican Republic and surreptitiously cross the border into Haiti before U.S. troops arrived. Higher-ups at the Pentagon withdrew their approval, fearing Willey might be taken hostage.) According to a former top Clinton administration official, in dealing with the media in Haiti, the military was "much more sophisticated" and more willing to be open than the civilian side of the U.S. government. On the other hand, he said, since Vietnam, "The press hasn't gone to school on the military at all."[62] Many other officials whom I interviewed concurred.

In its fullest expression, this proactive view of the military's relations with the media comes down to the old saw, "If you can't beat 'em, join 'em." For better or worse, the military, particularly the Army and the Marines, are learning the basics of public relations. Some military public affairs officers have trained at major commercial public relations firms such as Fleishman-Hillard, as well as at CNN. In an article entitled "Winning CNN Wars," published in fall 1994, psychological operations expert Frank J. Stech argued that national leaders and the military should use the same symbolic, emotive images employed by the broadcast news media to tell the story of what U.S. troops are doing and why:

The "government knowledge machinery" that supports the leadership must be ready to prepare both information and compelling communications as quickly, readily and flexibly as CNN provides news video and analysis. . . . The biggest obstacle, however, is philosophical: the sentiment that the solution to the problems of CNN wars is to "turn out the lights"; to get the CNN spotlights pointed elsewhere, dimmed, switched off. Or, if you are a policymaker, to turn your back on them.[63]

Such statements, of course, immediately raise questions about propaganda and the triumph of image over substance, questions that haunted the military-media relationship in Desert Storm. Stech criticized the coercive, us-versus-them approach to the media still entrenched in much of the military. But at the same time, he counseled the active use of symbols, news "frames," and the war of images, such as U.S. Patriot missiles dueling in the night sky with Saddam Hussein's Scud missiles. This *perception* of success, he suggested, is more important than the fact that the Patriot was not nearly as effective as it seemed to be to viewers of CNN.[64] Ironically, Desert Storm was responsible for much of the changed thinking that Stech expressed. Many Army officials now feel that because of overly strict control of the news media, the service wasted an opportunity to show the American public how well troops and equipment performed as they swept across the desert. While the Army did most of the fighting, it was the Marines, led by Lt. Gen. Walter Boomer (a former public affairs officer), who were most open to the media—and got the best press.[65] Such interservice rivalries open huge doors for the news media. In Haiti, according to one network producer with long Pentagon experience, by playing on the "psychic fear" that one service would get better exposure than the others, the television networks were able to persuade the Army and Navy to permit correspondents to travel with individual units, and thus break away from the pool system.[66]

To summarize, in peace operations, unlike in traditional combat missions, the U.S. military's operations are highly transparent to the international news media: "The instinctive military need for control is irrelevant in the face of an institution which can field, depending on the size of the operation, thousands of reporters who are equipped with instantaneous communications capabilities and who often understand alarmingly little about the stories they are covering."[67] This media scrutiny is combined with a mission definition in which *political* objectives, for which wars have always been fought, take on added significance over purely *military* considerations.[68] The U.S. military is moving toward a more proactive approach to media relations in peace operations, using new technologies (including the Internet) as a "weapon" in the same manner it has used new technologies for decades to develop more conventional armaments.[69] But so far military public affairs officers have been outgunned by the news media in the crucial early hours of peace operations. In Somalia and Haiti, they depended on reporters or other military units for vital communications equipment, such as satellite phones.[70]

The future of the press pool remains unclear. Many reporters and officials believe that, even if U.S. and allied forces had not overwhelmed the Iraqis so quickly in the Persian Gulf War, the pool system would have broken down shortly after the start of ground combat. The national press pool going to Haiti would have disbanded after the first six hours. After his experience in Haiti, David Wood believes the pool system "has reached the end of its useful life. . . . It didn't work, won't work, can't work." He argues that news organizations took many of their best national security and foreign affairs reporters out of the pools and sent them directly to Haiti, leaving third- and fourth-string reporters, who were neither eager for the assignment nor ready to cover combat in the pool. As a result, military commanders were loath to take on the burden of having to worry about unprepared journalists on the "front lines" and shifted pool reporters into the more out-of-the-way assignments. Wood says, "the fault at this point, I am sorry to say, lies almost entirely with the press."[71] But Wood is far more experienced in covering combat and more knowledgeable about military procedures than many reporters who cover the U.S. military in peace operations. As the previously quoted network producer acknowledged, the television networks simultaneously despise the pool system and accept it, because it affords them access and protection. Col. Willcy said: "I felt very helpless the first few days" in Haiti. "Then I realized how many media were dependent on us."

Information Warfare

Thus far, this chapter has examined the relationship between the news media and different sets of actors—the NGOs, the United Nations, the U.S. military—that are part of what might be called the "peace operations team," helping to conduct the operation and attempting to achieve policy goals. However, according to Stech, "events in CNN war do not unfold as monologues, but in dialogues, with allies, neutrals, and opponents."[72] Peace operations, regardless of whether they are mandated by Chapter VI or VII of the UN Charter, take place in areas where conflict may be ongoing, where various factions may not welcome the peacekeepers' presence, and where there is close contact with civilian populations who may be uncertain or misinformed (perhaps deliberately by their leaders) about the peacekeepers' role and plans. Under these conditions, communications technology becomes a weapon, and because troops' use of force may be severely restricted or inadvisable for political reasons, information becomes a primary (at times, even *the* primary) means of warfare.[73] The revolution in communications technology allows potential or actual parties to a conflict to send messages to the local populace and to the world at large in ways that significantly affect the mission and how it is reported by journalists. Mohamed Farah Aidid and his rivals in Somalia, Radovan Karazdic and the government of Alija Izetbegovic in Bosnia, and Gen. Cédras in Haiti all used television outlets, especially CNN, to try to influence world opinion and the outcome of peace operations in their countries. The very nature of peace operations also plays a role in the ability of antagonists to communicate with the world at large. In wartime, governments traditionally demonize the enemy, pressuring the news media to adopt a similar view. Even in the Persian Gulf War, while Saddam Hussein spoke to Western leaders and publics via CNN, the Bush administration had by then cast him as a villain on a par with Hitler. Some lawmakers in Washington vilified CNN correspondent Peter Arnett for broadcasting Iraqi-censored reports from Baghdad. In peace operations, there is no "enemy" in the usual sense and the news media do not have problems gaining access to key antagonists.

CNN, in particular, gives other actors, such as sectarian leaders or warlords, a two-way communications tool with which they can monitor and affect events. Developments in Somalia in early October 1993, including the killing and capturing of U.S. Army Rangers and President Clinton's subsequent Oval Office address declaring a U.S. withdrawal from Somalia by March 31, 1994, were broadcast by CNN to elites around the world. In Haiti, four days after Clinton's October 7 address, thugs loyal to Gen. Cédras rampaged at the Port-au-Prince dock as the USS *Harlan County* waited offshore with unarmed U.S. and Canadian engineers and police trainers aboard. The rioters numbered less than two hundred and their actions were carefully staged to be menacing, but not deadly. They threatened to create "another Somalia." Prior to the demonstration, Cédras had seen a CNN poll that found two-thirds of Americans opposed to sending U.S. troops to Haiti. The Clinton administration turned the *Harlan County* around.[74]

This seeming ubiquity of images and information puts a premium on the close monitoring of policy and the *effective communication of that policy*. This holds true at the highest levels of U.S. foreign-policy decision making and in the field before and during peace operations. The military's Civil Affairs and Psychological Operations (PSYOPS) units take on special importance in peace operations. While both involve communications, rather than force, to improve the political terrain on which U.S. forces operate, there are differences. Civil Affairs tasks include reconstruction, civil administration, liaison with different ethnic groups or factions, and the like. PSYOPS, while usually thought of in wartime as propaganda aimed at hostile forces, play a different role in peace operations.[75] They are defined as messages targeted at selected foreign groups that are designed to favorably influence their perceptions of U.S. forces or to disseminate information on public health and safety. The usual media employed by U.S. military PSYOPS units are portable printing presses, radio broadcasting equipment, or loudspeakers.[76] Often, the goal is to minimize misunderstandings between the peace operation forces and the local populace that could lead to violence or loss of life. While PSYOPS do not directly target the U.S. and international media, they are designed to counter hostile propaganda that could otherwise make its way into media reports.[77]

Information warfare does not have to be high tech. In Rwanda, the extremist Hutu radio station, Radio Mille Collines ("A Thousand Hills"), played a key role in inciting the mass slaughter of an estimated half-million Tutsis and moderate Hutus. The station also incited attacks on Belgian civilians and the small UN Assistance Mission in Rwanda (UNAMIR). The death of ten of its soldiers and six civilians on the day the mass slaughter began prompted the Belgian government to withdraw its contingent of 440 troops. At about the same time, the UN Security Council voted to scale back UNAMIR. The radio's impact did not reflect its size: when its site near the presidential palace in Kigali was destroyed in a bombing by the Tutsi-led Rwanda Patriotic Front (RPF), the broadcasts resumed from a mobile transmitter, probably located on the back of a truck. After the RPF dislodged the Hutu government in July 1994, radio broadcasts urged Hutus to flee to Zaire, a journey that killed many. Later, the radio urged the new refugees to stay in camps on Rwanda's borders, saying they would be slaughtered in revenge attacks if they returned home. UNAMIR took no action to knock the radio off the air, saying it was not in its mandate.[78] That was also the reaction of U.S. forces in Rwanda, who reluctantly helped the new RPF government repair the destroyed broadcast facilities in Kigali, bringing in technicians from Germany, where the radio equipment had been manufactured. But the station lacked resources, and the new government had other things to worry about. "On a scale of effectiveness from one to ten, I would say the radio . . . was probably a five," said a U.S. officer who had been in Rwanda.[79] The United Nations had its own radio in Rwanda to counter anti-UN propaganda, but its effectiveness was limited. A review of the Rwanda mission concluded that the United Nations needs to develop its own public affairs and psychological operations strategies for peacekeeping and humanitarian operations.[80] The international community puts hundreds of millions of dollars in a small country, and "[w]e don't even have the capability to talk to them," a senior UN peacekeeping official said. "This is [expletive] ridiculous."[81]

In Somalia during Operation Restore Hope, wrote American diplomats John Hirsch and Robert Oakley, the airwaves and presses were key weapons. Radio stations operated by Aidid and rival warlords helped spread the word not to interfere with the Marine landing and told their followers that, after December 26, "technicals"—the makeshift trucks mounted with machine guns that prowled Mogadishu's streets—would be destroyed if spotted out of their cantonments.[82] Within a week of the landing, a small U.S. Army PSYOPS team from Fort Bragg began publishing a newspaper and operating a radio station. Both media used the Somali language and both were named *Rajo*, or "Hope." The operations had multiple purposes: to explain U.S. policy and actions in Somalia, to counter propaganda by faction leaders, and to rebut inaccurate stories in the international mass media. Both the newspaper and the radio station were sensitive to the Somalis' Islamic faith (the station began broadcasts with appropriate verses from the Koran) and focused on the operation's progress in rebuilding Somali society.[83] Former AID official Andrew

Natsios credited the newspaper's reports on Aidid with pressuring the reluctant warlord to sign the Addis Ababa agreements for a cease-fire and political reconciliation in Somalia. Aidid "thought he could play games and nobody would know about it," Natsios said. At times of tension, Aidid would lash out at the newspaper and radio, which he called "Radio Trouble."[84] Later, when Aidid decided to confront UNOSOM II, the UN mission that followed Restore Hope, he used his own Radio Mogadishu as a weapon, prompting UN authorities to decide to close it. Pakistani peacekeeping troops entered the Radio Mogadishu building on June 5 as part of a weapons inspection (the radio was located at a weapons depot). That action sparked intense fighting that left twenty-four Pakistanis dead and prompted the UN Security Council to launch the ill-fated manhunt for Aidid. Hirsch and Oakley pointedly note that the PSYOPS units that ran the radio station and newspaper were not replaced when the United Nations took over command of the Somalia mission from the United States.[85] Natsios found a much more relaxed public relations operation after the United Nations took charge. The UN spokesman, a career bureaucrat, rarely left the UN compound. He "actually had a sauna bath in his bathroom in Mogadishu," said Natsios, along with what must have been one of the few flush toilets in all of Somalia. It was "all new stuff from Italy."[86]

Limit to Freedom (I): Reporter as Target

Aside from the constraints of time and money that were discussed in the previous chapter, another factor can limit journalists' ability to cover a peace operation fully: sheer physical danger. Sometimes, reporters are caught in the middle of fighting. But more and more often, in an arena where images and information warfare are crucial, reporters become specific targets. Reporters may be unable to get to the scene of the action when important events occur or may be forced to seek the protection of UN or national armed forces. This scenario occurred most frequently in Somalia and Bosnia.

In Somalia, as violent confrontations escalated between Aidid's militia on one hand and U.S. and UN forces on the other, reporters became targets as well. On July 12, 1993, four journalists—a British-American photographer, a Kenyan photographer and a Kenyan sound technician working for

Reuters, and a German photographer working for AP—were shot, beaten, and stoned to death by a mob after U.S. warplanes launched air strikes against Aidid. The incident prompted major U.S. news organizations to pull their staffers out of Mogadishu. The *Washington Post,* the *New York Times,* and the *Los Angeles Times* left Somalia, joining the three major U.S. broadcast networks, which had shut down the huge operations they had set up to cover Operation Restore Hope after President Bush's visit to Somalia in January. CNN withdrew its American correspondents in September after five Somali drivers and bodyguards were killed by gunfire in cars clearly marked "CNN."[87] For those correspondents who remained, moving around Mogadishu became dangerous, if not impossible, making it difficult to cover the story. AP pulled its last staffers out in late September because of threats by Aidid supporters to kidnap Americans, threats that brought back memories of the seven-year captivity of AP correspondent Terry Anderson in Lebanon. As a result, by the time of the politically most important event in the mission—the October 3–4 firefight that killed eighteen U.S. soldiers—no American reporters were in Mogadishu. The video footage of a dead U.S. soldier being dragged down a street in the Somali capital and of captured U.S. Army pilot Michael Durant was taken by Somali stringers; still photographs were taken by Paul Watson of the *Toronto Star.*

For journalists, the former Yugoslavia has been even more murderous than Somalia. As of May 1995, at least forty-four local and international journalists had been killed in the Balkans in the preceding four years, making it the most dangerous conflict for the news media since Vietnam (which lasted far longer). Many journalists have been specifically targeted by Serb, Croat, and Muslim forces because of their profession or because of specific stories. After *Newsday's* Roy Gutman pieced together the story of UN peacekeepers' alleged wrongdoing at Sonja's, he could no longer visit the site, which was just six miles north of Sarajevo. His earlier stories on ethnic cleansing had earned him the enmity of most Bosnian Serbs. "I couldn't cross into Serb lines," Gutman recalled. "It would have been a one-way trip." A colleague went for him.[88] The advice of a survival guide for journalists covering the Balkans is telling: always wear flak jackets, including flaps to cover neck and groin. If you are a cameraman, consider getting even more protection. For extensive overland travel, get an armored vehicle, such as a Land Rover with special cab and undercarriage protection that costs $37,500. Don't wear military-style clothing, lest you be mistaken for a combatant. Television crews should bring a small video monitor and extra-long video cables, so they can monitor camera shots away from hotel windows, where the glow might attract sniper fire. Displaying the word "Press" on the outside of a vehicle is no guarantee you will be left alone—it may even draw fire. Displaying "TV" is even worse, because it is seen as more powerful and is the main propaganda weapon for all sides. ABC News producer David Kaplan was killed on August 13, 1992, while riding in a convoy in Sarajevo with Serbian premier Milan Panic. The sniper's bullet entered their van between the "T" and the "V" taped to the exterior.[89]

The sheer number of deaths as well as the many more injuries or close calls is evidence that physical danger is not necessarily a barrier to "getting the story." Indeed, some freelance journalists seem almost reckless. Yet the danger and obstructionism of all three belligerents meant that in Bosnia many areas of the battlefield were out of reach. Information on conditions in these zones was based largely on unconfirmed reports and propaganda from the belligerents themselves. For television, especially, danger and the logistics of modern electronic media meant that Sarajevo, with its good communications and strong UN presence, received much of the most dramatic television coverage. "Some of that was predetermined by the danger, the access, the logistics," said Laura Logan, who oversaw coverage of the former Yugoslavia from 1989 to 1993 as ABC News deputy bureau chief in London. "It was very frustrating for people because it was very difficult to get out in the countryside." Sarajevo itself was far from danger free, so television networks instituted a pool system in which all news organizations had access to any video that was taken.[90] Covering the rest of Bosnia became increasingly dangerous as time went on. Other horrors, arguably worse than those suffered by Sarajevans, were never captured on video. Some were recorded only because of the bravery of correspondents like the BBC's Jeremy Bowen, who reported on the Croat siege of Mostar, or, in the case of Srebrenica, Tony Birtley.[91]

In spring 1993, Serbs besieged the Bosnian city of Srebrenica, whose population was swollen by Muslim refugees who had fled Serb ethnic cleansing elsewhere in eastern Bosnia. Journalists could not get to the city, so reports of the desperate conditions there were vague, based largely on secondhand reports from humanitarian-relief organizations. Two people changed that: French Gen. Philippe Morillon, who led a UN convoy into the city without orders from UN headquarters in New York, and Birtley, a freelance reporter on contract to ABC News. Birtley sneaked into Srebrenica aboard a Bosnian government helicopter after previous attempts to get there on foot and on a donkey had failed.[92] Armed only with a small videocamera like those found in millions of homes, Birtley captured scenes of residents' desperate, nighttime scramble for food as U.S. military aircraft dropped surplus MREs (meals ready to eat) outside the city. Later images showed the medieval conditions in the city itself—people dressed in rags and living in the streets, children drinking sewer water. Morillon's actions and Birtley's reports put Srebrenica on the international agenda, forcing world leaders to pay attention to its fate. Soon, Logan found herself besieged by news organizations the world over for copies of Birtley's video. Birtley had no way to transmit directly from Srebrenica. Instead, his tapes were smuggled out with help from UNMO personnel, who in at least one instance unscrewed a taillight from one of their vehicles and hid the tape in the crevice; they took it to the city of Tuzla. Although his shocking reports got out, Birtley could not. Once the reports began appearing around the world, he became a "wanted man" and dared not cross Serb checkpoints. Stranded in Srebrenica for nearly a month, Birtley ran out of food, and the batteries in his camera ran low. He depended on the United Nations for a tent to sleep in and food, which caused some tensions since UN peacekeepers were themselves low on rations. ABC tried to smuggle food, clean clothes, and fresh videotapes in UNHCR convoys from Belgrade. Some of the supplies were pilfered at Serb checkpoints. Communications were covert and difficult. After a few days, Birtley discovered an amateur radio operator on the outskirts of Srebrenica, who contacted a fellow radio operator in Sarajevo. ABC News personnel in the Bosnian capital managed to hook the radio into an INMARSAT phone and dialed London. At a predetermined time each day, Logan could talk to Birtley and make plans for coverage. She had to shout to be heard, but spoke in code for the benefit of any eavesdroppers. She felt a little like a spymaster, "like it must have been when you had someone behind the lines." Meanwhile, Logan was in daily phone contact with Birtley's wife and was phoning UN officials across Bosnia, asking for help. She was told by public affairs officers with the British contingents at Tuzla and Vitez: "We are not responsible for journalists." But Morillon promised to get Birtley out safely, although ABC did not know how or when. Then, on a Sunday afternoon, Birtley was with UN peacekeepers at an observation post when it came under Serb mortar attack. His leg was hit, shattering it in four places. An emergency operation saved the leg from amputation. A German still photographer, the only other Western journalist in Srebrenica, filmed the operation with Birtley's own camera. The doctor told Birtley that he would have lost the leg if he were a soldier, because he could not have expected proper aftercare. After first denying permission, the Bosnian Serbs allowed a UN helicopter to land, and Birtley, loaded aboard as if he were a UN peacekeeper, was evacuated to Split, Croatia.

In Bosnia, the very real danger to reporters caused them to fall back on the traditional protection of military units in wartime. A similar shift occurred in Somalia after the October 1993 firefight, when U.S. news organizations asked the Pentagon to provide access—and protection.[93] In both places, at times of intensified fighting, the television networks relied on trusted stringers and freelancers rather than sending in their own correspondents. Bosnia, especially, caused ABC News to change how it covered lethal civil wars in Somalia, the Caucasus, Afghanistan, and elsewhere. Bulletproof vests and medical kits became standard equipment. The network learned "after we made mistakes," Logan acknowledged. Kaplan's death—he was not wearing his bulletproof vest at the time—had a huge impact. New rules dictated traveling in armored vehicles and wearing a helmet while in Sarajevo. Logan learned to weigh the dangers to her personnel against the news value of the story—and senior-level producers' interest in having it on *World News Tonight*. "There's no sense in sending someone into a dangerous place unless there's a market for it," she said. ABC correspondents were sent to conflict zones only voluntarily. ABC benefited from its relationship with the BBC, which had long experience in covering Northern Ireland and set the standard for protecting journalists in Bosnia. In 1993, following the BBC's lead, ABC began requiring correspondents going into a danger zone to attend a battlefield school in the English countryside operated by the British military. The course for journalists and NGO personnel simulates the modern battlefield: militias, snipers, car accidents, serious wounds. After his experience in the much different (and less dangerous) environment of Haiti, David Wood also argues that journalists should accept military training. He proposes that pool reporters meet physical fitness standards, train with military vehicles and weapons, and take a battlefield survival course: how to behave in a firefight or ambush, rudimentary first aid, "creative MRE cuisine." Wood acknowledges the dangers of what might amount to military "licensing" of journalists. He writes:

> Journalists, to state the obvious, are not soldiers. But like any other assignment, we do have an obligation to come prepared to report the story: to be knowledgeable about the military; to fit unobtrusively into the military environment; and to be self-sufficient enough as to not require the military to provide the minders and keepers we profess not to need.[94]

Limit to Freedom (II): The Camera

In reporting on peace operations, as elsewhere, the camera is a double-edged sword. The presence of a camera often seems to change the event being recorded or prevents it from being recorded at all—and many things that are recorded are deemed too terrible to be shown on the evening news. Yet pictures and video give a story certain powers that words alone cannot.

Although much of the recent debate over television has focused on its powers to show graphic and disturbing images from around the world, there are real limits to this power. Many studies have found editors and television producers reluctant to use the most graphic photos or footage of war: "an editorial preference rooted in their relations with the audience, advertisers, military families and the military, as well as cultural norms."[95] This self-restraint was confirmed by a producer at one of the major networks. The network did not air some of the most graphic footage, including scenes of decapitated torsos, it had from the February 1994 marketplace massacre in Sarajevo. "You must make decisions about what is too gory to put on the air," the producer said. "There is a self-monitoring process. Any producer who says there isn't is not being truthful." A similar filter was used when the Iraqi regime used chemical weapons on its Kurdish citizens in the town of Halabja in March 1988. "Some of the pictures were horrific. You would just not put them on."[96] This phenomenon can also be seen in the public's reaction to U.S. newspapers' use of Paul Watson's photograph of the dead U.S. soldier being dragged through the streets of Mogadishu. A survey found that of thirty-four major U.S. dailies, eleven ran the photograph on the front page, fifteen used it on inside pages, and eight did not use it at all. Newspapers that did run the picture received hundreds of complaints. Among the complainants to the *Norfolk Virginian-Pilot* was the soldier's mother, who discovered her son's fate when she saw the picture.[97]

Print reporters know that their stories do not have the same impact without pictures, still or moving. "You had to package the story. It's not enough to come upon it. You have to make it credible. . . . You have to have the pictures," Roy Gutman said of his reports on the concentration camps in Bosnia. In mid-July, Gutman went to northern Bosnia with freelance photographer Andree Kaiser, who covertly took pictures of Muslim prisoners having their heads shaved at the Manjaca camp. By that time, Gutman had heard reports of mass killings at another camp, in a former iron-mining facility at Omarska. The reporter-photographer team could not get to the site. Gutman's dispatch detailing what was happening at Omarska was published, without any pictures of the camp, on August 2, 1992, a Sunday. On August 6, Britain's ITN broadcast the first, shocking television images of emaciated inmates at the Omarska and Trnopolje camps, images that immediately recalled the Nazi concentration camps. Both Gutman and Ed Vulliamy of *The Guardian*, who accompanied the ITN team, believe that television greatly increased the impact of their stories. Yet it is unlikely that obtrusive television cameras would have been able to break the story on their own, Gutman noted. Cameras "can't find out what's really going on. They can show you what seems to be going on. . . . It's only if you don't have the television cameras and the lights on, you can go around asking questions, quietly."[98]

When ABC News tried to follow up on another part of Gutman's stories, the rape of Muslim women in detention camps, it ran into difficulties. Though Gutman found the experience painful and difficult, he had been able to interview some of the women. ABC found it "virtually impossible" to cover their story, according to Logan, even though the network sent in female reporters and camera crews. "It's sometimes easier to talk to people when you don't have a camera," she said. "We are picture-driven."

Keith Richburg was critical of television crews' intrusiveness in Somalia and wrote an article about the problem for the *Washington Post*.[99] But he said there was another side to television as well. "I didn't mind TV showing up at some [event], because it meant my story had a better chance of getting on the front page." Richburg knew his editors would be watching.[100]

4

The Push

The News Media and Intervention

> "The dictatorship of the fourth power, the dictatorship of the TV picture, horrifying millions of people with images of mass violence, urges us to adopt humanitarian decisions and to avoid political ones."
> —*Georgian president Eduard Shevardnadze*

This chapter examines the news media's role in shaping U.S. government decisions about post Cold War interventions overseas. First, I review some cases in which the media seemed to help propel the dispatch of American forces abroad on peace operations. Next, I examine several cases in which the power of news media reports was far weaker or even negligible. The findings suggest that the news media's impact is highly dependent on the nature of the proposed intervention and the degree to which government policy is in flux, and that this impact may decline over time. Finally, I discuss the news media's past—and, in all likelihood, future—failure to provide early warning of crises.

The First Post–Cold War Peace Operation: Northern Iraq

On April 16, 1991, President Bush announced at a White House news conference that he was sending U.S. troops to northern Iraq to aid hundreds of thousands of Kurdish refugees. The Kurds had fled to the forbidding mountains along the Iraq-Turkey border, and east to Iran, to escape bombing and strafing by Saddam Hussein's army. Bush's announcement was a clear change of policy: at least half a dozen times in the previous two weeks he had set the limits of what the United States could do to help the Kurds. He wanted to bring American troops home from the just-concluded Persian Gulf War as quickly as possible and, as he put it as early as April 3, not "see us get sucked into the internal civil war inside Iraq."[1] Bush's action and that of the British and French governments also represented a turning point for the international community's response to humanitarian crises. Although not specifically authorized by the United Nations, Operation Provide Comfort was launched under the umbrella of UN Security Council Resolution 688 of April 5, which for the first time deemed a sovereign state's repression of its own citizens a threat to "international peace and security" under Chapter VII of the UN Charter.

Western reporters and cameras already in the region to cover the Gulf War dramatically captured the Kurds' plight. The video and still images they showed to the world—mothers burying sons and daughters on the rocky mountainside, children burned by napalm, miles-long lines of refugees snaking up the snowy mountains—were critical to Bush's policy switch, according to news accounts at the time and subsequent statements by the president's top aides. Bush himself alluded to these images at the April 16 news conference, saying: "No one can see the pictures or hear the accounts of this human suffering—men, women, and most painfully of all, innocent children—and not be deeply moved."[2] Said Richard Haass, director of Near East and South Asian affairs on Bush's National Security Council staff: "I would be the very first to admit that I think television probably had the greatest impact at this time in pushing us through the various phases of policy than at any time during the [Gulf] crisis.... The political and the human desire to respond to what was unfolding on the screen had a sizable impact." Haass was echoed by Paul Wolfowitz, the undersecretary of defense for policy: "I do think the vividness of TV images probably heightened the sense of urgency.... I think the inescapable fact was that you had a half a million people who, if nothing was done, were liable to all die and start dying rather quickly."[3] Those same images also jolted British prime minister John Major.[4] He became the moving force behind the establishment of encampments protected from Saddam by Western militaries that patrolled a "no-fly" zone over northern Iraq and designed to draw the Kurds out of the perilous mountains and back toward their homes.

There were factors in play that made the images of suffering more politically potent than they otherwise might have been. On several occasions, Bush had called on the Iraqi people to take matters into their own hands and remove Saddam from power. While he never specifically mentioned the Kurds in the north or the Shiites in the south, those groups did rise up and were mercilessly suppressed by the remnants of Saddam's army that had survived the U.S. onslaught of Desert Storm. Spokesmen for the Kurds pointed to radio broadcasts over the U.S.-supported Voice of Free Iraq and said they had been encouraged to revolt, only to be abandoned by Washington in the face of Saddam's assaults. Throughout the first half of April, reporters repeatedly questioned Bush about his responsibility for the Kurds' fate. The administration was "taking on a lot of water," recalled State Department spokeswoman Margaret Tutwiler. While not admitting responsibility, "[w]e did have to act," she said. "We acted with a symbol, which was a picture."[5] The Bush administration thus entered the public arena with its own counterimages. The picture was Secretary of State James A. Baker III visiting the remote camps of human flotsam, showing that the United States cared about the fate of the Kurdish refugees. The visit was Tutwiler's idea. "It was not only the visual I knew would come out of there," she said. "It was sending a symbol . . . to all of our allies" that the United States was committed and would act.[6] Baker and his staff went to considerable trouble to ensure that the symbol was seen. A stop in Turkey was added to a previously planned trip to the Middle East. Baker, his staff, and accompanying journalists flew from Ankara to Diyarbikar in southeastern Turkey, where they switched to helicopters for the long flight into the mountains. At the village of Cukurca, they took jeeps up muddy hillsides to the encampments. Baker's April 8 arrival coincided with the White House's first, limited response to the tragedy: a U.S. Air Force airdrop of food, blankets, clothing, and other relief supplies to the desperate Kurds that had been announced three days before. The secretary of state spent a total of seven minutes with the refugees. Like many reporters, Alan Elsner of Reuters wire service mentioned the brevity of the visit in the middle of his story. But Elsner's dispatch—one of the first accounts of the visit to be transmitted around the world—was headlined: "Baker Spends Seven Minutes at Site of Kurdish Refugee Tragedy."[7] The dispatch enraged Baker and his aides; its content was clearly antithetical to the message of caring they had hoped to send. Tutwiler recalled it without prompting four years later. "I was semi-livid. . . . Taking the press with you is not always a guarantee" of positive coverage.[8]

Andrew Natsios, then director of OFDA, saw less of a media impact during the crisis. Two major geopolitical considerations drove policy at the time, Natsios said. The first was concern for Turkey, one of Washington's closest Muslim allies, which had played an invaluable supporting role in the coalition against Iraq. Turkey, with its own Kurdish "problem," had no desire to take in hundreds of thousands of destitute Kurdish refugees. The second consideration affecting policy was that other groups in Iraq seeking to oust Saddam Hussein might think again if the Kurdish rebels were abandoned completely. Even if the cameras had not been there, the Bush administration "would have made the same decision," Natsios said. But the news media accelerated the decision-making: it "simply brought it to [the president's] attention much faster." The policymaking process was telescoped into six to ten days, which was "fairly rapid" given the complicating factor of Iraq's sovereignty over the area, he noted.[9]

The emotive images from the mountains put President Bush between two competing priorities, as unwelcome TV images so often do. On one side was his fervent desire to bring U.S. troops home and end the Persian Gulf War cleanly, while staying out of a potential civil war in Iraq. On the other side was the need to respond to the pictures and the pressure from the Washington press corps that came with them. The images did not appear in a policy vacuum but reinforced other geostrategic motivations and a sense of U.S. responsibility. Bush chose to act, first with the airlift and then by establishing "safe zones," in a manner that would meet both his policy goals. As Haass put it, "This was an attempt to meet *a pressing humanitarian need without getting physically involved on the ground. There was a fear of getting bogged down.*"[10] The images helped push the president toward a different policy, one with which the military in particular was uncomfortable.[11] But the images' effect went only so far—Bush had a firm, frequently articulated policy on the civil war in Iraq, and the United States stayed out of it.

Finally, if the images from northern Iraq did help initiate humanitarian action but nothing more on Bush's part, that effect of the news media was in tune with public opinion. Fifty-three percent of respondents to a *Newsweek*/Gallup poll opposed taking military action to help either the

Kurdish or Shiite rebels; 78 percent favored providing them with food and medical aid.[12] The U.S. public, as it has many times before and since, opposed involvement in another country's internal affairs but favored providing humanitarian aid. Bush aptly captured the public mood in an exchange with reporters on April 11: "We are going to do what is right by these refugees, and I think the American people expect that, and they want that. But I don't think they want to see us bogged down in a civil war by sending in the 82nd Airborne or the 101st or the 7th Cavalry."[13]

The Role of Images: Somalia 1992

"CNN got us into Somalia, and CNN got us out." That is the popular explanation of television's role in the U.S. military intervention in Somalia, an explanation accepted by many government and media leaders in the United States.

One would expect television's policymaking impact—especially that of CNN's round-the-clock, real-time broadcasts—to be found in Somalia if it is to be found anywhere. Indeed, many officials of the Bush administration who participated in the decision making on Somalia in the summer and fall of 1992 said they felt that the graphic, often pitiful television images of famine victims helped change U.S. policy and overcome the military's strong resistance to involvement. But these officials were deeply divided over how crucial television's role was, some saying it was the deciding factor, others saying it was but one of many factors in the decision-making process. Clearly, a closer examination is needed. Precisely what role did the images play? Why were they able to have an impact? What other factors were involved? How did those images make their way onto the television screen in the first place? No conclusion about television's impact—and that of other media—can be reached without looking at the broader context surrounding President Bush's decisions in 1992 regarding Somalia.

Bush's first major action in the Somalia crisis was to launch a massive U.S. military airlift, overruling a reluctant Pentagon.[14] Operation Provide Relief was to get food to the Somali interior (as well as northern Kenya), bypassing clan violence that had blocked earlier attempts to deliver relief supplies. Bush decided on the airlift August 12 and announced it two days later. What role did televised images play in Bush's decision? Prior to the

August 14 announcement, the three major U.S. television networks had broadcast reports that mentioned Somalia only fifteen times in 1992 (Figures 4.1 and 4.2). Thirteen of those reports showed scenes of suffering, but nearly half (six) showed only fleeting glimpses of Somalia's plight as part of one-minute or forty-second news roundups that covered many other subjects as well. CNN's coverage was equally skimpy prior to the White House's announcement.[15] This low level of reporting, evidence that television networks did not accord Somalia a high priority before mid-August 1992, raises questions about how large an influence televised images had on Bush's first major decision regarding Somalia.

Of course, senior decision makers, including the president, do not rely solely on television for information on foreign crises. In Somalia, other media had an impact on the policymaking process, if not on policy. In late June 1992, U.S. ambassador to Kenya Smith Hempstone, visited northeastern Kenya, along the border with Somalia, to survey the desperate famine conditions there. He described the conditions in a powerful cable (it came to be known as the "Day in Hell" cable) that reached Washington in early July. The cable found its way to Bush's desk. According to Natsios, the president wrote in the cable's margins: "This is very, very upsetting. I want more information." The National Security Council staff passed Bush's instructions on to Natsios and Herman Cohen, the assistant secretary of state for African affairs.[16] That same month, Acting Secretary of State Eagleburger told his staff that the president wanted the State Department to be "forward leaning" on Somalia.[17] Bush is also thought to have been affected by Jane Perlez's account of Somalia's desperation that ran on the front page of the *New York Times* on July 19.[18]

The influence that the U.S. government's own relief agencies exerted on the decision-making process, directly and indirectly through the media, was substantial. The role of relief organizations and U.S. relief officials discussed in the last chapter bears additional examination here since they played a particularly important—perhaps even decisive—role in generating media coverage of the Somalia famine and influencing internal policy debates. Natsios had long taken an activist approach toward the news media, treating the press corps as a "resource of government." He lunched monthly with reporters over lasagna and wine and "developed a cadre of people I could rely on to report on [disaster relief]." In late 1991 and early 1992, at a time when OFDA already was launching a traditional response

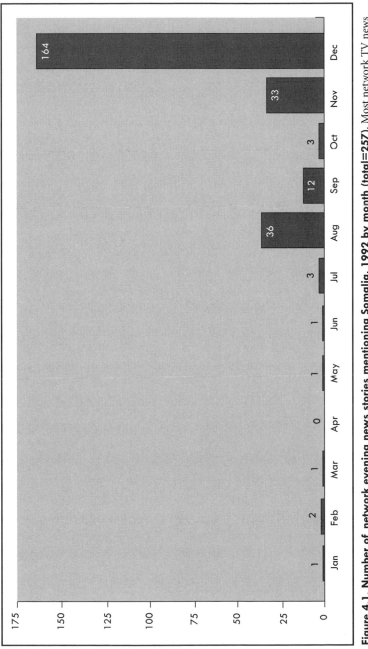

Figure 4.1. Number of network evening news stories mentioning Somalia, 1992 by month (total=257). Most network TV news reporting on Somalia in 1992 followed rather than preceded policy actions by President Bush (in August and November). The networks paid little attention to Somalia in the first seven months of the year, even as hunger and disease in the country worsened. Data source: Network Evening News Abstracts, Television News Archives, Vanderbilt University.

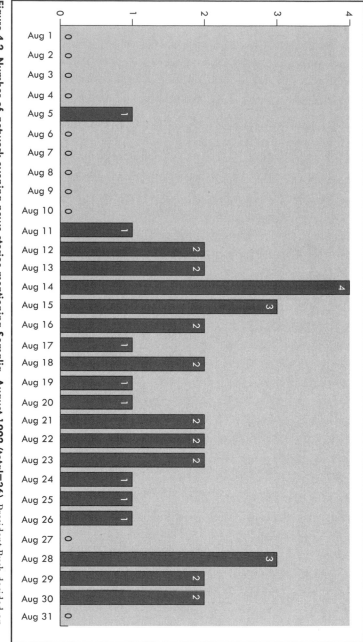

Figure 4.2. Number of network evening news stories mentioning Somalia, August 1992 (total=36). President Bush decided on an airlift to Somalia on August 12, 1992, and announced it publicly on August 14. Network news coverage rose just prior to the announcement and then continued as television devoted its first sustained attention to a problem that Bush had now deemed worthy of a military intervention. Data source: Network Evening News Abstracts, Television News Archives, Vanderbilt University.

to the famine, Natsios tried to draw public and government attention to
what was happening in Somalia with interviews and press briefings. The
briefings were sparsely attended. Throughout the first half of 1992, according to Cohen, the official position of the U.S. government was that Somalia's problem was one of food, not one of security that might require forceful action by the United Nations or the United States. Both Cohen and
Natsios, who was by now an assistant administrator of AID, disagreed with
this policy. Cohen recalls his colleague's strategy: "What does Natsios do?
He starts giving monthly or weekly reports" on how many people are
dying or at risk in Somalia. Natsios would hold weekly meetings with representatives of the NGOs. "They all are in there, planning strategy: . . . how
do you inform the world?" said Cohen, who, as an ally, attended one such
session. Because Natsios focused on the suffering and dying, he could
depart from the official policy "in a way that he couldn't be called on the
carpet," Cohen said. "This is a clear example of the government using the
media—elements of the government."[19] As the situation in Somalia worsened over the summer, these efforts began to bear fruit. News media coverage was beginning to snowball, as major newspapers, including the *New
York Times* and the *Washington Post*, began to devote more resources to the
story. (It appears that television followed newspapers in covering Somalia,
not vice versa.) OFDA director Jim Kunder traveled to Somalia in July. His
August 3 press conference upon returning to Washington was well attended.
He told the reporters that one-fourth of the Somali population was at risk
of starvation and one-fourth of children under five already had died.[20]
Much later, Natsios and Kunder were at a ceremony to receive awards for
their service to AID. As he presented the awards, Acting Administrator
Scott Spangler told Natsios: "You and Jim, Andrew, manipulated the media
to get us into Somalia. . . . The reason AID has been so involved is because
you used the media to drive policy, including us." Spangler was only half
joking.[21] "It's [a question of] who's manipulating who," Cohen said. "It
started with government manipulating press and then changed to press
manipulating the government." If the images had an impact, it was because the U.S. government had pressured itself into acting.

Another source of pressure came from members of Congress, particu-
larly Senators Paul Simon and Nancy Kassebaum, the chairman and senior
Republican, respectively, of the Senate Foreign Relations Committee's
Africa subcommittee. Kassebaum, who had visited Somalia in early July,

testified on July 22 before the House Select Committee on Hunger. "I strongly support sending a United Nations security force to Somalia," she said. Over the next three weeks, both the House and the Senate passed resolutions urging the United Nations to dispatch forces to Somalia. This congressional activity provided much of the basis for the modest increase in television reports on Somalia in late July and early August 1992. Once again, television did not lead, but followed policy action or proposals.[22]

Bush's decision to mount Operation Provide Relief is more important than generally realized and merits more attention than it has received.[23] It "created an activist consensus in the national security bureaucracy where none had existed earlier."[24] It altered the dynamics for the news media as well. Beginning on August 14, the media's attention to the story increased greatly and, for the first time, planeloads of journalists began heading to Somalia to cover the increased U.S. military activity. A close look at the patterns of reporting on Somalia indicates that, throughout 1992, the attention of the news media—television in particular—was cued by policy statements or actions by the U.S. government. In other words, sharp increases in media coverage *followed*, rather than *preceded*, the administration's actions. The policymakers affected the media more than—or at least before—the media affected them. The lesson here is that by taking the first step into Somalia, the Bush administration opened itself up to greater potential influence from the news media. Once the decision was taken, reporters and camera crews from around the world began to converge on Somalia and report back on a tragedy that had been going on for many months while the world paid only sporadic attention.[25]

Television reporting patterns (Figures 4.1 and 4.2) bear out this tendency of the news media to follow rather than lead. From Bush's August 14 announcement of the airlift to the end of that month, there were thirty network evening news reports on Somalia, roughly five times the number in the first two weeks of August. In September, network news attention cooled, returning to the early August level. Somalia almost disappeared from the map in October and early November, no doubt because of the 1992 presidential election. There were eighteen reports between the election and Bush's November 25 decision to launch Operation Restore Hope. That decision leaked to the media almost immediately, prompting coverage that was far above previous levels. There were ninety-five reports between November 25 and December 9, the day U.S. troops landed near

Mogadishu. The level of network coverage fell within a few days of the landing, although it remained relatively high through year's end. CNN's reporting patterns are similar to those of ABC, CBS, and NBC. If anything, CNN's reporting seemed to be even more closely tied to political debate and action.

I now turn to President Bush's decision in late November 1992 to send twenty-eight thousand U.S. troops to Somalia to secure delivery routes so that food and other supplies that were being stolen or impeded could reach desperate Somalis. Bush, who at that point had been defeated for a second term in office, opened another new chapter in humanitarian-relief interventions. It ended ultimately in the deaths of thirty U.S. servicemen, the withdrawal of U.S. troops, and a sea change in the country's political debate about participation in peace operations. But it is important to remember that, in making the decision, Bush and his senior advisers thought that the United States could achieve great benefits at low cost and then quickly hand the burden over to the United Nations. According to interviews with senior policy officials, as well as written accounts, many factors went into Bush's decision. Televised images of suffering were just one factor, albeit a persistent and important one. I will examine each of these factors before coming to some conclusions about television's role in pushing the United States into Somalia.

Somalia Was Not Bosnia

Throughout the summer and fall of 1992, the Bush administration's policy toward Somalia was closely linked to its policy in another crisis—Bosnia. The pressure to act in Somalia came from two fronts.

First, there was growing restiveness among Islamic nations and the developing world in general about the West's failure to come to the aid of Muslims in either Bosnia or Somalia. The Bush administration had resisted pressure for military intervention in Bosnia following the outbreak of fighting there in April 1992, when the Bosnian Serbs launched a brutal campaign of ethnic cleansing against Bosnian Muslims. U.S. hesitancy to protect the Muslims contrasted with its active use of the UN Security Council to go to war against Iraq, a Muslim nation. According to Bush's national security adviser, Brent Scowcroft, UN secretary general Boutros Boutros-Ghali had told the president that there was growing unrest among developing nations at the developed world's use of the Security Council to tackle only the problems it was interested in. Somalia was black, Muslim, and outside the developed world. "Here was a way to restore faith" in U.S. foreign policy, Scowcroft said.[26]

Second, the policy attention that the former Yugoslavia was receiving in Washington and New York contrasted with the lack of attention to Somalia, a much deadlier tragedy purely in terms of lives lost and at risk. This contrast was a persistent theme in news reports and comments by opinion makers and major international figures in the weeks leading up to Bush's earlier decision on Operation Provide Relief. In late July, Boutros-Ghali had accused the Security Council of "fighting a rich man's war in Yugoslavia while not lifting a finger to save Somalia from disintegration."[27] That challenge weighed on Bush's mind in August, according to Scowcroft. Boutros-Ghali's critique was echoed by members of Congress and by both the print and television news media at the time Bush decided to launch the airlift. On August 12, the day of the decision, the *Washington Post* printed a dispatch by Richburg, headlined "Somalia's Overshadowed Tragedy: World Anxious about Balkan Turmoil, Aloof to That in Africa." That same day, the *New York Times* carried a column by Anna Quindlen with the same theme.[28] The next evening, ABC News aired a lengthy report comparing the differences in the U.S. reaction to Bosnia and Somalia. Whether these news reports, coming as late as they did, could have affected the decision-making process is an open question.

The Bush administration chose intervention in Somalia because it was judged to be "easier" (that is, it carried fewer risks) than Bosnia and deflected unwanted pressures for taking action in the Balkans. Comparing Somalia and Bosnia, former secretary of state Lawrence Eagleburger said the administration could act in Somalia "because we knew the costs weren't so great and there were some potential benefits." Eagleburger said his own mind was made up after reading a pair of November 12 memos from Robert Gallucci, the assistant secretary of state for politico-military affairs, arguing for forceful U.S. action in both Bosnia and Somalia. Eagleburger said he called Gallucci in, listened to his arguments, and told him: "I don't agree with you on one, but you're right on the other." "Gallucci's memo was what decided me," Eagleburger said.[29] This was the second time, following the Hempstone cable, that an internal written communication had a significant impact on the decision-making process regarding Somalia. Gallucci said he was affected by television images, but even more so by increasingly dire reports from officers in his bureau who coordinated airborne relief efforts in both Bosnia and Somalia. "It's not only the images," he said. "It's that you actually have contact" with conditions on the ground. Frustrated that U.S. efforts were helping only around the edges of the two crises, Gallucci delivered to Eagleburger two one-and-a-half-page memos prepared by his staff. One argued for providing a safe environment for delivering food in Somalia. The other made the case for a "reasonable" U.S. military presence in Bosnia, which would attract more European troops, creating pockets of security and thus a chance for a peaceful settlement. In the meeting, Gallucci acknowledged that Bosnia represented a higher risk for U.S. forces and that it might be more difficult to limit the military mission there. A few days later, Eagleburger called him back following a White House meeting. "He said, 'You're one for two. We're going to do Somalia,'" Gallucci recalled.[30] Gen. Colin Powell, chairman of the Joint Chiefs of Staff, had predicated his support for Restore Hope on the condition that the United States would attempt no such mission in Bosnia.[31]

The Mission Seemed "Doable" at Low Cost

Senior Bush administration officials were unanimous in saying that, when they decided to intervene in Somalia, they were taking on a mission they believed and intended would be low cost and limited in duration and would achieve great benefit. In other words, even if one concludes that televised images forced the Bush administration to act in Somalia, *the images worked along a narrow portion of the spectrum of foreign and national security policy concerns*: a massive humanitarian disaster that seemed to be amenable to a quick solution without U.S. forces being engaged in major combat.[32]

Moreover, the Bush administration already was invested in Somalia by virtue of the airlift and other relief programs. By mid-October, it had become clear to administration officials that the airlift and other piecemeal approaches were not stemming the hunger and violence in Somalia. The UN peacekeeping mission, UNOSOM I, was not fully deployed, with the first five hundred Pakistani soldiers pinned down at the Mogadishu airport. "We were faced with acknowledging defeat and letting all of the areas where the refugees were starve to death . . . or do[ing] something," Scowcroft said.[33] With the presidential election over, the White House in November came under more intense pressure from a variety of sources to take stronger action. Television and other news media again began to pay attention to Somalia, the worsening conditions there, and the failure of ongoing efforts to stop the dying. Congress was again calling for action. Relief groups were also active: InterAction sent the letter to the president that was mentioned in the previous chapter. As these pressures added up, the question became, "What could we do about it, and what were the consequences?" according to Eagleburger. "We decided we could do something about it."[34] It was at this point, in mid-November, that the option of a major deployment of U.S. ground forces to secure relief delivery routes became the focus of discussion. "It looked like that was doable. It was doable in a relatively short period of time," Scowcroft said. "There was an easy consensus on doing something in Somalia."[35]

The final precondition for Bush's decision fell into place when the U.S. military hinted it would not oppose a large-scale American intervention. Senior military officials never actually recommended this step. But in a meeting of the Deputies Committee, the subcabinet body that was considering policy alternatives, the military representative, Gen. Barry McCaffrey, stated the Pentagon's belief that the United Nations was not up to the task. If there was a mission to be done, the U.S. military would rather be in command.[36] This statement shifted the focus of policy debate to a U.S.-led intervention in Somalia, and it represented a "complete turnaround" in Pentagon thinking from five months earlier.[37] At a November 21 Deputies Committee meeting, Adm. David Jeremiah, deputy to Joint Chiefs of Staff chairman Powell, shocked all present by stating that U.S. ground forces "can do the job" in Somalia.[38] Four days later, Bush met with his senior advisers, including Scowcroft and Gen. Powell, to decide which of the options to choose. According to Scowcroft, Powell gave a military briefing in which he "went through all the negatives, as a good military officer would do." These included concerns over whether there could be a smooth, rapid handoff to UN peacekeepers once the mission of establishing security for relief operations was complete. However, Scowcroft said, Gen. Powell was "quite obviously" on board.[39] Bush accepted the military's recommendation, choosing a mission that all concerned thought would be limited in time and scope.

The Role of the President's Personality and Experiences

Ultimately, it was President Bush who made the decision to dispatch U.S. troops to Somalia.[40] If the pictures affected him, they did so on the basis of the president's personality, experiences, and strongly held views of the United States' role in the world. Bush's written instructions on the margins of Hempstone's July cable are evidence of presidential concern and engagement on the issue. Bush had a long-standing interest in Africa, having made eighteen trips there as vice president. And, in the wake of the Persian Gulf War, he had campaigned for a greater role for the United Nations and multilateralism as part of his New World Order.

Natsios recalled being present at a December 1992 meeting between Bush and Phil Johnston, president of the relief organization CARE and acting director of UN humanitarian operations in Somalia. During the discussion, Bush recalled a visit that he, as vice president, and his wife made in the mid-1980s to a CARE feeding center in the Sudan. "Barbara and I will never forget all those children who were dying," Natsios quoted Bush as saying. "I know why Bush made that decision," Natsios said. "He then said, 'No one should have to die at Christmastime.' . . . It's not more complicated than that."[41]

The Role of Images

"Every American has seen the shocking images from Somalia." With those words, President Bush informed the nation on December 4, 1992 that he was dispatching American troops to the Horn of Africa.[42] Bush's words can be seen two ways: as imputing cause or as an effort to explain the action he was taking, relating it to what many viewers already had seen.

It is clear that the effect of the images broadcast on CNN, ABC, NBC, and CBS is far less—and much different—than is widely assumed. The pictures of the dead and dying, the refugees, and the hopelessness in Somalia did not push the United States into that country in the summer and fall of 1992. Indeed, given the patterns of reporting, they could not have. Rather, television took its cue from elsewhere—the actions of the U.S. government, the well-crafted public diplomacy of some government officials, statements by members of Congress and relief groups. The media's role in Somalia was remarkably similar to that described by Daniel Hallin in Vietnam—it reflected the tone of the policy debate in Washington.[43]

Yet this does not mean that television played no role whatsoever in the decision. Brent Scowcroft, Lawrence Eagleburger, Herman Cohen, and others questioned whether the U.S. government would have taken the same action in the absence of the gripping images on American TV screens. As Scowcroft put it, "I'd like to say, 'Yes, we would have done it anyway.' But I don't know."[44] The images were a necessary, but not a sufficient, condition for U.S. action. Although it was not by accident or media independence, once those images appeared, they accentuated the other factors that went into the decision. Along with internal communications, they helped bring the urgency of the issue to the attention of senior decision makers, including the president. Perhaps the best way to describe the role of images is that, rather than determining the direction of U.S. foreign policy, they shaped the environment in which decisions were made. Eagleburger expressed this best, saying that Gallucci's argument for action in Somalia had extra power because of the pressure coming from the media and Congress in mid-November 1992. "It fell on fertile soil," he said.[45]

The cases of northern Iraq and Somalia illustrate how, in specific circumstances, televised images can reinforce other policy considerations that point to the launching of a peace operation for humanitarian purposes. The two cases had several important factors in common. The United States already had a policy stake in northern Iraq (by virtue of having just fought the Persian Gulf War) and Somalia at the time of the November 25 decision (an airlift and other relief efforts already were under way). Those previous policy actions meant that the news media already were present in force in the affected areas. Their presence should not be surprising, given the findings of the preceding two chapters about parachute journalism, new communications technologies, and the open environment that peace operations offer to reporters. More important than this, however, is that in each case, the Bush administration responded to a narrowly drawn (but in human terms, massive) humanitarian problem. The policy decisions specifically excluded any combat role for U.S. forces in the civil wars that plagued the two countries. The Somalia mission began that way, even if it did not end that way.

Reflecting on his experiences with Bosnia and Somalia, Gallucci said that pictures "don't come anywhere near" forcing a deployment of U.S. ground troops when it is known they will be in harm's way. "When you're short of that, then the pictures are very useful in getting people to focus on it as a basis for humanitarian support." Pictures of suffering can bring the far away closer, Gallucci said. But for anything more than that, "It's gotta answer the question, Why us?"[46]

The Limits of Television's Power: Rwanda and Bosnia

In early July 1994, the Tutsi-dominated RPF seized control of Kigali, sparking the flight of an estimated two million refugees, mostly Hutus, across Rwanda's borders. It was one of the swiftest mass movements of people in history. There seems little doubt that televised images of this flood of humanity and the refugees' desperate condition helped propel President Clinton to announce on July 22 that the U.S. military would immediately begin a massive effort to assist the UNHCR and other relief agencies in dealing with the tragedy. Several officials spoke of feeling a strong sense of public pressure to "do something" as pictures filled the television screens. "The public awareness of what was going on clearly motivated us," said a Defense Department official. While the U.S. government's first inclination was to stay out of Rwanda, "[i]t just seemed impossible to stand back and not do anything."[47]

On July 14, AID administrator J. Brian Atwood had just returned to his Jerusalem hotel after becoming the first senior U.S. official to meet in the Gaza Strip with Palestine Liberation Organization chairman Yasser Arafat. With an hour to himself, he turned on CNN, hoping to see how the visit was playing. A CNN lead-in announced that the story would be broadcast at the top of the hour. Atwood waited, with increasing frustration, as "one story after another about this Rwanda situation" was reported instead. "What was becoming obvious was that Rwanda was becoming a huge story in this country." Then the White House called. Atwood was instructed to go to Goma, Zaire, site of one of the largest refugee camps. There he found "an encampment of cameras." He surveyed the situation, did an interview with NBC, and then flew to Nairobi. The White House called again. "We got word it would be useful to do some more television out there to describe the problem," Atwood recalled. He returned to Goma and did four more television interviews, including *CBS Morning News*, NBC's *Today*, and *The MacNeil/Lehrer NewsHour*. Like Baker during his visit to the Kurds, Atwood and his superiors were both being influenced by television and using it as a tool of influence. The American people wanted a response "because they saw these pictures. If the administration had decided that we weren't going to respond, I think there would have been tremendous pressure" and criticism, Atwood said. "I wanted to show President Clinton's interest in this terrible situation."[48]

Yet what is most notable about the Rwanda case is not the power of television images, but the shallow and limited nature of that power. The crisis in central Africa broke into the world's consciousness on April 6, 1994, when an airplane carrying the Hutu presidents of Rwanda and Burundi crashed mysteriously near the Kigali airport. In Rwanda, an apparently well-planned mass slaughter of Tutsi and moderate Hutus was unleashed, urged on by Radio Mille Collines. The three major broadcast networks gave fairly heavy coverage (Figure 4.3) to the slaughter and related international developments. In fact, Rwanda was covered more heavily on the network evening news during April and May 1994 than Somalia was in any month during 1992, excluding December, when Bush announced his decision to deploy U.S. troops. Yet the images from Rwanda of ethnic warfare and its grisly results held no power to move the U.S. administration to intervene or to move the public to demand that it do so. Referring to widely seen footage of corpses floating down a Rwandan river, a senior U.S. official said:

> None of those provoked or provided the kind of catalyst for a U.S. military intervention. . . . The [later scenes of refugee] camps were a different matter. . . . The mind-numbingness of it all was almost a made-to-order operation for what the U.S. can do and do very quickly. But it was into a basically benign environment.[49]

Atwood said he felt sure the public would not have supported an earlier U.S. deployment to halt the civil war, a sentiment echoed by many other officials. A U.S. Army officer who went to Rwanda as part of Operation Support Hope said: "The mission was to stop the dying. . . . Has that solved the problem in Rwanda? No. It's a civil war, and it's still going on today." He added: "It's disheartening. It's really disheartening. But I know the military can't solve that civil war. And I know the American people wouldn't want us to solve that civil war. Is that selfish? No."[50] Policymakers probably read the public mood correctly. Julia Taft, president of InterAction, the coalition of U.S.-based NGOs, said that when pictures were shown of Rwandans being hacked to death, private relief groups "got virtually no money whatsoever" from the viewing public. That did not change until the refugees flooded into Zaire and there were "pictures of women and children, . . . innocents in need."[51]

More powerful than the images in determining U.S. policy in Rwanda were the recent experience in Somalia and the new, more restrictive U.S.

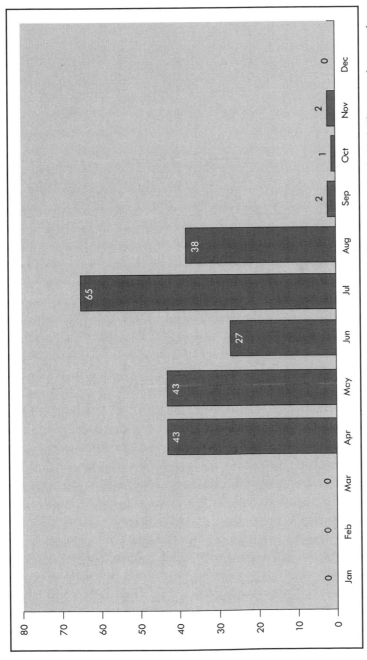

Figure 4.3. Number of network evening news stories mentioning Rwanda, 1994 by month (total=221). The networks covered the slaughter in Rwanda in April and May 1994 more heavily than they covered Somalia in 1992, excluding the U.S. troop deployment in December of that year. But the images from Rwanda had no impact on U.S. policy until their content changed in July, when hundreds of thousands of helpless refugees fled for the country's borders. Data source: Network Evening News Abstracts, Television News Archives, Vanderbilt University.

position on engaging in peace operations that was shaped by that experience. The new policy was made public in May 1994, as the slaughter in Rwanda was under way.[52] It provided the rationale for the U.S. government's decision not to intervene in central Africa as the fighting was taking place and to oppose the dispatch of 5,500 UN peacekeepers, contributing to a long delay in assembling the force.[53] When the problem in Rwanda became less about slaughter and more about sick and hungry refugees, Clinton ordered a massive U.S. airlift and dispatched 2,350 soldiers to help the United Nations and NGOs halt the deaths. A senior Defense Department official confirmed the impact of the new policy and the Somalia experience on these decisions. Especially potent was the criterion that U.S. forces participating in multilateral peace operations have a clear "exit strategy."[54] "'Exit strategy' was the mantra," the Pentagon official said. "Those two words—I can't overemphasize how those two words drove policy on intervention after Somalia." A huge logistical effort by the U.S. military in support of humanitarian relief also met the new policy's criterion that U.S. forces should be deployed only if they were uniquely necessary for the operation's success. "Everyone felt comfortable enough that that was a specific job that we could" perform, the official said. Before, during the slaughter, "we didn't see that clear picture."[55] In short, the presence of a firm policy moderated the potential effect of the images, keeping the administration to a narrow course of action its advocates and critics still bitterly dispute.

In this environment, the news media themselves were an additional factor in keeping the United States *out* of Rwanda in anything more than a highly circumscribed way. Officials knew that the television cameras would instantly transmit news of U.S. casualties or other setbacks. The Pentagon adopted what one official called "the Souter strategy"—a reference to President Bush's quiet, uncontroversial Supreme Court nominee—that called for U.S. troops to be behind the scenes as much as possible. Fears about a backlash from the media and the public "limited us to only being involved in the humanitarian operation and not the peacekeeping operation," the official said.[56]

Before the cease-fire in Bosnia and the introduction of U.S. troops in late 1995 as part of the Implementation Force (IFOR) to carry out the Dayton peace accords, there had been numerous points during the preceding four and a half years at which the Bush and Clinton administrations might have intervened with U.S. combat forces in an attempt to stop the wars in the former Yugoslavia. A detailed study of recent U.S. foreign policy toward the Balkans is beyond the scope of this study. Rather, I will focus on the late summer and fall of 1992, when, arguably, media pressures on the U.S. government for action were most intense.

On Sunday, August 2, 1992, under the headline, "Death Camps," *Newsday* published Roy Gutman's dispatch that reported for the first time in detail how the Bosnian Serbs were engaged in a "systematic slaughter" of Muslims and Croats in a manner not seen in Europe since Nazi Germany.[57] The resulting furor rose to a new level four days later, when Britain's ITN negotiated access to Serb-run camps at Omarska and Trnopolje. Here, captured on video, was the evidence: emaciated men, skin stretched against their ribs, staring in quiet desperation from behind barbed-wire fences. The images immediately rekindled memories of what had awaited the liberators of Hitler's death camps. Officials and journalists involved agreed that the ITN video gave the story a power it would not have had otherwise.[58] The international reaction—from the rest of the news media, from Congress, and from Bush's rival for the presidency, Gov. Bill Clinton—was intense.

Interviews with many officials involved in U.S. policy toward Bosnia lead to the conclusion that the administration's response took two forms. First, the images and their consequences did not change the Bush administration's predilection not to get more deeply involved in what it saw as a potential Balkan quagmire. Second, the administration devoted considerable effort to addressing not the human rights abuses themselves *but the political problem created by the images.* In other words, U.S. government officials believed they had to be seen to be reacting, even as they kept policy virtually intact. I will look at each of these responses in turn.

By August 1992, President Bush and his top aides had reached the unanimous conclusion that to be meaningful, a U.S. intervention in Bosnia would have to involve the deployment of hundreds of thousands of American ground troops on a mission that had no clear end point. That same year, images from Somalia were helping break down resistance to a humanitarian-relief mission that seemed to have relatively few costs and risks; by contrast, the images from Bosnia did not affect officials' calculations. According to Scowcroft, "We did some marginal things, but there was a real consensus—and I think probably an unshakable consensus—[that] to make a real difference . . . would require an American or a NATO intervention that we did not see justified." Referring to the storm of media pressures to stop the killing, Scowcroft said that once policy was determined, "then we just sort of rode it out."[59] Eagleburger spoke in almost identical terms:

> Through all the time we were there, you have to understand that we had largely made a decision we were not going to get militarily involved. And nothing, including those stories, pushed us into it. . . . I hated it. Because this was condoning—I won't say genocide—but condoning a hell of a lot of murder. . . . It made us damn uncomfortable. But this was a policy that wasn't going to get changed no matter what the press said.[60]

Warren Zimmermann, the last U.S. ambassador to Yugoslavia, concurred, citing the consensus among Bush, Powell, Scowcroft, and Eagleburger: "It wouldn't have mattered if television was going twenty-four hours around the clock with Serb atrocities. Bush wasn't going to get in."[61]

As in Rwanda, the very fear of the news media's potentially negative impact once an intervention was under way proved a deterrent to a more activist policy. According to Eagleburger, if something went wrong, if U.S. soldiers were killed or hopelessly bogged down, the same media that pushed the government in would be demanding that it pull out. He explained this dread of the media's fleeting nature:

> Those who got you in won't defend you. They will turn on you. . . . There is no institutional responsibility as to what they've done [compared] to what they were doing. . . . What you're worried about is that you'll orient the United States to a policy and you'll have to reverse it. And that's terrible if you're worried about world stability.[62]

With this firm policy in place, how then did the Bush administration respond to Gutman's stories, the ITN video, and the pressures on policy that soon accompanied them? Indeed, what did the administration already know about gross human rights abuses in Bosnia? I explore these questions, not to determine responsibility or whether there was a cover-up, but because in examining the effects of the news media on intervention, it is important to know precisely how government foreign policy officials respond.

At first, the resistance to action translated into a lack of interest in the details of what was going on in the Bosnian camps, for the very reason that they represented a potential challenge to established policy. This fact became clear to Gutman and his colleagues in *Newsday*'s Washington bureau in July 1992, when they began to discover what the Bosnian Serbs were doing and tried, in Gutman's words, to alert "every major government agency. No one responded."[63] George Kenney, at the time a State Department desk officer for the former Yugoslavia, encountered the same attitude. When Gutman went to the U.S. consulate in Zagreb, Croatia, to share his fears about the camps and find out what the U.S. government knew, Zagreb sent a cable back to Washington. Kenney received a copy. "I saw fireworks going off," he said. He showed the cable to his colleagues. They were uninterested. On Tuesday, August 4, with the controversy over the camps in full swing, *Washington Post* diplomatic correspondent Don Oberdorfer conducted an interview with Deputy Assistant Secretary of State Ralph Johnson, the point man for Yugoslavia in the State Department's European bureau. In preparation, Kenney put a stack of materials, including the Gutman story, on Johnson's desk. Yet Oberdorfer found Johnson "altogether complacent and utterly lacking in energy, I thought, about a desperate situation," he wrote later in his private journal. "I was angry and in a very rare outburst spoke sharply to Johnson about why he and State didn't do more. My piece that day was rough on State and the administration—rougher than any I can recall in a long time."[64] Kenney concludes: "Political insensitivity to the Nth degree" got the State Department into trouble.[65] This series of incidents is consistent with the foreign policy bureaucracy's disregard for the news media that was noted in chapter 2. (Spokeswoman Margaret Tutwiler, a political appointee and one of Baker's closest aides, was an exception. Earlier in the year, frustrated by the lack of media—especially television—focus on Bosnia, Tutwiler used her daily press briefings to draw attention to the plight of besieged Sarajevo, knowing that provocative statements about conditions there would draw reporters' questions. She also called network news bureaus, urging more coverage. "Early on, there were no pictures. . . . There was zero interest," Tutwiler said. "I thought if more people knew about this, governments would be stronger" in taking action. Tutwiler was hoping not for U.S. military intervention, but for diplomatic and symbolic steps against the Serbs.[66] Tutwiler left the State Department on July 31, two days before the pivotal *Newsday* report.)

On Monday, August 3, at the first State Department briefing after *Newsday*'s explosive story appeared, State Department deputy spokesman Richard Boucher answered reporters' persistent questions by saying:

We do know from our own reports of information similar to the press reports that the Serbian forces are maintaining what they call detention centers for Croatians and Muslims. And we do have our own reports, similar to the reports you've seen in the press, that there have been abuses and torture and killings taking place in those areas.[67]

For any reporter, that statement was the equivalent of adding fuel to the story's fire. "I had rarely seen the State Department press corps—or what was left of it in August—so agitated," Oberdorfer wrote in his journal. Boucher's statement, unaccompanied as it was by any signal of a policy change, provoked a political uproar. Presidential candidate Clinton and his running mate, Senator Al Gore, demanded that the United States call a special session of the UN Security Council and use military force if necessary to stop the abuses. Many lawmakers from both parties echoed the call. Bosnia had vaulted to the top of the political agenda.[68] Oberdorfer was told by a National Security Council official that his four front-page reports in the *Post* that week, detailing the effects of the *Newsday* report, played a major role in putting the issue at the forefront.[69] Oberdorfer's report is another example of the enduring impact of the print media, as opposed to television.

The day after Boucher's briefing, on August 4, Thomas Niles, the assistant secretary of state for Europe, tried to take back the impact of the spokesman's statement. Niles told a shocked and indignant House Foreign Affairs Committee, "We don't have, thus far, substantiated information that would confirm the existence of these camps."[70]

Numerous officials have confirmed that Niles's statement was intended to reduce the pressure for action. In other words, top officials saw the news media reports of death camps and the pressures that they generated primarily as a political problem, not as an event that should call U.S. policy into question. "We took too much time to deal with it. . . . We kind of waffled around a little bit," Eagleburger recalled. "All of us were being a little bit careful . . . because of this issue of whether or not it was going to push us into something that we thought was dangerous."[71] A senior State Department official said the pressure for action was mounting too swiftly as a result of Boucher's statement, which was officially approved. "Our intention was to move the ball forward one step, and the (news) reports moved it forward two steps," the official said.[72] According to Ambassador Zimmermann, "Niles was sent up to the Hill to basically deny this. This deniability was not possible." There also was an aversion to using the word "genocide" in public statements, Zimmermann said, because if genocide was occurring in Bosnia, the United States was obligated under international law to take action.[73]

Two questions remain: Was Gutman's report a surprise to the administration, or did it merely raise on the public agenda something that already was known to U.S. officials? And what actual change in policy did it bring about? The evidence regarding the first question is mixed. "Well ahead of media revelations," according to John Fox, a State Department policy planning official, "the U.S. government had in its possession credible and verified reports of the existence of the camps—Serbian-run camps—in Bosnia and elsewhere as of June, certainly July, 1992."[74] But other officials said that Gutman's vivid firsthand reporting was well ahead of the fragmentary reports from other sources being compiled at the State Department. Kenney, who kept a personal file on Bosnia, said the first reports began to trickle in during May, with fifteen to twenty in June and no more than two dozen in July. The sources were mostly political contacts at the embassy in Belgrade or western Europeans who had been in the area and passed on second- or thirdhand accounts. None of the evidence was considered conclusive. By the time Gutman's story broke, "we really didn't know that much," Kenney concludes.[75] There were other indications of what was occurring from lists of camps provided by the Bosnian government; from Bosnian lawyer Zlatko Hurtic, who collected 120 statements from witnesses of alleged mass murders of Muslims; and from periodic press reports, including a June 24, 1992 front-page story in the *Philadelphia Inquirer*.[76] Yet, as already noted, senior officials displayed little interest in these reports.

Newsday and ITN changed that. Their coverage set the agenda for the Bush administration's foreign policy in August 1992, forcing senior officials to pay attention to an issue they previously preferred to ignore and demanding some sort of public response. On August 6, the day the ITN footage first aired, President Bush demanded that the international community be given access to the camps and said the United States would push for a UN Security Council resolution authorizing the use of "all necessary means" (that is, including military force) to ensure that humanitarian supplies were delivered throughout Bosnia. Bush repeated the demand for access to the camps in a news conference the next day. But asked whether the United States would use force unilaterally to ensure aid deliveries, he repeated the Vietnam-based justification he had used to stay out of the Iraqi civil war: "I do not want to see the United States bogged down in any way into some guerrilla warfare. We lived through that once."[77] On August 13, the Security Council passed Resolution 770, demanding unimpeded outside access to the camps and calling on member states to use "all measures necessary" to ensure the delivery of humanitarian aid.[78] Under international pressure, the Bosnian Serbs gradually closed the concentration camps. The printed and televised news reports also played a part in the establishment of the first war crimes tribunals in Europe since World War II. On December 16, 1992, Eagleburger publicly named Serbian and Bosnian Serb leaders who should stand trial for war crimes.

But had U.S. policy toward Bosnia really changed in any significant way? According to several officials, the response of the Bush administration (and, it should be noted, of other governments at other times) to news media pressures was to *appear* to be acting and perhaps even to take action in minor ways. According to a senior Bush administration official, the president and his foreign policy aides could not ignore the emotional issue of the camps, and Bosnia in general, but at the same time did not want to do anything that might presage greater involvement in the war. "I know you can do halfway things," the official said. "We did do halfway things."[79] According to Kenney, government concern for the media "only extended to the appearance of maintaining we were behaving responsibly," while in reality maintaining a hands-off policy toward Bosnia.[80] Similarly, a British official told Nik Gowing: "TV almost derailed [Bosnia] policy on several occasions, but the spine held. It had to. The secret was to respond to limit the damage, and be seen to react without undermining the specific focus" of policy.[81] As in northern Iraq, President Bush's actions in response to images were limited to the humanitarian. Where the humanitarian and the military converged, caution prevailed. Resolution 770 never was fully implemented because of the fears of entanglement that underlay the administration's thinking about the Balkans. Roy Gutman believes that his and others' reports had a major impact inside the former Yugoslavia, saving perhaps thousands of lives that might have been lost had the camps remained open. But when asked to assess the media's impact on U.S. foreign policy, he brings his thumb and finger together to form a zero. "Really," he said, "what you had is a lot of reaction to reports, but never any policy change."[82] The statements of senior Bush administration officials themselves are testimony to their desire to resist involvement. To protest this lack of action, George Kenney resigned from the Foreign Service on August 25, 1992. Graphic images of the worst human rights abuses in Europe in forty years did not have the power to move governments in directions in which they were determined not to be moved.

Bosnia also provides a specific case in which the power of televised images to pressure U.S. foreign policy officials diminishes over time, especially when the leadership itself does not act or send some other signal of the issue's significance. "This is the limited influence the media have," said Gutman. "You actually can have impact at times." But if governments do not take action, "it dissipates."[83] By March 1995, Deputy Secretary of State Strobe Talbott could say that "the 'don't just stand there, do something!' instinct"—the public's unspecific demand for some kind of policy action —no longer applied to Bosnia. It is not that officials felt some countervailing pressure, he said, but that public pressure was absent altogether. After four years, he said, Americans now knew where Bosnia was and that there were no simple solutions. This, Talbott believes, diminishes the CNN effect.[84] The United States did send troops to Bosnia later that year to enforce the Dayton accords, but—as will be seen—did so for reasons that had little to do with media or public opinion pressures.

A Different View of Real-Time Television's Influence: The February 1994 Marketplace Massacre

Just after noon local time on Saturday, February 5, 1994, a 120-millimeter mortar shell was fired into the central market in Sarajevo's old city. The shell tore through the corrugated tin roof of a stall and slammed into a table, exploding before it hit the ground. This happenstance had two important consequences: it made it impossible to tell who had fired the shell, and because it exploded at waist level the destruction was all the more gruesome. The shell turned the crowded marketplace into a charnel house, dismembering and decapitating bodies with its powerful explosion. Sixty-eight people were killed and nearly two hundred wounded in the deadliest single attack in Sarajevo's twenty-two-month siege. Within minutes, television cameras caught the horrible carnage and broadcast the scene around the world. At the Wehrkunde security conference in Munich, attended by recently appointed U.S. defense secretary William Perry, along with European defense ministers and parliamentarians, the images came in on the hotel television system's CNN channel. The impact was immediate. Perry emerged from a closed-door session only to be greeted by reporters demanding to know what his government would do about an event he did not yet know about. The ministers "perceived both through the pictures themselves and the questions at the press conferences, and perhaps in calls from capitals back home, that this was something that would intensify pressure among their voters or constituents for something to happen," said one journalist present.[85] In New York, Madeleine Albright, the U.S. ambassador to the United Nations, was in a meeting with her staff when the telephone rang with the news. As noted in chapter 2, she "did what anyone would do. I turned on CNN." Later that afternoon, she appeared on CNN to begin explaining the Clinton administration's response.[86] ABC News anchor Peter Jennings happened to be traveling in the former Yugoslavia when the shell hit, and his report that evening showed U.S. jet fighters overflying Sarajevo but taking no action, underscoring the West's impotence.[87] Four days later, on February 9, NATO gave the Bosnian Serbs a ten-day deadline to remove their heavy weapons from within a twenty-kilometer radius of Sarajevo or risk having them destroyed by NATO air strikes; the threat was backed up with strong U.S. and French support. The Serb weapons were indeed withdrawn, giving Sarajevo an aura of normalcy it had not known for nearly two years. Eventually, NATO's threat of air strikes would lead to the alliance's first use of offensive force in Europe since it was formed forty-five years earlier. At the same time that it supported a more aggressive military posture, the Clinton administration abandoned its hands-off diplomatic stance on Bosnia. It joined the Europeans in a five-nation "Contact Group" that would give new momentum to the search for a political solution to the conflict. And it persuaded the Bosnian government and Bosnian Croats to join in a federation.

Here we seem to have a case where graphic and disturbing television images from a war zone, transmitted in real time, produced a sharp change in U.S. foreign policy, pushing policymakers to intervene where they previously had feared to tread. But once again, as with Somalia, a closer examination of the events regarding Bosnia in the first two months of 1994 yields a much different conclusion.[88] According to a half-dozen senior U.S. officials in several government agencies, the pictures did *not* produce a sharp policy swing. Rather, the images accelerated and catalyzed a policy evolution that was already under way. In internal Clinton administration deliberations, they provided ammunition for those officials arguing for a more forceful American policy toward Bosnia. Perhaps most interestingly, in terms of officials' perceptions of what public opinion would permit them to do, the images provided a moment of increased public attention to Bosnia that could help justify the administration's policy response. "It was a short window. We took advantage of it. We moved the policy forward, and it was successful," recalled Dee Dee Myers, White House spokeswoman at the time.[89] Of course, one has to take into account the possibility, here and elsewhere, that government officials are consciously or unconsciously minimizing the impact of the news media. If the media does have a significant impact on policy, it would tend to derogate officials' own latitude for policymaking. Yet the unanimity of officials' responses and a close look at the events themselves argue against this. Furthermore, as we shall see, while Perry and others in the U.S. leadership were forced to give a near-instant rhetorical response to the event as captured on television screens, they did not respond with an instantaneous change of policy.

The evidence that the U.S. government was moving toward a more proactive policy in the Bosnian conflict prior to February 5 comes from many sources. On January 24, 1994, Secretary of State Warren Christopher met in Paris with French foreign minister Alain Juppé. Christopher was virtually browbeaten by his French counterpart, who complained of the damage being done by U.S. policy and urged the United States to help seek a solution to the worsening conflict. (At this point, the United States was taking little part in Balkan diplomacy, having declined to endorse the Vance-Owen proposal for a territorial division of Bosnia and refusing to pressure the Muslim-led Bosnian government into signing any accord.) The Christopher-Juppé encounter was followed by a similar warning in Washington by British foreign secretary Douglas Hurd a week later. At the same time, other senior U.S. officials, including Ambassador Albright and National Security Adviser Anthony Lake, were independently coming to the conclusion that a more forceful policy was needed. On February 4, the day before the mortar attack in Sarajevo, Christopher concurred with these opinions in a long position paper that he sent to Lake and Perry. In a cover letter, he wrote: "I am acutely uncomfortable with the passive position we are now in and believe that now is the time to undertake a new initiative."[90] Christopher's proposal was for a renewed diplomatic effort, combined with the threat of force.[91] "We had a real sense that we didn't have a Bosnia policy that was going anywhere," said a senior State Department official. "We had already made the psychological determination [about] the direction we wanted to go." This official was in a series of meetings on revamping the Bosnia policy around the time the mortar attack occurred and recalled worrying that the new policy would be seen, incorrectly, as an instant response to the massacre.[92] A primary motivation behind the policy change, then, was not the images, but an assessment that the status quo was damaging U.S. credibility, the NATO alliance, and transatlantic relations generally. The policy deliberations were caught in midstride by a single mortar shell.

The Clinton administration's immediate reaction to the shelling was not action, but caution. President Clinton's "instinct was to ask the allies what to do."[93] Nearly a year before, the administration had determined there would be no unilateral U.S. action in Bosnia, following western Europe's rejection of Clinton's proposal to "lift and strike"—lift the UN arms embargo as it applied to the Muslim-led Bosnian government and conduct air strikes against Bosnian Serb positions. The president's advisers also were unwilling to recommend retaliation while it remained officially unclear who had fired the deadly mortar shell.[94] (This is evidence that officials do not always react immediately to dramatic news media reports that may turn out later to be inaccurate or incomplete.) The president had not been awakened early February 5 with news of the marketplace deaths, and by the time he went to give his Saturday radio address, he had seen only a brief glimpse of the carnage on CNN. Over the ensuing hours and days, he kept to a previously set schedule of work and recreation, conferring periodically with his senior advisers. Senior lawmakers of both parties, including Senate Republican leader Robert Dole and Representative Lee Hamilton, chairman of the House Foreign Affairs Committee, called on the president on Sunday and Monday to order air strikes to retaliate for the shelling. However, Clinton rejected immediate retaliation. In Houston that Monday, he said: "Until those folks get tired of killing each other over there, bad things will continue to happen."[95] But at the same time, the president and his advisers were moving toward embracing the threat of air strikes as a way to prevent a recurrence of the massacre and to push the peace process forward.[96]

At this point, "[t]he pressure came not from television images but on the phone from the French government." The images from Sarajevo helped make France's case for more aggressive action in the Balkans.[97] France's change of position in favor of potential air strikes was critical, since Paris contributed the largest contingent of ground troops to UN-PROFOR. France had rejected previous proposals for the use of air power, fearing for its troops' safety. Juppé spoke with Christopher by telephone on Saturday and Sunday, arguing that NATO should seize the moment and use the threat of force to create a demilitarized zone around Sarajevo. NATO ultimately adopted this French proposal, which was modified by Washington. The scenes on television similarly helped Christopher—who was now a leading advocate of forceful U.S. action in the Balkans—make his case both publicly and within the administration. During this period, Christopher took the lead in publicly denouncing the shelling and suggesting a strong Western response. Thus the real-time television images accelerated the decision-making process and forced decisions out of the bureaucracy, according to Michael McCurry, Christopher's spokesman at the time. "It could have taken weeks or months," he said. "The impact of the marketplace bombing . . . was to force there to be a response much quicker than the U.S. government" would normally produce one.[98] "In some ways, it kind of jelled with exactly the direction we were going," another top State Department official said. The marketplace massacre "gave us a chance to come in, be responsive to the Bosnian [government's] concerns, strengthen our credentials."[99] These descriptions of the news media's role concur with previous studies of far different kinds of policy decisions—namely, that the media can have their largest impact when the decision-making process is incomplete; that it speeds up that process; and that coverage, particularly negative coverage, propels the issue up the bureaucratic ladder to higher-level officials.[100]

The question of whether the United States and Europe would have taken more decisive action in Bosnia in early 1994 without the driving force of the horrible images from Sarajevo borders on the existential. Clearly, the event, as captured on videotape, put the suffering of Sarajevo and the inadequacy of Western policies at the top of the agenda. This was despite the fact that, in some sense, nothing had really changed. "People had been dying day after day after day," a senior U.S. official said. But once the images came on screen, viewers "think something new or different has happened . . . a discrete act that needs to be responded to."[101] It is an open question whether the Clinton administration could have explained a more forceful policy in the Balkans to the American people, or convinced reluctant allies such as Britain and Canada to go along, without the action-inducing atmosphere the pictures created.[102] Even if true, this view of television's impact is far different from the cause-effect relationship that often is cited.[103] Far from pushing policymakers where they fear to tread, dramatic television images can open the door to action that was desired but might not have been possible before. It is equally valid to ask what effect the images from the shattered marketplace would have had if U.S. and European policy had been moving in the opposite direction—away from further engagement in Bosnia. Several officials cited a belief that images play a role only when events are already moving in the direction that the images suggest. "There have been two images that, at least in terms of television . . . have been most vivid since I've been here [in the Clinton administration]," a senior U.S. official said. One was the image from the Sarajevo market; the other was that of a U.S. soldier's corpse being dragged through the streets of Mogadishu in October 1993, an event that will be analyzed in detail in chapter 5.

> In both of those instances, there seemed to be an intersection of an event with a growing mood, frustration, policymaking decisions being imminent. They propelled policymakers to take certain steps. . . . For the media to have a dramatic impact on policy, there almost has to be a convergence of certain factors for that to happen.[104]

Finally, the Sarajevo marketplace provides further evidence of how the impact of television images, no matter how dramatic, declines over time. On August 28, 1995, another mortar shell fell in the same marketplace, killing at least thirty-six Sarajevans and horribly wounding dozens more. A UN investigation left no doubt that the Bosnian Serbs had fired the shell. Several weeks before, following the fall of the Srebrenica and Zepa "safe areas" to the Serbs, NATO's defense ministers had gathered in London and pledged to protect the remaining safe areas, including Sarajevo, from attack. The international community's already reduced credibility was on the line. These nonmedia factors—the strategic and diplomatic environment—determined U.S. intervention policy in this instance far more than the television images did. The only question was, "were we going to make good on those commitments?" said McCurry, who by now had become White House press secretary. NATO did, launching a massive air campaign against Bosnian Serb targets. According to McCurry, the equally horrifying images from the marketplace played a much smaller role in the policy process than they had in February 1994. "Because it's the second time around, it had less shock value," he said.[105]

Television, Preventive Diplomacy, and Early Warning

With growing policy and academic concern over destabilizing internal conflicts in many parts of the globe, the United Nations, government officials, and scholars have increasingly turned to the concept of *preventive diplomacy.* UN secretary general Boutros Boutros-Ghali defined preventive diplomacy as "action to prevent disputes from arising between parties, to prevent existing disputes from escalating into conflicts and to limit the spread of the latter when they do occur." He also called for consideration of *preventive deployment* of UN peacekeeping forces when inter- or intrastate conflict threatens to break out.[106] Such early intervention by governments, it is hoped, would save lives and the physical and human environment, and do so at a cost that is insignificant compared with the cost of action once a conflict is full-blown. A related concept is that of *early warning,* the dissemination of information that a conflict is about to occur or escalate, or that disaster looms in a humanitarian crisis. These concerns have, in turn, raised the question of whether the news media can and should provide more timely warnings of incipient crises to policymakers and the public.[107]

The track record of the news media, especially television, in early warning is not good. Of the four cases examined, this fact is seen most clearly in Rwanda and Somalia. Rwanda was absent from U.S. network television screens throughout the early 1990s, when the developments that led to the slaughter were occurring both there and in neighboring Burundi. There were two network reports concerning Rwanda in 1993, one of them dealing with mountain gorillas. Nor was there any television coverage (or much newspaper coverage) of an October 1993 massacre in Burundi—whose ethnic disputes are similar to Rwanda's—that left 50,000 to 300,000 dead.[108] If the news media had paid attention to that event, what occurred later in Rwanda "might not have been such a big shock," said the *Washington Post's* Richburg.[109] Nor did television give any attention to Somalia as civil war raged there in the aftermath of President Mohamed Siad Barre's fall in January 1991; that event would lead directly to famine and, ultimately, U.S. military intervention. There were four network news stories in January 1991—three of them covering the evacuation of U.S. and other foreign nationals, the other a ten-second report from the CBS studio on Siad Barre's flight from Somalia. During the remainder of 1991, there were three network reports that mentioned Somalia; during the first half of 1992, there were six.[110]

One of three network stories that aired during February–December 1991 is instructive. In a lengthy report (three minutes, ten seconds) broadcast on Sunday, March 3, ABC News briefly mentioned the Somali civil war in a review of significant news developments that had *not* been thoroughly covered because of the attention given to the Persian Gulf War. This case is far from the only example of a major event that has all but drowned out other significant stories. Richburg suggested that the October 1993 massacre in Burundi might have received more coverage had it not been for the deaths of eighteen U.S. soldiers in Mogadishu that same month. In 1995, the O. J. Simpson trial pushed aside a lot of other news.[111]

Many other media observers, including Cohen and Reston, have noted the media's tendency to focus on one "continuing big story" at a time.[112] Commenting on newspapers, Cohen added that they focus almost exclusively on observable events that are already in the past: "By its own cannons, the press does an unsystematic, haphazard job of stimulating or structuring discussion of ideas or possibilities in advance of issues, crises or events."[113] Television, today's dominant medium, is even more constrained by the finite limits of airtime and the need for dramatic visual images. These constraints make for a cruel irony regarding early warning of famines and other humanitarian disasters: "Famines don't become visually newsworthy until people die, which only takes place in the advanced stages of a drought cycle."[114] Television, then, is ill equipped to provide early warning of potential ethnic conflicts or humanitarian emergencies, two types of crises likely to give rise to peace operations. And the medium's limited capacities in this area will constantly be under the threat that a "big story" will appear, swamping most others.

As has been seen throughout this study, in Vietnam, in the Persian Gulf crisis, and in Somalia, journalism is a less independent institution than is commonly perceived, being cued instead by political debate or policy action in the executive branch. The attempts by relief organizations to cue the news media in cases such as Somalia also have been noted. But in the early and even middle stages of a crisis, these attempts can go only so far in the absence of high-level executive branch communication, by word or deed, of the issue's importance. Even under the determined Andrew Natsios, OFDA did not fare well in its initial attempts to draw international media attention to the Somalia disaster through congressional testimony in December 1991 and press conferences in January and February 1992. Nor is media attention a prerequisite for humanitarian relief or other policy actions.[115] On August 18, four days after Bush announced the airlift of supplies to Somalia, Natsios told a crowded State Department briefing: "I get the impression sometimes from some of the media coverage that all of a sudden this started three weeks ago and that nothing has happened before. And that is certainly not the case."[116] Action by the executive or political debate in Congress is by far the strongest catalyst for media attention.

In short, the news media's own standards of what is "news" make it an inappropriate focus for attempts at improving the international response to emergencies: "Focusing attention on the decision-making apparatus of the U.S. government would probably be more productive than on attempts at reforming errant media behavior."[117] Moreover, as we have seen in this chapter, officials of the U.S. government do not depend on the news media to bring them first warning of developments in places such as Bosnia or Somalia. (The exception, of course, is fast-breaking crises such as Sarajevo's marketplace massacre, where real-time television may inform officials before other sources of information do.) These findings suggest that early warning and preventive diplomacy are primarily a matter of political will on the part of national and international leaders, who have to use their leadership, their time, and other crucial resources to build support for action. In Rwanda, "[a]mple early warning signaled an impending disaster. Lacking was the will to take preventive action."[118]

Summary

Where popular debate sees a powerful and pervasive role for television in the decision-making process on U.S. interventions in the post–Cold War era, television's effect is in fact quite narrow and specific. Put differently, the decision on whether to launch a peace operation for humanitarian or political purposes remains largely in the hands of government officials. Television alone has no power to push U.S. foreign policy to the extent that policymakers *knowingly* incur significant risks, such as sending American combat forces into another country's internal war, in the absence of a major threat or national interest. Television and other media do seem to shape the policymaking environment in such a way that they can enhance other factors already highlighting the need to deliver humanitarian relief to areas suffering large-scale crises. Yet even this does not necessarily represent the "loss of policy control" that some have used to measure the CNN effect.[119] Pictures and other news media products can help explain the need for intervention to the public, making officials' task of persuasion that much easier. To recall former State Department spokesman Richard Boucher's comments in chapter 2, news media reports of humanitarian disaster can help government officials explain interventions they wanted to pursue anyway.

It also is clear that television images in and of themselves are not sufficient to move U.S. intervention policy. A firm, preexisting policy against intervention in a conflict, as in Bosnia in the fall of 1992 or Rwanda in the spring of 1994, diminishes or negates the effect of images. When the United States already has staked its prestige and military forces on an operation's outcome, as it did in the airlift to Somalia, the potential impact of television and other news media seems to be enhanced. This phenomenon will be examined further in the next chapter. But it underscores the news media's predilection, unchanged by technological advances, to follow rather than lead—whether it be following the troops as they deploy abroad or following political debate in Washington.

Finally, we have seen several instances where written communications, both those internal to the administration and those produced by the news media, played a role in the decision-making process on intervention. These instances include the July 19, 1992 front-page account in the *New York Times* of Somalia's desperate straits and Roy Gutman's articles in *Newsday* about the detention camps in Bosnia.

Even with all these caveats, the finding that televised images of innocents' suffering can be a factor in moving policy is significant nevertheless. This is because of the news media's very emphases on the humanitarian dimensions of crises that were discussed in chapter 2. It suggests a synergy between those stories that the media, particularly television, are most drawn to and the ones that have the greatest potential to affect policy-makers. Every conflict examined in this chapter has involved a mix of humanitarian and political factors, and government officials were more willing to address the former than the latter. To reformulate the quotation from Eduard Shevardnadze at the beginning of the chapter: the "symptoms" (famine victims, refugees, civilian casualties) are attended to, but not the "disease" (the fundamental political causes of conflict), which might require a different, and more risky, type of intervention. Officials sometimes seem to engage in a *minimalist response*, which can be defined as an attempt to defuse media or public pressures for action, usually through measured humanitarian assistance and rhetoric, while in fact minimizing real policy change. Many of the officials interviewed for this study believed this occurred with regard to U.S. policy in Bosnia in 1992. Even if policy-makers are determined not to become involved, they strike a pose of indifference at their political peril.[120]

This points to several problems for making foreign policy in a democracy infused by television. First, it could lead to a distortion of policy that concentrates purely on the outward face of human suffering, to the detriment of other concerns. (However, as already noted, the impact of dramatic, emotive images seems to decline with repetition.) Second, actions that follow the minimalist response pattern may suggest to the media and the public that an administration has altered its policy toward intervention more than it really has. In fact, the rhetorical responses and minor policy shifts that officials undertake in reaction to television images may account for the widespread perception that television determines policy. Third, humanitarian relief, while vital to those who receive it, may have little effect on the root causes of conflict. It is worth pondering whether this feeds the American public's cynicism about the inability of its leaders to solve the problems before them. Finally, the flicker of increased attention by the media and the public to those in need of help can be snuffed out at any time.

The humanitarian intervention in Rwanda, while it came late, undoubtedly saved tens of thousands of human lives. Yet six months later, the television cameras were long gone, and donations to the United Nations Children's Fund operations were falling far behind the need. "Andy Warhol's fifteen minutes of fame are over, and Rwanda is no longer flavor of the month," a senior UN official said.[121] Relief groups are intimately familiar with the dichotomy of the media's power. In summer 1995, a solicitation for funds from Médecins sans Frontières highlighted the group's work in Uganda, Kurdistan, and Mozambique. It was entitled, "Beyond the Cameras."

5

The Pull

Public Opinion and Peace Operations

> "Once the commitment is made and the soldiers go,
> the minicams will be there, and we must prepare the
> troops for the roll (and the role) of the CNN video.
> If policymakers and military leaders hold no vision of
> the human face of our commitments, if they tell no
> stories from the heart of the how and why of our
> military actions, then others will do it for them,
> and the results may not be to their liking."
> —*Frank J. Stech*

This chapter examines the news media's impact on public support for peace operations once the president has deployed U.S. military forces abroad. I first examine two cases where U.S. ground troops were engaged in combat: Somalia and Haiti. The NATO-led peace operation in Bosnia is not covered. It began as this study was being completed and, as of this writing, is still under way. Special attention is given to Somalia because of the media's presumed role in curtailing the mission and Somalia's profound impact on later peace operations. Two related questions are posed in both the Somalia and Haiti cases: How did the news media's reporting affect the conduct of the mission itself? How did it affect public support and leaders' ability to sustain the mission? I then briefly examine the news media's role in strictly humanitarian-relief operations. The second half of the chapter examines potential media impacts that are broader than just the reporting of a single incident or incidents: What role do wildly fluctuating levels of media coverage play in sustaining support for a mission? What role do the media play in the final assessment of a peace operation as a success or failure?

I argue that the *potential* for media impact is far greater once a mission has begun than it is prior to the decision to intervene. The media have a stronger effect of *pulling* a peace operation out of a crisis-ridden country than they do in *pushing* one in. Many factors contribute to this difference in effects, including the risks to American lives that a deployment poses, the political prestige an administration invests in a particular operation, the media's proclivity to follow the troops in great numbers, and journalists' relative freedom in covering peace operations. Peace operations are particularly vulnerable to media impact because they involve no or relatively minor national interests and, at the same time, merge political and military, as well as tactical and strategic, concerns. These media impacts on the policymaking *process*, and to a much lesser extent on policy, are neither predetermined nor inevitable. But if political leaders do not use the tools of communication and persuasion at their disposal, the news media—and, perhaps through it, an adversary—will fill the vacuum quickly, with predictable consequences for public support for the operation.

Somalia, 1993

On Monday, October 4, 1993, the American body politic received a profound and unexpected blow, made all the worse in the view of many officials by Operation Desert Storm's legacy of sanitized images of battle. The attention of Washington's policymakers and journalists on the attempted coup in Russia was ripped away to another part of the world. In Somalia, eighteen American soldiers had lost their lives and nearly eighty were wounded in the deadliest single battle the nation had fought since Vietnam. Somali casualties were estimated at three hundred dead and seven hundred wounded. There was no video of the battle itself, but the images of its aftermath were almost too much to bear: the body of a dead American soldier was poked at with sticks and dragged down a dusty road in Mogadishu as crowds of Somalis cheered and jeered. Another soldier, Chief Warrant Officer Michael Durant, was in captivity. On TV, his face was battered and bruised, his eyes uncertain. While the public had strongly supported President Bush's decision to send U.S. troops to Somalia to stop the starvation, support had now almost vanished. On Capitol

Hill, mounting calls for a withdrawal of U.S. troops rose to a level that President Clinton could not ignore. After an urgent policy review, the president on Thursday, October 7, stated a series of policy changes. In a nationwide address, he announced that U.S. combat troops would be withdrawn from Somalia by March 31, 1994. In the meantime, extra troops and armaments would be sent to better protect the remaining U.S. forces. Clinton would make an intensified push for a political solution to Somalia's problems.[1]

In the previous chapter, we saw how the notion that the news media, unabetted, pushed the United States into Somalia was inaccurate. Now I turn to the news media's role in pulling American military forces out of the same country. Did images, both televised and photographic, force the United States out of Somalia, as many commentators maintain?[2] In addition to the two questions posed at the introduction to this chapter, this examination of the events of May–October 1993 seeks to answer *why* the media—via the October images—seemed to play such a powerful role. I argue that the impact of those images was a consequence not of the news media's actions but of failures in the administration's policy and, even more important, in communicating that policy to Congress and the public. U.S. policymakers changed the goals of the Somalia mission but failed to clearly tell Congress and the American public about these changes and their potential costs. They did not ensure that their new policies had public and congressional support; indeed, that support had ebbed long before the tragic events of October 3–4.

At the heart of what happened in Somalia in the summer and fall of 1993 was a huge gap between the way the mission was perceived at home and the realities in Mogadishu. That gap at times caused U.S. officials in Somalia to complain about the news media's reporting. The target of their anger, by and large, was not the press corps in Mogadishu, with whom they were in daily contact. Officials believed that the reports of journalists in Washington, which were based on official sources, failed to reflect the difficulties of the conflict. This feeling was reminiscent of Vietnam, when official Washington's optimism was not matched by that of the soldiers and reporters in the field. Those in Somalia were *not* shocked by the October images. One officer with long experience there said his despair upon seeing the images was tempered by this hope: "Maybe now the world will see this place for what it is."[3] If anything has changed in a generation, it is the speed with which the news media can fill such gaps and the shrinking distance between the home front and a war without any front.

Washington

On May 5, 1993, President Clinton held a ceremony on the South Lawn of the White House to honor troops returning from Operation Restore Hope. In an address to the troops and their commander, Marine Corps Lt. Gen. Robert B. Johnston, the president told them that "the mission is accomplished" and that "America opens its arms in a hearty welcome home." The president acknowledged that there was "a significant American component" to the UN peacekeeping mission, UNOSOM II, which had assumed responsibility in Somalia with an expanded mandate the day before.[4] But from that day forward, the administration, in its public statements, repeatedly referred to the mission in Somalia and to the decisions made in its name, as being under the aegis of the United Nations, with the United States playing only a supporting role.[5]

In fact, the U.S. government strongly supported UNOSOM's vastly expanded mandate, which included promoting reconstruction of national and local government throughout the country and encouraging political reconciliation.[6] Madeleine Albright, the U.S. ambassador to the United Nations, called it an "unprecedented enterprise aimed at nothing less than the restoration of an entire country."[7] Yet UNOSOM was being asked to carry out this expanded mission with far less capable troops than the United Task Force (UNITAF), the U.S.-dominated military component of Restore Hope, had.[8] UNOSOM's only potent firepower in the event of a crisis was relatively small, and it was American—the thirteen-hundred-man Quick Reaction Force (QRF) from the U.S. Army's Tenth Mountain Division. The administration's emphasis on the United Nations and the reality of the continued pivotal position of the U.S. military in Somalia would plague the mission, both on the ground and in the administration's explanations to the American public and Congress about who was in control of the operation.[9] That, in turn, contributed to a backlash against U.S. participation in peace operations and, in some quarters, in the United Nations itself.

After May 4, 1993, Somalia largely dropped off the screen in Washington, no longer considered a top-level problem by the administration nor accorded sustained attention by the news media. The American public had never considered Somalia a major issue on the national agenda. Media and public attention did not return until U.S. casualties began to occur in large numbers.[10]

The second major alteration in the mission occurred on June 5, when a Pakistani patrol conducted a weapons inspection at Radio Mogadishu, controlled by clan leader Mohamed Farah Aidid. As it withdrew, the patrol was ambushed by members of Aidid's Somali National Alliance (SNA), who took cover behind a crowd of women and children (a tactic that would later become all too familiar to the U.S. military). When the fighting ended, twenty-four Pakistani peacekeepers had been killed. The next day, the UN Security Council passed a new resolution calling for the "arrest and detention for prosecution, trial and punishment" of those responsible.[11] This action was strongly supported by the United States. Like U.S. Navy Admiral Jonathan Howe, the new UN envoy in Somalia, the Clinton administration feared setting a precedent in which peacekeepers could be attacked with impunity. "There was . . . general support for trying to respond to thugs that would kill UN peacekeepers," said Deputy National Security Adviser Samuel "Sandy" Berger.[12] U.S.-UN retaliation began on June 12, with strong and public backing from the Clinton administration.[13] Yet there was little high-level debate within the administration over the suddenly changed nature of UNOSOM's mission, or whether the U.S. forces in Somalia were appropriate for the task. Nor was there a sustained effort to explain to the American public the new direction of UNOSOM and the risks of this change. The view from Washington had begun to diverge from what was really happening in Mogadishu.

Mogadishu

By May 4, the international news media had long lost their appetite for the story that was Somalia. Most of the hundreds of journalists from around the world who descended on the Horn of Africa to cover Operation Restore Hope departed after President Bush's New Year's Eve visit to U.S. troops. The three U.S. broadcast television networks (ABC, CBS, and NBC) left along with the bulk of U.S. troops; CNN remained. Reporting on Somalia by CNN and ABC fell precipitously from January until the deaths of the Pakistanis and the UN retaliation in June.[14] By the end of February, only a hard core of reporters remained, including representatives of AP, Reuters, CNN, the *Washington Post,* and the *New York Times.*[15] The media

in Mogadishu now consisted largely of seasoned members of the Western
press corps based in Nairobi, Kenya, who had covered Somalia throughout most of 1992. Being familiar with Mogadishu and possessing numerous Somali contacts, they were not dependent on UN or U.S. officials for
much of their information. "They didn't need me to go get the action. I
had no control, and they knew that," said U.S. Army Maj. David Stockwell,
UNOSOM's chief military spokesman. The media contingent grew again
as full-scale fighting began. Many "celebrity" reporters "parachuted" in for
brief visits.[16] Journalists' freedom was limited only by the increasing physical danger in Mogadishu as summer wore on.[17]

As previously described, UNOSOM did not accord the same degree
of importance that UNITAF did to public communication, in either the
public affairs or psychological operations areas of the mission. An Italian
lieutenant colonel who was to be the mission's chief military spokesman
failed to show up. Maj. Stockwell, who went to Somalia as public affairs
officer for Maj. Gen. Thomas Montgomery, deputy UNOSOM commander
and commander of U.S. forces in Somalia, was selected. Stockwell wore
two hats, retaining his role as chief spokesman for U.S. military forces in
Somalia and, later, for Task Force Ranger, whose job was to capture Aidid.
Stockwell was widely liked and respected by the Mogadishu press corps,
but he was, in his own words, outnumbered. His predecessor, UNITAF
spokesman Marine Col. Fred Peck, had a JIB of as many as sixty people,
some of whom were detailed outside of Mogadishu. When hostilities
broke out in mid-June, Stockwell was alone. The U.S. forces in UNOSOM II
did not have their own public affairs staff, an oversight Gen. Montgomery
would later regret.[18] Meanwhile, the UN civilian spokesman in Somalia
was judged by both the press and other officials to be ineffective.[19]

I will now examine how reporters' freedom and officials' actions toward
the media affected both military operations in Somalia and the strategy of
the Somali clan leader Aidid. Throughout the Somalia mission's various
phases, the news media were able to report on events faster than the U.S.
military's own internal reporting channels. Reporters came to Peck and
later to Stockwell to get the military's reaction to events or the military's
side of the story. In Somalia, and later in Haiti, a reversal of the traditional
roles occurred, and the military became dependent on journalists, who
were more mobile, for valuable information and intelligence. The television
networks gave Peck small handheld radios so that he could communicate

with them. The radios allowed Peck to follow camera crews' movements, alerting him if a major event was unfolding. It was information he passed on to headquarters. The media were "another intelligence source," he said. "I probably got as much from them as they got from me."[20] After open conflict began in June between Aidid's SNA and UNOSOM, which offered a reward for Aidid's capture, journalists could travel to places that the U.S. and other militaries could not. Two British reporters, Mark Doyle of the BBC and Mark Huband of *The Guardian*, were the first non-Somalis to see Michael Durant in captivity. They interviewed him five days before the ICRC secured access. "It was just a terrific service. They were able to tell me the extent of his injuries," Stockwell recalled. "I was passing messages through them to Durant and vice versa. . . . I did ask them where he was held. And they didn't tell me."[21]

Once hostilities began, with U.S. military forces leading the attack on Aidid and his allies in response to the Pakistanis' deaths, the news media became more of a complicating presence. There is no evidence that journalists in Mogadishu breached operational security by reporting impending U.S. military actions. But they were a factor in mission planning and execution. Numerous aircraft sorties were launched, so that neither Aidid nor the media would know which were real and which were training exercises. Before authorizing a strike against the SNA, Gen. Montgomery would ask his subordinates where journalists were congregated and how they might cover the action.

The media's speed and pervasiveness is illustrated by an incident on June 14, when a U.S. Army Cobra helicopter overflying Mogadishu spotted a Soviet-made rocket launcher near one of Aidid's enclaves. The helicopter crew fired a TOW missile and destroyed it. At the first of his twice-daily briefings in the UN compound, Stockwell was asked how many missiles the helicopter had fired. "Just one," he replied. Reporters knew the "destroyed" rocket launcher was in fact a rusted, useless hulk; they walked by it almost daily. But there was something more important they knew that Stockwell did not. They asked the spokesman if he would like to see their videotape of the engagement. It showed two missiles being fired. The first had gone awry, slamming into a tea shop and killing a Somali woman and her daughter. Stockwell checked, and repeatedly was told that just a single missile had been fired. He repeated the information at his second, afternoon briefing to a room full of incredulous and angry reporters.

When the cameras were turned off, Stockwell, whose credibility was now at stake, assured them he would get a straight answer. At the noon briefing the next day, he said: "I can officially confirm that two TOW missiles were fired."[22] The media had gotten there first, and the appearance was that the military had told the truth only because it had been confronted with videotaped evidence.[23]

The news media, along with the NGO community, became increasingly critical of UNOSOM tactics and the escalating number of Somali casualties, many of them civilian. Task Force Ranger, composed of four hundred men under U.S. control, arrived in Mogadishu in late August with the goal of capturing Aidid. Its first strike, on a compound occupied by the UN Development Program and a French NGO, prompted widespread media and NGO criticism. Three days later, the Rangers conducted a second mission, trying to locate a militia's mortar firing position thought to be hidden in a compound housing the headquarters of the NGO World Concern. This time, the troops knocked on the gate and asked permission to enter. "Media coverage had influenced that patrol's conduct," Stockwell concluded.[24]

On September 9, Aidid's militia ambushed U.S. and Pakistani peacekeepers, sparking a pitched battle in which the SNA took heavy casualties. But the news media's focus was not on the ambush or the setback for Aidid, but on the large number of Somalis, including women and children, who were killed by Cobra helicopter gunships while they served as human shields for the SNA shooters. Under pressure from CNN, whose personnel were by now staying on the UNOSOM compound with their seven-meter satellite dish, Stockwell for the first and last time held a live briefing. Reporter after reporter asked about the slain women and children. Stockwell's widely reported statement, "In an ambush there are no sidelines or spectator seats," was an accurate description of Somali tactics. But it further contributed to the brewing storm in Washington, where there were inevitable comparisons to controversial American tactics in Vietnam.[25] The battle and civilian casualties fanned growing discontent in Congress and the administration over the mission's course. President Clinton was among those disturbed by the battle.[26] Stockwell felt the military never had the time to present its case—a microcosm, perhaps, of media-military relations in Somalia, where the media's speed and scope repeatedly put the military on the defensive or embarrassed it. "The media has the upper hand, because their agenda is so much faster. It gave us the appearance of being inept," Stockwell said.[27]

The September 9 incident raises the important question of whether Aidid was able to manipulate attitudes in the United States via CNN and other global media outlets. Aidid clearly favored CNN as a tool of communication, particularly at key points, such as the October 14 release of Durant and a Nigerian soldier. The clan leader and his lieutenants appeared on CNN in one form or another twenty-nine times between June and December 1993.[28] Aidid and his allies "learned very quickly how to play the CNN factor. They didn't want to talk unless CNN was there," said journalist Michael Maren, who discussed the activities of the Western news media with Aidid several times.[29] The SNA repeatedly tried to draw reporters' attention to the casualties and destruction caused by the escalating U.S. raids. In the aftermath of such attacks, militia members frequently came to the four-story Sehafi ("Press") Hotel, where journalists stayed, encouraging them to come view the devastation.[30] Sometimes, these efforts involved heavy-handed attempts at manufacturing "damage" done by the U.S. military, ruses that were more often than not seen through by reporters.[31]

In the view of many journalists and officials who spent time in Somalia, the news media failed to give adequate coverage to Somali leaders other than Aidid. Some of these leaders opposed Aidid's actions and were less antagonistic toward U.S. and UN forces. Following the deaths of the eighteen U.S. soldiers, Aidid's chief rival, Ali Mahdi Mohamed, organized pro-UN demonstrations of as many as fifteen thousand people in northern Mogadishu. The protests received some international media coverage, but they took place in a part of the capital that was dangerous for journalists to travel to and were overshadowed, in any event, by the U.S. casualties and the reaction in Washington. From June to October, journalists focused on the confrontation in south Mogadishu between the SNA and U.S. and UN forces.

Some U.S. officials began criticizing the media's narrow focus. In early July, Ambassador Albright visited Kismayo. Speaking to journalists based in Mogadishu, she rebuked them for ignoring the relative calm in the countryside outside the capital. Journalists, who faced increasing physical danger, were enraged; they pointed out to Albright that she had toured Kismayo from the safety of an armored personnel carrier. The *Post's*

Richburg wrote an angry letter to Albright's spokesman.[32] The news media were not setting the agenda; they were following the one established by UN headquarters and the Clinton administration, whose chief political representatives, Adm. Howe and U.S. envoy Ambassador Robert Gosende, made capturing Aided a virtual obsession. Aidid's effort to portray himself as Somalia's rightful leader and the only force that could stand up to the "imperialist" outsiders was aided less by the media than by Howe's decision to launch a highly public manhunt. Howe's efforts included putting up wanted posters that offered a $25,000 reward for Aidid's capture, which had the effect of boosting Aidid's stature among Somalis, even among the many who did not support him, an effect he skillfully nurtured.[33] It also set up a dramatic contest of the type the news media are drawn to. The contest became increasingly embarrassing for Aidid's U.S. pursuers as he eluded them, only to appear on international television. Many in the U.S. military were deeply uneasy about the hunt for Aidid. None of the spokesmen wanted to be the ones to unveil the wanted poster offering a reward for his capture. Said one senior officer: "What's the media going to do? We set the roots of the conflict. . . . The story was in Mogadishu. There was no story out there (in the countryside)."[34] More than Aidid's propaganda or the media's focus on conflict, the *fact* of U.S. casualties was responsible for the decline in support from the public, which had neither expected nor been prepared for such costs in a humanitarian-relief mission.[35] Following the watershed July 12 UNOSOM attack, in which twenty to seventy of Aidid's clan members were killed, Aidid decided to kill American soldiers.[36] When that happened, the Clinton administration had no ready explanation as to why or what U.S. interests were at stake.

Both this communication vacuum and the power of television, in particular, to fill it are highlighted by the likelihood that the mission to Somalia would have collapsed from lack of public and congressional support long before October 1993 had other events been widely reported to the American people. One senior U.S. officer expected the end to come when one of the many mortar shells fired by the SNA hit a barracks, killing large numbers of U.S. soldiers—a rough replay of what had happened in Lebanon a decade earlier. The incontestable evidence of an American soldier's body being desecrated in Somalia was new, in the sense that it had not appeared on U.S. television before. The reality of such mistreatment was not. This leads to two conclusions. First, the media, and especially television, do have an impact on policymaking depending on whether they "capture" and report events. But it also shows that any CNN effect depends on the environment that policymakers put in place, inasmuch as reports of other events would have had similar impact:

- On August 8, four American soldiers were killed when their vehicle was destroyed by a remote-controlled bomb placed under the road. That afternoon, Somalis allied with the SNA came to the Sehafi Hotel with a gruesome trophy—a piece of flesh that they claimed came from one of the soldiers. They posed, encouraging photographers to take pictures. Journalist Michael Maren, on assignment for the *Village Voice*, videotaped the incident with a handheld videocamera that belonged to Reuters. The videotape was shown in Europe but not in the United States.[37]

- On September 5, seven Nigerians were killed on the first day of more than a week of intense battles between the SNA and UNOSOM. CNN shot footage of the Nigerians' bodies being desecrated. But this vivid account of what was happening in Somalia was broadcast only once on CNN's domestic U.S. service; it was bumped by the news that pop star Michael Jackson had been accused of child molestation.[38] Within a week, U.S. reporters had abandoned Somalia in the face of Aidid's threat to take Americans hostage.

- In the early morning of September 25, Somalis fired a rocket-propelled grenade into the belly of a U.S. Blackhawk helicopter—a forewarning of what would happen ten days later. The damage was catastrophic; three crew members were killed, and the pilot and copilot were badly wounded. Stories began to circulate that the body parts of the soldiers were being displayed in Mogadishu's main market. The Pentagon denied the reports, which were true. The three caskets that left Mogadishu did not contain full sets of remains.[39] Paul Watson, a reporter with the *Toronto Star*, had seen the gruesome displays in the marketplace. Watson began carrying a pocket camera. He was not thinking of winning a Pulitzer Prize, but of proving what Somalis were doing to the dead.[40]

The beginning of the end came on Monday, October 4, when Stockwell got a telephone call from Atlanta.

The United States

The voice on the other end of the phone belonged to the president of CNN, Tom Johnson. Although CNN had pulled out of Mogadishu, its Somali stringer, Hassan Mohamoud, was still there with a HI-8 video-camera. Mohamoud had lived in Detroit for well over a decade and spoke impeccable English. His video of the dead soldier and of Durant in captivity was put on the "Pony Express," an NGO flight to Nairobi, and then on to London, where it was beamed back to CNN headquarters in Atlanta. By the time Johnson called, Stockwell already had a good idea of what the video would show. Johnson said that it would run at 3 p.m. Eastern Time (10 p.m. Mogadishu time). He wanted Stockwell on live with anchor Frank Sesno. He was open to guidance about how to use the material. Stockwell asked for two favors: He wanted Durant's family notified beforehand, and he asked that CNN not show any view of the dead soldier from which his family might identify him. Johnson called back later, after talking to the Pentagon: "It's done. Durant's family knows." Said Stockwell: "I'll forever be indebted to him. He didn't have to do that." CNN did not run some of the most offensive parts of the videotape. Other networks that obtained the footage were not as careful in how they used it.[41]

As the October 3 Ranger raid to capture Aidid turned into a daylong firefight, the administration's information on what was occurring remained sketchy. That Sunday, White House spokeswoman Dee Dee Myers wandered into National Security Adviser Tony Lake's office. "There's some sort of pitched battle under way in Somalia. We don't really know what's happening," Lake said.[42] The CNN video began running on American television screens on Monday, October 4. "We had a lot of trouble just getting basic information," said a senior Pentagon official, who recalled seeing the body and "not even knowing it was [a] U.S. [soldier]."[43] Once again, the news media's speed had outstripped the administration's other sources of information. A "very angry" President Clinton saw the video while in his room at the Fairmont Hotel in San Francisco and immediately began discussing with his senior aides how to respond.[44] Millions of other Americans saw the images of the soldier and Durant over the next twenty-four hours, either on television or in their morning newspapers, where Watson's photograph was published.[45] Many protested the media's use of the images.[46]

To reiterate the questions posed at the beginning of this chapter, what was the impact of the images and why? The setbacks for the mission, as portrayed in the news media, caused an immediate emotional reaction. In Congress, where alarm over the mission in Somalia had been growing over the previous month, dozens of senators and representatives took to the floor to demand an immediate U.S. withdrawal from Somalia. Many Clinton administration officials said that, with support for the mission already ebbing, the deaths of eighteen U.S. soldiers alone would have provided the final blow to policy, whether or not the events were reported in gut-wrenching, real-time television images. But the graphic way in which the setback was portrayed and the ability of political opponents to use the images meant that the administration now had little time in which to act. Images "amplify and accelerate . . . time pressures in which you have to make a decision," Berger said. "This was a catalytic event."[47] Myers said that in the hours and days after the battle in Mogadishu, the administration was under pressure to respond publicly to events and political opponents within the same news cycle. The White House had to ensure that its views and actions were "out there" alongside those of its opponents. "That definitely speeded up the process," Myers said. "You couldn't let it go on indefinitely."[48] The Clinton administration had to do something—and more quickly than it preferred.

The news media helped drive the speed of the policy response, but did it also drive policy, determining that response? In other words, did the real-time television report of a military setback, including casualties and a POW, force the administration to bow to public opinion and terminate military operations? The evidence is mixed. There was significant pressure to withdraw U.S. troops from Somalia immediately. But as in Korea and Vietnam, public opinion was not the specific source of pressure it is often portrayed to be. It offered policymakers little firm guidance. There was strong support for immediate withdrawal (43 percent), but also significant backing (38 percent approval versus 57 percent disapproval) for Clinton's decision to send additional troops and armored vehicles. The public also supported capturing and punishing Aidid. Those who had seen the image of the soldier being dragged down a street were more supportive of both the withdrawal and the escalation options.[49] Clinton administration officials unanimously agreed that they were responding to pressures from Congress during this period, not to mass public opinion. "That drove the policy response," Myers said. "It had to have something that had a reasonable chance of succeeding on the ground and also to respond to Congress."[50]

The president's advisers opposed heeding the calls in Congress for an immediate withdrawal of U.S. troops, fearing that a retreat in the face of casualties would have disastrous consequences for U.S. prestige worldwide. "We very quickly came to the judgment that was a mistake under the circumstances," Berger recalled.[51] The administration preserved some policymaking leeway for itself. By this time, Congress already was on record as wanting the mission terminated by November 15 unless Clinton received its explicit approval to continue. On the morning of October 7, President Clinton met with congressional leaders and made the case for a respectable interval before U.S. troops left Somalia; in the meantime, he said, he would send additional troops and weapons to allow U.S. troops in Somalia to better protect themselves. He announced his policy decisions later that day, including the withdrawal date of March 31, 1994. While the administration avoided the full-scale retreat that officials so feared, Clinton nonetheless was forced to set a precise withdrawal date: "If he hadn't set one, Congress would have, and it probably would have been earlier."[52] Without the images, "I think we probably still would have gotten out. But it wouldn't have been considered the disaster it was," said a high-ranking Pentagon official. The president felt that "we did have to come up with a plan to get out."[53]

But the images from Somalia do not support the contention that televised casualties will automatically force an end to military endeavors. The images revealed less about the effects of the news media than about the mission itself and how its developments had been communicated to the public. A different policy option—massive retaliation—was considered briefly by Clinton and his senior aides when they met October 5. They decided that the risks of such a step did not measure up to the threat to U.S. security. "The decision was made [that] it wasn't worth a lot of American lives to go after this guy," according to Myers.[54] "The lack of perceived security stakes ended up shaping things more than anything else," said Jeremy Rosner, who at the time was the National Security Council staff's chief liaison to Capitol Hill.[55] By this late date, the administration had discovered that there was a gap between the costs of the mission to Somalia on the one hand and, on the other, what costs the United States was willing to bear for what the public had been told was a humanitarian mission.

Nor was the Clinton administration's policy change in Somalia the instantaneous shift it seemed when the images brought events to such a swift conclusion. The effect of television images in October 1993 was remarkably similar to their effect four months later during the Sarajevo marketplace massacre. As in the former Yugoslavia, U.S. policy in Somalia already was moving in the direction that the mission's events, and images of them, would soon suggest. All the concerns that would explode on October 3–4 had already been in place for months. In midsummer 1993, largely in response to unexpected difficulties in Somalia and continuing problems with UNPROFOR in the Balkans, the administration began scaling back a draft policy on U.S. support for multilateral peace operations. It effectively limited the scope of the administration's future support to the United Nations and abandoned Albright's "assertive multilateralism."[56] In August, even as Clinton dispatched Task Force Ranger and stepped up the hunt for Aidid, the administration began to look for a way out of Somalia. Officials were concerned that there was too much emphasis on the "military track" and wanted to reenergize the search for a political solution.[57] These policy changes were made in response to pressures from Congress, where opposition to the Somalia mission was on the rise. Public approval had begun to fall as well.

The sudden increase in U.S. casualties in August and September 1993 did occasion additional media reporting on the mission. But the increased Washington policy debate over Somalia took place without any dramatic images like those the nation would see on October 4. And much of the reporting focused not on the casualties themselves but on the growing debate in Congress and elsewhere over the value of the Somalia mission.[58] Once again, media reporting was influenced by policy actors as much as or more than it influenced them. The congressional discontent, with Democratic Senator Robert Byrd of West Virginia in the lead, culminated in passage in the Senate (September 9) and the House (September 28) of a nonbinding resolution directing the president to report to Congress on the mission by October 15 and to seek congressional authorization for continued deployment of troops to Somalia after November 15.

Another factor in the policy shift was former president Jimmy Carter, who had met and corresponded with Aidid. He talked at length with Clinton on September 12, advising that the only solution in Somalia was a political one.[59] On September 20, a revised U.S. policy was presented by Secretary of State Christopher to Boutros-Ghali, who was also told of Washington's desire to withdraw its troops quickly from Somalia. Boutros-Ghali was unhappy with the plan. There was "fairly strong resistance on the UN's part."[60] The new policy contained elements of what Clinton eventually would announce to the nation on October 7. It called for enlisting Somalia's neighbors, Ethiopia and Eritrea, in a new effort to find a diplomatic solution. The new policy was made public during Clinton's late-September trip to New York to address the UN General Assembly. In sum, the Clinton administration was moving toward disengagement from the confrontation in Somalia long before October and had taken active steps in that direction in the second half of September. These policy changes were motivated primarily by factors other than the news media, especially congressional pressure. Viewed in this light, the images of October 3–4 were merely the coup de grâce for a policy that already lacked wide national support and was in the process of being revised. Rather than causing a sudden change in policy, the televised and printed images accelerated the inevitable.

As many officials would later acknowledge, the images had the impact they did because the Clinton administration did not secure strong prior support for its course of action in Somalia:

> When events went bad, the Clinton administration lacked credible news frames for the images and perceptions. Faced with the darker side of CNN war, it was unready to defend policies and events which formed no coherent story. The outcome of the Rangers' fight was militarily insignificant; the TV images and lack of a media plan to explain Administration policies made the losses politically overwhelming.[61]

This truly was reminiscent of what we saw during the Vietnam War and the Tet Offensive, as discussed in chapter 1.

In Somalia, policymakers at the top levels of the Clinton administration did not closely monitor the mission. Partly because of this, when the mission changed, they did not communicate those changes to Congress or the American people. On the first point, the lack of attention, one senior official said that after October 4, "I never heard many discussions of options beyond, 'What the hell are we doing there?'"[62] Somalia was not considered a high-level issue like Russia, Japan, or international trade. The mission's key policy issues were not decided at the top level of administration policymakers, but one level down—in the interagency Deputies Committee. "We were not sufficiently attentive," Christopher said.[63] There was no principals meeting beforehand to discuss the ramifications of Security Council Resolution 837, which provided the legal underpinnings for the hunt for Aidid. Nor was there a meeting of high-level officials to discuss the president's August 22 decision to dispatch Task Force Ranger to Somalia.[64] Most of all, officials said, there was no realization of the huge departure from traditional UN peacekeeping that the nation-building mission in Somalia—and its risks—would entail. According to Rosner, President Clinton's policy toward Somalia was a logical continuation of Bush's expanded support for the United Nations as a security instrument in the wake of the Cold War's end. "It was much more that there was a casualness in assumptions across the political spectrum, in both parties, about what you could do with peacekeeping," said Rosner.[65] Once the new mission was under way, the administration did not have a clear sense of the growing risks, Aidid's ability to sustain and rearm himself, or the extent to which the hunt for Aidid had overshadowed humanitarian-relief efforts in Somalia.[66]

This lack of internal debate relates to the second point, the administration's failure to explain the changed nature of the mission, and the risks of the new course, to Congress or the American public in anything approaching a comprehensive way. "They did not pay enough attention to the difficulty of an objective like taking on Aidid and his faction and did not pay close enough attention to what was necessary with regard to the press and the Congress if you're going to take on a military action like that," Rosner said.[67] Also, President Bush had never sought congressional approval for the relief mission to Somalia, a gesture that might have secured deeper support and given Congress more of a stake in the mission's outcome. From May 4 on, Clinton and his aides made few attempts to explain the broader context of U.S. policy in Somalia or to mobilize support for the mission. "The administration never came forward and said, 'This is why we're staying, here's what we hope to accomplish,'" acknowledged a senior administration official.[68] This lack of communication fed congressional and public unease about what was happening in Somalia.

In late August, the administration attempted to address this unease. In a major speech on August 27, just a few days after Task Force Ranger was dispatched to Mogadishu, Defense Secretary Les Aspin explained the decision to step up operations against Aidid. Aspin said that the U.S. mission's purpose in Somalia was limited to security; the United Nations would undertake nation-building. But he set three criteria for a U.S. troop withdrawal: restoring calm to south Mogadishu, taking heavy weapons away

from the warlords, and establishing credible police forces in major population centers. The new criteria were widely interpreted as leaving the mission open-ended.[69] There were few other attempts by the administration to
explain U.S. policy or mobilize public and congressional support. Immediately after the deaths of the U.S. troops on October 3–4, a Gallup poll
found that slightly more than half (51 percent versus 47 percent) of the
respondents said it was not clear why the United States was in Somalia.[70]
The confusion over those events was increased by the fact that, little more
than a week before, Clinton and his aides had made it known they were
shifting from a military to a political strategy. Yet the Rangers' hunt for
Aidid was not called off. "The message was not handled properly from the
administration," said one officer. The images of Durant and the slain soldier being dragged down a street in Mogadishu were "a graphic illustra-
tion of the futility of what we were doing."[71]

In the course of interviews, more than one official volunteered a comparison between the impact of the images from Somalia and the less dramatic, but nonetheless graphic, media portrayal of the friendly fire incident over northern Iraq in April 1994, when two U.S. Air Force F-15 jets
shot down two American helicopters, killing twenty-six U.S. and foreign
personnel. There was no significant pressure to end U.S. participation in
patrolling the no-fly zone over northern Iraq, a senior official said. "In that
case, the policy itself was one already widely discussed and accepted, and
a war [in the Persian Gulf] fought over it," the official said. In other words,
the effect of media reports depends on the stability of the policy and public opinion they impact upon. In the case of Somalia, the reports brought
public frustrations to a head: *Why were U.S. soldiers dying in a country
whose people they were supposed to be feeding?* "Peacekeeping is an increasingly risky business," the official added. "You best have support in advance
of something going wrong."[72] The administration did not have that support when the Somalia mission encountered difficulties. It was this vacuum
that accounted for the power of the images of October 4. They appeared
bereft of any context or counterimages provided by the Clinton administration; they spoke for themselves. As was the case during the Marines'
mission to Lebanon in 1983 and the Tet Offensive in 1968, the events,
dramatized by images, could not be explained by policymakers in light
of what they had said previously. As if in a final confirmation of this,
the events in Somalia propelled the Clinton administration to consult

more regularly and actively with Congress and the American public on peace operations.

Aftermath

State Department, and later White House, spokesman Michael McCurry summed up the impact of the events of early October 1993 this way: "One lucky shot into the rotary tail of a Blackhawk helicopter changed perceptions of UN peacekeeping forever."[73] In the aftermath of the Somalia experience, Congress and the American public blamed the United Nations and the Clinton administration for allowing U.S. armed forces to be subordinated to UN command. Congress moved to impose restrictions on U.S. funding and participation in UN-led peace operations, going far beyond anything contemplated in the Clinton administration's more restrictive policy. These actions took on new vigor after the 1994 mid-term elections, in which the Republicans became the majority party in Congress. A persistent theme in congressional rhetoric and action was that U.S. military forces should not be placed under UN command.

Yet the perception that U.S. combat forces were responding to UN orders in Somalia was incorrect. Throughout the UNOSOM mission, U.S. forces, including the QRF and Task Force Ranger, were under the operational control of American military commanders.[74] The missions they undertook, including the repeated attempts to capture Aidid, were ordered and strongly supported by the U.S. government.[75] U.S. Army PSYOPS units prepared the wanted posters for Aidid.[76] Adm. Howe, the chief UN envoy, spent as much time talking on the telephone to Washington as he did consulting with UN headquarters in New York, which tended to blur the lines of authority.[77] Yet the public and congressional perceptions were a logical consequence of the Clinton administration's communications, which consciously put the United Nations in the forefront and, indeed, blamed the world body when things went wrong.[78] After the May 1993 handover to UNOSOM, the administration—whose policy at that point was to promote a greater role for the United Nations—downplayed the U.S. role, despite UNOSOM's dependence on American combat forces. The QRF and other U.S. forces were ordered to keep a low profile.[79] There was "a real attempt to make it look to the world that the Americans weren't leading this, when we truly were," according to one U.S. officer. Stockwell, as UNOSOM's chief military spokesman, gave the mission an American face, a fact that caused increasing consternation in Washington. In August 1993, he was joined by an officer from New Zealand and told to assume a less visible role.[80] After the tragedy of October 3–4, President Clinton and other administration officials did not make it clear that the U.S. troops involved in trying to capture Aidid had been carrying out a U.S.-approved mission and were acting at all times under U.S. command. Pentagon spokeswoman Kathleen de Laski told reporters, "The search-and-seizure missions are UN operations."[81] In his address to the nation on October 7, the president emphasized that the additional troops he was ordering to Somalia would be "under American command." But this had been the case throughout the mission, something the president and his aides were reluctant to acknowledge until much later.[82] Almost three years to the day after the fateful battle of October 3–4, in the first televised debate of the 1996 presidential campaign, President Clinton said: "I take full responsibility for what happened in Somalia, but the American people must remember that those soldiers were under an American commander when that happened."[83]

A backlash against U.S. participation in multinational peace operations may have been inevitable after the tragedy in Somalia. But the attacks on the United Nations were aided, unwittingly perhaps, by U.S. government officials, who failed to communicate the roles of the parties involved and left the impression that the United Nations, not the United States, was responsible.

Haiti, 1994

The U.S. intervention in Haiti in 1994 provides additional evidence that policymakers and other policy actors, rather than the news media, set the agenda prior to military action by the United States. But Haiti also shows, albeit far less dramatically than Somalia, the media's ability to change the course of a peace operation once it is under way. Finally, of all the cases studied, it was in Haiti that officials took the most proactive posture toward reporters, opening military operations to coverage in an unprecedented way. This openness, many officials felt, helped explain the mission to the American public and other audiences. There is insufficient evidence to determine how this coverage would have affected support for the mission had there been significant American casualties or other setbacks.

As in the case of U.S. policy on the Somali crisis, the critical policy correction that would set the United States on the path toward intervention in Haiti occurred several months beforehand. On May 8, 1994, President Clinton announced significant new policy initiatives toward Haiti, including the appointment of William Gray III as his special envoy; U.S. support for tougher economic sanctions against the junta that had seized power from elected president Jean-Bertrand Aristide; and a new policy that would allow Haitian refugees to have their exit interviews conducted at sea or in third countries, rather than in Haiti itself. The president refused to rule out other options (that is, U.S. military force) to remove the junta led by Lt. Gen. Raoul Cédras from power.[84]

Clinton shifted to a more activist policy under unrelenting pressure from his own natural political allies—notably, members of the Congressional Black Caucus and TransAfrica executive director Randall Robinson. On April 12, Robinson began a highly publicized hunger strike to protest the Clinton administration's policies toward Haiti, particularly the forcible repatriation of Haitian "boat people" headed for U.S. shores. Even though Clinton had harshly criticized the repatriation policy during the 1992 presidential campaign and just prior to his inauguration, he continued the policy upon entering the White House.

This domestic dissent from one of the president's core bases of political support—African-Americans—led to significantly increased levels of network news coverage of events surrounding the crisis in Haiti, whose prominence as a lead story in network newscasts had dropped off soon after the presidential campaign. Just prior to the Clinton administration's policy change, nearly two-thirds of the network stories on Haiti in April and early May featured criticism of Clinton's policies by Robinson, members of the Congressional Black Caucus (some of whom were arrested during their demonstrations outside the White House), and others. The media's coverage of the Haitian crisis during this period focused on the policy struggle in Washington that pitted the policy's opponents against the administration, which acknowledged that its policy was not working and would have to be changed. The president, in an unusually frank statement, admitted the salience of Robinson's tactics. "I understand and respect what he's doing," Clinton told a group of newspaper columnists on April 20. "And we ought to change our policy. It hasn't worked. . . . He ought to stay out there. We need to change our policy."[85] The president's statement and a similar one by White House spokeswoman Dee Dee Myers nine days later appeared to further whet television's appetite for the story as the prospect grew that the United States would adopt a new, tougher policy toward the Haitian junta.

In retrospect, it seems that the media's portrayal of Robinson's tactics helped push the Clinton administration into adopting a new policy that included a greater possibility of intervention. But once again, while they did not *determine* policy, the media were allowed to play a greater role in policy formulation because a vacuum of presidential leadership existed.[86] Moreover, contrary to the conventional view of the CNN effect, dramatic images of events overseas had a minor impact on policy in this case. Rather, television focused on the Washington policy struggle, which revived interest in the Haitian crisis after the presidential campaign (see Figure 5.1). In other words, the policy debate drove the coverage, not vice versa. Robinson's successful use of the news media to further his organization's agenda is strikingly similar to how members of Congress and NGO representatives put Somalia's plight high on the nation's agenda in 1992. Compared to Somalia, policy toward Haiti had two characteristics that made it even more salient to the media: the political combat between a president and a powerful constituency, and the country's proximity to the United States. The latter—appearing on American televisions as Haitian "boat people" headed toward U.S. shores—gave urgency to Haiti's crisis and the search for a solution.

In Haiti, the cameras once again followed the troops—or, more precisely, the cameras went where news organizations thought the troops would soon be. It was during the time of the administration's May policy review, when a military deployment was becoming more likely, that the U.S. news media first descended on Haiti en masse. "This was a signal for a mass influx of journalists," said Stanley Schrager, the U.S. embassy spokesman in Port-au-Prince. "They were clearly here to cover the invasion."[87]

Yet as the prospect of U.S. military action increased, the news media, both television and print, were anything but a force pushing Clinton in that direction. The U.S.-based media gave heavy coverage to opponents of Clinton's policy in Congress and among the foreign policy establishment.[88] Prestige newspapers such as the *New York Times* and the *Washington Post* editorialized against the administration's course of action in Haiti, including its decision not to seek congressional authorization for an inva-

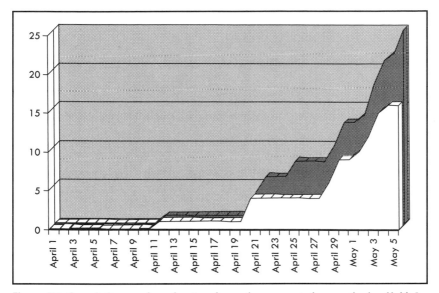

Figure 5.1. Cumulative number of network evening news stories mentioning Haiti, 1 April–5 May 1994 (total=25). In the weeks before President Clinton's decision to take a significantly tougher stand against the junta in Haiti, network news coverage focused on the struggle in Washington over Haiti policy rather than on the conditions in Haiti. This provides further evidence that the media follow rather than determine policy and that a lack of policy consensus piques media interest. (Unshaded area in foreground shows number of stories on domestic sources criticizing the Clinton administration's policy on Haiti.) Data source: Network Evening News Abstracts, Television News Archives, Vanderbilt University.

sion.[89] As Daniel Hallin would have predicted, the media reflected the lack of domestic consensus about Haiti's importance. Public opinion polls found that a majority of Americans (averaging around 60 percent) opposed sending U.S. troops to Haiti to restore Aristide. Support rose if the mission was to evacuate American citizens or stop the flow of Haitian refugees to U.S. shores.[90]

Clinton, acting in defiance of popular and congressional preferences, argued that the deployment of U.S. troops to Haiti was in the national interest. On the evening of Thursday, September 15, 1994, the president gave a nationally televised address from the Oval Office, outlining the reasons for the imminent action. Clinton defined U.S. interests in Haiti as stopping the junta's brutal atrocities against the Haitian people, securing U.S. borders (from refugees), promoting democracy in the Western Hemisphere, and upholding "the reliability of the commitments that we make and the commitments others make to us."[91] Clinton's speech boosted support for his policies slightly. In the immediate aftermath of his television appearance, those who heard it were slightly more likely (42 percent versus 31 percent) to favor a U.S.-led invasion of Haiti, but they were still in the minority. More important, Clinton failed to convince the public that U.S. interests were at stake in Haiti.[92] The speech was coupled with a White House campaign to highlight the junta's human rights abuses, but both came late in the domestic debate over Haiti. This may have been a factor in limiting their effectiveness. The administration was belatedly trying to "do a 'babies pulled out of the incubator' thing," a Defense Department official said. He referred to Bush's efforts in the months before Operation Desert Storm to highlight Iraqi president Saddam Hussein's abuses in Kuwait and portray Hussein as a present-day Hitler.[93] Opposition in Congress to a Haiti invasion had been building for weeks, and Clinton's speech did little to change minds there.[94] Lawmakers again called on Clinton to seek congressional authorization, a vote he might well have lost. Support for Clinton's handling of the situation in Haiti rose markedly in the aftermath of the diplomatic agreement reached September 18, in which the junta promised a delegation led by former president Jimmy Carter that it would leave power by October 15 and countenance the peaceful introduction of U.S. forces.[95] The first of 21,000 U.S. troops began landing in Haiti the next day. In early October, Congress decided not to impose a deadline for withdrawal of U.S. troops, as it had earlier threatened.

President Clinton and his senior aides were keenly aware of the lack of deep public support for the Haiti mission. This lack of support narrowed Clinton's room for making policy, forcing his administration to limit the scope and time of the mission and to put a major emphasis on keeping casualties to a minimum.[96] Even after control of the mission was handed over to the United Nations in March 1995, U.S. troops remaining in Haiti were prohibited from establishing any direct contact with the population and from touring Port-au-Prince. "These restrictions served to reduce even the slightest chance that an American soldier might lose his or her life during the course of this operation."[97] The lessons learned in Somalia after expanding a peace operation without congressional or public support infused virtually every aspect of planning and execution of the U.S. mission to Haiti.[98]

Given its tenuous domestic position regarding Haiti, the Clinton administration turned to a time-honored tool to help explain what it was doing and build public support—the news media. As one official said a few days before U.S. troops landed:

> It's no secret there's no great support for this mission coming from the American people. One of the keys to our success is for the American people to understand that the mission is a success. We can't do that with smoke and mirrors. It's in our interest to help reporters figure out how to tell the story.[99]

As noted in chapter 3, the news media were given almost unprecedented access to military plans and units during the Haiti incursion and the days that followed. One of the military's major goals was to secure media coverage of individual units and soldiers as they did their jobs. Officials hoped this would help explain the mission's progress and generate support and understanding for what U.S. troops were trying to accomplish. As chairman of the Joint Chiefs of Staff Gen. John Shalikashvili explained later: "The best salesmen of what our military does are the PFCs (privates first class)."[100] ABC News chief national security correspondent John McWethy and a camera crew became the first TV reporters ever allowed to accompany a U.S. Army special operations unit on a mission. McWethy's report followed the nine-man Army team as it landed outside the rural town of Miragoane, drove up to the local headquarters of the hated Haitian military, and took control of the town of 10,000, all the while attempting to keep the soldiers and people from exacting revenge on each other. The citizens of Miragoane joyously welcomed the U.S. troops. McWethy pointed out that during the initial deployment of troops to Haiti, virtually every U.S. military unit had a reporter attached to it, outside the formal pool system. "It allows the military to tell its own story" from a human point of view, McWethy said. "It's to their advantage to do it."[101] The military's strategy was helped immensely by the particular circumstances in Haiti—U.S. troops were warmly welcomed by the Haitian masses, and the initial deployment went forward with few hitches and no casualties. "The pictures coming out of Haiti are quite amazing," a Pentagon official said five weeks after the deployment began.[102]

As in Somalia, the international news media in Haiti were a pervasive presence on the streets of the capital. Col. Barry Willey, the chief military spokesman, found himself in a position identical to that of Stockwell in Mogadishu—he often found out about what was happening in the streets from reporters. Frequently, they asked him for an immediate response to an event, a response he frequently did not have. Inevitably, this fast and mobile news media played a role in how the mission was conducted.

On September 20, the day after the first U.S. troops arrived in Haiti, Haitian police viciously beat Aristide supporters. U.S. forces, lacking orders, watched from close by, but took no action. One Haitian, a coconut vendor, was killed. Videocameras and print accounts vividly captured the beatings, as well as the frustration of U.S. soldiers, some of whom cursed their own inability to intervene. Deputy Secretary of State Strobe Talbott was in his seventh floor office at the State Department when he saw the beatings on television. He said to himself: "Oh, Jesus. . . . What are we going to do about that?"[103]

Prior to the incident, and even in its immediate aftermath, Clinton administration officials stressed that American soldiers had no mandate to intervene in situations of Haitian-on-Haitian violence. There was a strong desire to avoid the "mission creep" that occurred in Somalia. Responding to questions later in the day on September 20, after scenes of the beatings had aired on CNN, Gen. Shalikashvili said that it was not the U.S. troops' mission to become a police force in Haiti. Yet within twenty-four hours, the administration announced that a thousand Military Police were in or on their way to Haiti and that these and other U.S. troops would be authorized to act to stop further abuses by the Haitian police. The rules of engagement now allowed U.S. soldiers to intervene with authorization of a senior commander, as long as it did not imperil the safety of American troops.[104] Military and civilian officials said that a major reason for the incident's impact was the policy vacuum created when Carter secured a last-minute diplomatic agreement. U.S. military forces had expected the junta to be gone, either through an invasion or of its own accord. They had not expected or been able to plan for a situation in which the junta would still be in place and U.S. troops would be patrolling the streets alongside the repressive Haitian police force.

Once again, the news media quickly and dramatically exposed a vacuum. The images forced the Clinton administration to come up with a response at a time when, officials said, the exclusive focus had been elsewhere—getting U.S. forces safely ashore. Given the administration's previous statements on the subject of Haitian-on-Haitian violence and its desire to keep the mission limited, it seems clear that the images did have a policy impact. However, several officials emphasized that the response was not, in Col. Willey's words, "a knee-jerk reaction," but awaited the arrival of more troops. They also said that the mission of protecting civilians was one the military inevitably would have undertaken now that U.S. troops were in Haiti. "We'd been there thirty hours when this happened," said Kenneth Bacon, whose first day as Defense Department spokesman coincided with the images from Port-au-Prince. "We would have gotten to that sooner or later."[105]

The tension between the administration's desire for a limited mission in Haiti and the media's reporting patterns continued over the next several weeks. On September 30, several thousand Haitians marched on the third anniversary of the military coup that ousted Aristide from power. Paramilitary forces, known as *attachés*, attacked the crowds, killing at least eight demonstrators and injuring others. U.S. troops, who were a few blocks away, again did not intervene. The U.S. troops' instructions were to establish and maintain roadblocks, or what was called "outer-perimeter security," while the Haitian police had the job of crowd control, or "inner-perimeter security." The Haitian police permitted the *attachés* to attack. This incident prompted what both Willey and Schrager described as the tensest confrontation with reporters during the time the U.S.-dominated Multinational Force was in Haiti. At Willey's and Schrager's joint news briefing, dozens of reporters demanded to know why U.S. armed forces had stood by as Haitian civilians were killed. Reporters did not find the spokesmen's explanations convincing. Willey was adamant that policing was not the job of U.S. forces. Schrager, the civilian spokesman, took a softer line, to the dismay of some at the Pentagon. The United States, he said, would not stand by and watch violence against Haitians, but would adjust its tactics. Military officers accused Schrager of making policy on the spot. He replied that if he had not seemed sympathetic in the face of what had happened, "the media would have pilloried us." Schrager's response suggests a media impact, both on U.S. rhetoric and the conduct of the mission. Three days later, on October 3, U.S. forces raided the headquarters of the main *attaché* organization, the Front Révolutionnaire pour l'Avancement et le Progrès d'Haïti (FRAPH), and carried out other searches for arms in a significantly more aggressive policy toward paramilitary groups. The media images and questions "led to a more assertive troop posture," Schrager said, forcing a change in tactics if not in overall policy.[106]

During this period in early October, some administration officials and members of Congress chastised the news media for focusing too narrowly on the violence and chaos in parts of Port-au-Prince, ignoring the calm throughout much of Haiti. They did so in terms nearly identical to Ambassador Albright's comments in Mogadishu. Rep. John Murtha declared after a visit that the media were "looking at Haiti through a soda straw" and voiced fears that the media focus on violence would push the U.S. military further into a dangerous police role.[107] Deputy Secretary of State Talbott said that for several days, attacks on civilians and other violence were the only stories about Haiti he saw on television. "It wasn't as though it was inaccurate. It was disproportionate," he said.[108] Several officials said that reports on CNN gave the impression that there was a lot more violence throughout Port-au-Prince than was actually the case. Schrager recalled a report by CNN correspondent Christiane Amanpour that included video of the mass looting of a store. The video showed Haitians swarming over the store's roof, and Amanpour's on-camera report implied a general lack of security throughout Haiti. But the store was the only scene of such violence at the time. Despite the pressures associated with these images, policymakers were not mindlessly driven by them. "Fortunately, we had this intelligence on the ground," said White House spokeswoman Myers. U.S. force commanders in Haiti "were saying don't react to CNN."[109]

In sum, the news media's pervasive presence in Haiti pressured the Clinton administration to expand, at least slightly, the parameters of the operation and become more involved than it had planned in protecting Haitians from violence by other Haitians. That pressure, however, pushed policymakers only so far. The Clinton administration did not undertake the massive and risky disarmament campaign that some in the media, at UN headquarters, and in Aristide's government were calling for. Instead, the military launched a voluntary buyback of Haitians' weapons. The real-world lessons of Somalia far outweighed the media's impact.

There are strong parallels between the opening weeks of the operation in Haiti and the aftermath of the Persian Gulf War. In both cases, a U.S. administration had, by previous actions, implicitly accepted responsibility for the fate of civilians. Bush executed the Gulf War and called on Iraqis to rise up against Saddam. Clinton sent troops to Haiti to stop human rights abuses against the Haitian people. He was now subject to the criticism that U.S. troops, because of their joint security responsibilities with the corrupt

Haitian police force, were cooperating with the very perpetrators of those abuses. In both cases, news media reports pressured policymakers to take stronger action on behalf of civilians. But several officials involved in Haiti policy said reporters also acted as a brake on mission creep by constantly bringing up real or imagined parallels with the Somalia mission. As Bush did in northern Iraq, Clinton delved farther into the civil strife than he probably wanted to, but only so far and no farther.

This was the media's impact on the conduct of the peace operation in Haiti. Now to the second question: How did the media's coverage of the operation, as open as it was, affect public support for the deployment of troops? There is anecdotal evidence that viewers tended to use the images of the beatings on September 20 to reinforce their existing attitudes toward the Haiti mission, whether positive or negative.[110] The Clinton administration, too, used the reports of human rights abuses for its own purposes —to underscore for the public and Congress why it had sent troops to Haiti in the first place.[111] Willey felt strongly that the military's press strategy ensured at least that the stories reported out of Haiti were balanced; journalists would have reported the news with or without the military's help. This open strategy did not change when there was bad news. After a U.S. soldier committed suicide on October 16, the third to have done so, the military allowed reporters to speak with psychiatrists who were sent to Haiti to provide counseling to the troops.[112] It seems unlikely, however, that this proactive media strategy would have helped maintain the limited public support for the mission if it had encountered serious setbacks or large numbers of U.S. combat casualties.

Haiti offers no additional evidence about the impact of televised reporting of American casualties on support for a peace operation. There were no television images of the event when the first and, to date, only U.S. soldier was killed in Haiti. When the soldier was gunned down and another injured at a checkpoint outside the town of Gonaives on January 12, 1995, most reporters already had departed Haiti. Despite the increase in support for the Haiti mission once it was under way, that support did not appear deep. The public saw little national interest in Haiti worth sacrificing for, and the foreign policy establishment was, at best, deeply divided over Clinton's actions. Some lawmakers actually threatened additional legislative action if the mission did not remain limited. It seems likely that large numbers of casualties would have prompted these opponents to restart the national debate over the Haiti intervention. If reporting from Vietnam and Somalia is any guide, the media would have accorded more attention to the debate than to the casualties themselves. In addition, the public expected few casualties and a short mission.[113] It appears likely that public support would have dropped quickly if the costs had risen sharply or the U.S. military presence in Haiti had stretched out. Previous cases indicate that the most important factor here would not have been television reports, but the state of congressional and public support.

Humanitarian-Relief Operations

The two cases examined thus far involve peace operations mandated under Chapter VII of the UN Charter, missions in which U.S. military forces were actually or potentially involved in conflict. Somalia and Haiti accounted for most of the postdeployment media effects identified by the officials who were interviewed. Every peace operation involves a mix of political, diplomatic, military, and humanitarian endeavors; indeed, this mix is what separates them from traditional warfare. When the major focus of an operation is relief activity, the media's impact on mission execution and public support once troops have been deployed appears to be less than it is in more complex and politically risky nation-building or peacemaking operations. While this is hardly surprising, it is worth examining.

When U.S. forces are conducting humanitarian-relief operations, the cameras, notepads, and reporters who carry them are largely a beneficial presence, bringing information on local conditions to military commanders, informing the local populace of operation activities, and relaying an intrinsically positive story to the U.S. public. Even by the open standards of peace operations generally, relief efforts take place with few, if any, restrictions on reporters' work. According to Gen. Shalikashvili, the media pose little threat to mission conduct and the safety of U.S. troops during these operations. During Operation Provide Comfort in northern Iraq, the normal tensions between the media and the military "were practically nonexistent." In Rwanda (as well as in Haiti), Shalikashvili said: "We received, with very few exceptions, excellent press—and the operation and the country benefited."[114]

However, as in other operations, the media sometimes create pressure on both military commanders and civilian officials to take on new or expanded missions once troops are in the field. As shown in this and the previous chapter, it is usually policymakers or other policy actors (such as Congress or NGOs) that initially cue the media to begin paying attention to particular events abroad. But once the media's interest has been aroused, and once armed forces have been deployed, the potential for media impact increases. This is what happened after the Persian Gulf War (reporters already were present in the region, could report on the plight of the Kurds, and—wrongly or rightly—held Bush responsible) and with Operation Provide Relief, the Somalia airlift (the action drew the media to Somalia, where they reported further on famine conditions and the inability of the airlift to meet the needs of starving Somalis). During the UNITAF phase of the Somalia mission, Col. Peck, the chief spokesman, identified one impact that reporters had early on. Once American troops and equipment began landing, Peck said, he was bombarded with questions from the press (and pressure from the NGOs, too) about when American forces would deploy to Baidoa, the so-called "City of Death" in the center of Somalia's famine belt. As a result of these pressures, despite the fact that UNITAF's forces were still arriving in Somalia and there was concern about going "a bridge too far," the Marines accelerated their deployment to Baidoa, arriving there on December 16. This deployment was "a couple of weeks earlier than they originally anticipated," Peck said.[115]

Several officials identified incidents during humanitarian-relief operations in which they said inaccurate or distorted media reports pressured them to shift attention and resources toward the "crisis" portrayed by the media, away from more pressing problems. This pressure hampered the effectiveness of the operations. According to AID official Andrew Natsios, at the outset of Operation Provide Comfort, the news media (including the *Washington Post*) reported on a meningitis epidemic in the Kurdish camps and U.S. disaster response teams' refusal to inoculate the population. The military began inoculating everyone—although public health guidelines advise meningitis inoculations only for children under five years of age. Meanwhile, the real problem—cholera—was missed. "We got the disease wrong because the media report was wrong," Natsios said. "It hurt people . . . affecting the response in a very destructive way." Changing the approach championed by the media took a week, and the effort included visits with congressional staffers, including Peter Galbraith, whose boss, Senate Foreign Relations Committee chairman Sen. Claiborne Pell, had a longtime interest in the Kurds.[116] In central Africa in 1994, media reports of a cholera epidemic among Rwandan refugees in Goma, Zaire, meant that "efforts needed in the South and West were drawn away to the cameras. The lack of aid for locals while displaced refugees were fed and cared for increased the tensions and violence."[117]

These incidents involved tactical, as opposed to strategic, impacts of the media on peace operations. They may have made the relief work less effective or more difficult to carry out, but they did not alter the fundamental nature of the mission or U.S. public support. Pressure from the news media or other actors to take on new tasks in relief operations can be resisted, as it was in Rwanda. There, the fears of "another Somalia," whether well grounded or not, outweighed pressures generated by journalists' work. Most officials felt that reporters' ability to do harm was far less than their ability to help, that "the international media was one of the force commander's most powerful allies."[118] This role of the news media in humanitarian-relief operations was discussed in chapters 3 and 4. For UNAMIR's commander, Maj. Gen. Roman Dallaire, guaranteeing reporters access and helping them transmit their stories home meant that he "was able to garner additional resources for his mission."[119] In Haiti, Willey and others felt that the mission's support at home benefited from having images on American television sets of the relief portion of the operation—soldiers caring for Haitian children, providing aid and assistance during floods, and the like.

In northern Iraq, Rwanda, Somalia, and elsewhere, the American public favored the provision of humanitarian aid and opposed the use of U.S. troops to settle the internal conflicts that spawned tragedy. It seems reasonable to conclude that these views reflect a willingness to help but not to incur high costs in doing so. The news media reinforce these preferences—as long as a mission begun as a humanitarian endeavor remains so and does not incur unexpected costs.

Sustaining Support

It was the spring of 1991. U.S. Marine Col. Gary Anderson had been in Bangladesh for some time as part of Operation Sea Angel, the relief effort to help that impoverished country recover from Cyclone Marian.

The devastating storm killed an estimated 140,000 people, left more than a million homeless, and destroyed much of the country's agriculture and livestock. Anderson was on his way to the port of Chittagong, when he met a crew from CBS News. "We're going to India," a crew member said. Someone had assassinated Indian prime minister Rajiv Gandhi. Anderson tried to convince the CBS representatives to come with him instead. There were still a lot of good stories about the relief effort in Bangladesh, he said. "Colonel, you're wrong," the journalist replied. "There isn't a story. There *was* one. You made it go away. . . . We're leaving. And if you're smart, you won't be too far behind us."[120] In October 1994, a few weeks after the U.S. intervention in Haiti, Deputy Secretary of State Strobe Talbott visited Port-au-Prince. On his way home, Talbott shared his airplane with a crew from CNN. The network was shutting down its Haiti operation and shifting its resources to a "better" story: Iraqi president Saddam Hussein was making fresh threats against Kuwait.[121]

It is clear by now that the news media, and especially the time- and picture-constrained medium of television, follow events more than they create them. The media are, to recall Walter Lippmann's apt phrase, "like the beam of a searchlight that moves restlessly about."[122] This is at least as true today as it was to Lippmann, James Reston, and Bernard Cohen. Parachute journalism and other similar news media practices were examined in chapter 2. How do they affect peace operations?

Any soldier will testify that war means hours and days of sheer boredom, followed by moments of terror. And even more than traditional warfare, peace operations can involve flurries of activity that generate intense media coverage, which soon give way to periods of calm and media disinterest. The phases of an operation differ depending on the goals of the operation itself, the resources brought to bear, and the nature and site of the crisis. But from the U.S. military's perspective, these phases generally might include the outbreak of a crisis; the initial international response, usually carried out by NGOs or UN agencies; deployment of U.S. and other national military forces; beginning of activities; sustained operations; handover to the United Nations, a regional military force, or humanitarian-relief organizations; and exit. The operating environment is dynamic and can change rapidly from benign to hostile and back again.[123] The news media are usually present in large numbers at the beginning (especially if U.S. troops are involved), but most of the press corps leaves after the immediate crisis is over. Reporters (not necessarily the same ones) return only when dramatic events occur.

This uneven coverage was most evident in Haiti and Somalia, although media attention to Bosnia has fluctuated significantly as well.[124] Rwanda seems to be a case of massive, one-time attention, which evaporated after a few months. The peaks and valleys (Figures 5.2 and 5.3) show that the tempo of television coverage of Haiti and Somalia correlated directly with dramatic developments.[125] Commenting on peace operations, a senior Defense Department official with extensive experience in dealing with reporters said: "There's not the rah-rah kind of coverage you got with the Gulf War, for instance. It only becomes news when people die, or when there's a fight."[126] The latter observation seemed to be confirmed, at least regarding broadcast television, when U.S. troops landed in Haiti on the morning of September 19, 1994. Once it became clear the landing would be unopposed, the three broadcast networks quickly cut off live coverage and switched back to regular daytime programming. Only CNN stayed with the story. "Had there been violence, we would have stayed on the air," said CBS News vice president Joe Peyronnin.[127]

Officials' frustrations with this aspect of the news media (those frustrations extend far beyond peace operations) were aptly summed up by veteran diplomat Robert Gallucci, in what might be called Gallucci's Laws: "Good news is bad news. Bad news is good news. Complicated news is no news. Simple news is good news. Simple bad news is the best news."[128]

Government officials' complaints about the shallow and fickle nature of the media are hardly new. Nor are these characteristics likely to disappear, short of fundamental changes in the standards and economics of the information industry. Nonetheless, they have important implications for peace operations and public support. In peace operations, it is harder for policy-makers to hold the media's attention and, through it, to attempt to inform or influence the public. Numerous officials strongly expressed the opinion that after the initial flurry of coverage in Haiti and Somalia, reporters paid attention only if the news was "bad" (that is, a crisis of some kind). Most significantly, they said that when the missions were going well, efforts to keep the media interested (through public communication, press briefings, and so forth) met with journalistic skepticism and had limited effect.

Haiti provides a good lens for viewing the media's fickleness. From the time of the U.S. intervention in mid-September until President Aristide's return in October, between one thousand and thirteen hundred journalists went to Haiti. As in Somalia, these journalists departed quite quickly (in this case, after mid-October) and left behind a handful who had covered the story for years. The population of journalists peaked again at between four hundred and five hundred for President Clinton's March 31, 1995 visit to Port-au-Prince to witness the change of command from the U.S.-dominated MNF to UNMIH. There was another lull in media attention and then a small upsurge during the June 1995 parliamentary elections. Deputy Secretary of State Talbott said that once critics' "apocalyptic predictions" of a difficult and bloody entry into Haiti failed to materialize, "the press kind of loss interest." In March 1995, he said, "Haiti is every bit as good a story today as it was before the Multinational Force went in. There's a lot less coverage than it merits."[129] Willey, the U.S. military spokesman, pointed out that Aristide's October 1994 return to Port-au-Prince occurred without the violence that was expected because of the earlier beatings. "It was a wonderful event. But it was a nonevent as far as the media was concerned," Willey said.[130] "You're not going to get a feature story saying things are going fine in Haiti," said Schrager, the U.S. embassy spokesman. The face-off between U.S. troops and Haitian thugs was a relatively two-dimensional story, easy to cover and generally favorable to the United States, Schrager said. "We were on the good side before. . . . It was good versus evil. It was like a morality play." But as the operation progressed and Aristide returned, the story became more complex, demanding more sophisticated coverage from journalists, Schrager said. Reporters' focus shifted to the problems facing Aristide and Haiti, including the ineffectual justice system and the setbacks in preparations for parliamentary elections. "They're legitimate stories," he said. "That's one of the frustrating things now. It puts us on the defensive."[131]

These officials said their own ability to generate media interest, thereby communicating the importance of the mission, was limited when the operation was going well. Talbott, himself a well-known former journalist, said: "We try. . . . You know how much skepticism there is when we're trotted out at the noon [State Department] briefing. . . . There's limits to what you can do." If the news is positive, he said, "[y]ou sense a kind of turn-off on the part of the press." Willey stressed the need for more creativity: offering journalists helicopter rides; making generals available for interviews; "peddling" videotape from the military's own combat cameras to local

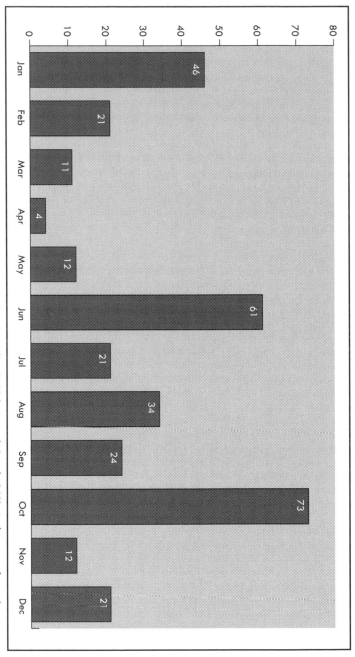

Figure 5.2. Number of network evening news stories mentioning Somalia, 1993 by month (total=340). As the network evening news coverage of Operation Restore Hope shows, television news reporting on peace operations can be highly erratic. Attention fluctuated significantly, falling during periods of calm and rising as hostilities occurred. This trend supports the contention of government officials involved in peace operations that it is hard to sustain public and media attention when the operation is going well. Data source: Network Evening News Abstracts, Television News Archives, Vanderbilt University.

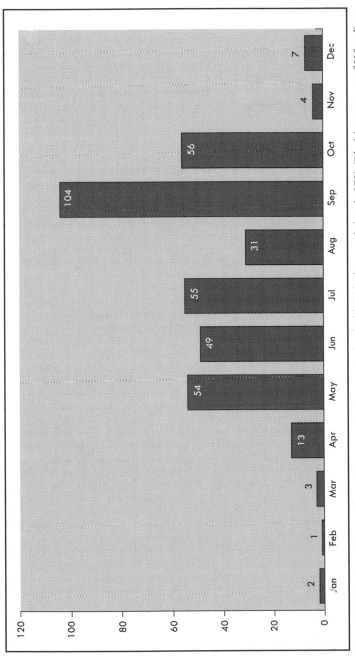

Figure 5.3. Number of network evening news stories mentioning Haiti, 1994 by month (total=379). Television coverage of U.S. policy toward Haiti followed a general upward trend, beginning in April and May, when the Clinton administration's policy was in flux. Coverage reached its peak during September's landing of U.S. troops in Port-au-Prince for the beginning of Operation Uphold Democracy. When the major broadcast networks saw no armed opposition to the peace operation, coverage declined precipitously. Data source: Network Evening News Abstracts, Television News Archives, Vanderbilt University.

U.S. television affiliates, who "will scarf it up in an instant." He saw reporters' departure en masse from Haiti as a mixed blessing. On the one hand, it signified that there was no conflict or violence. On the other, "[y]ou don't want the moms and dads, the American people, to forget about what they [the troops] are doing." A senior Defense Department official was most adamant on this point. Prior to the March 31, 1995 U.S. handoff of the Haiti mission to the United Nations, the Clinton administration debated internally about how best to get the message across that this transition from U.S. to UN leadership was going to be different from the outwardly similar transition in Somalia. This official was among those who argued that the president had to go to Port-au-Prince and lend his stature to the event. Clinton went, but the media's response was not what the official had hoped: "It got almost no coverage, even with the president going. It didn't do very much to educate the public about what was different."[132]

Here again we see the news media's, and especially television's, propensity to choose conflict or drama as the subject of coverage. Clearly the picture transmitted by television to viewers at home is distorted, inasmuch as it largely ignores Sir Brian Urquhart's "99.9 percent normality of life" in favor of the violent, chaotic, or unexpected. How does this uneven media attention affect the public's attention to peace operations? More important, how does it affect the public's view of a peace operation's salience?

On the first question, the relationship between media reporting and public attention is not clear-cut. In Bosnia, the level of public interest in the conflict has borne no relationship to the nature and extent of network television news coverage.[133] In Somalia, there did seem to be a rough correlation between the coverage and public attention to the U.S. mission there.[134] One plausible explanation for this difference is that U.S. ground troops were present in Somalia, which would raise the level of public interest or anxiety, whereas they were not in Bosnia during the period I examine.

In Somalia, the fluctuating levels of media coverage had only a minor impact on the public's view of the salience of the problem. Despite the changing patterns of coverage, the public was consistent in viewing Somalia as low on the list of international problems facing the United States.[135] The public supported the noble humanitarian goals behind Operation Restore Hope, but gave every indication that it expected the tangible costs—chiefly American combat casualties—to be low.[136] Again, there was a relationship between news media reporting levels and public attention to Somalia, although both the media and the public may have been cued as much by the rising policy debate over Somalia in Washington in August and September as they were by the incidents of U.S. casualties themselves.[137] But media reporting patterns had no significant effect on the public's view of what was at stake for the nation in the Horn of Africa. This observation puts officials' complaints about wayward media attention in a different light. *Even if the Clinton administration had been able to sustain greater media attention toward Somalia (or, for that matter, toward Haiti), it does not follow that such efforts would have caused the public to view the crisis there as worthy of more attention and national sacrifice in terms of U.S. troops and foreign aid.* The best time for U.S. leaders to make their case to the public is immediately before troops are first deployed on a peace operation, when public opinion may not have solidified but media attention is high.[138] Given the nature of peace operations, media attention is almost certain to fluctuate. This helps explain the remarks, though not ameliorate the frustration, of the senior Defense Department official who complained: "The only time we were able to get any coverage of Somalia was when there was some kind of fighting on the ground." The Clinton administration did have the public's attention after the tragic events of October 3, "[b]ut then it's too late to explain your policy."[139]

As mentioned at the beginning of the chapter, the Clinton administration's failure to inform the American public of the changed nature of the Somalia mission and the potential costs associated with that change helped determine the impact of the images of a dead U.S. soldier and a captured one. "Such a discussion or debate could well have insulated the administration's policy from some of the consequences of the mounting deaths."[140] Yet at the same time, the American public's view of ends and means—costs and benefits—is probably not "infinitely elastic."[141] In other words, there are finite limits to the executive branch's ability to marshal public support for new, potentially more costly goals that go beyond those the public already has accepted. In Somalia, the news media—or, for that matter, any other factor—did not change what seemed to be the public's basic view of the Somalia mission. That view was the one initially espoused by the president himself. He recalled the nation's tradition of aid to the world's needy, summoned up views of U.S. world leadership by saying that "America must act," acknowledged that the military would have "a difficult and dangerous job," and said the United States would not remain in Somalia with combat troops, nor "try to dictate political outcomes."[142]

What was true in Vietnam (see chapter 1) was also true in Somalia: public support declined not because of the news media, and specifically televised images of casualties, but because the costs, duration, and outcome of the missions began to diverge from what the public had expected. The televised images of casualties fell into this gap; there is no evidence that they created it. In both Somalia and Vietnam, costs began to outweigh perceived benefits to such an extent that members of Congress, columnists, and members of the foreign policy establishment, *followed* by the public, began pressuring the government for a new policy.

This finding further underscores the difficulty and political danger U.S. administrations face if they attempt to change the purposes of a peace operation involving U.S. military forces once the operation is under way or if the nature of the operation changes dramatically because of circumstances beyond their control. Peace operations are by definition limited uses of resources to achieve limited objectives that may touch U.S. national interests, but fall short of being vital interests. In the predeployment and early deployment phases, leaders can use the news media to frame the issue and marshal public support. Beyond that, more basic interests are needed to sustain public support and news media attention. One longtime observer of the media said of humanitarian crises such as those in Ethiopia in 1984 and Somalia in 1992: "That's episodic concern. It's not something that's sustainable."[143]

Success . . . or Failure?

There is one final potential media impact that is unique, or at least common, to peace operations and limited wars generally. Peace operations do not, as a rule, result in the clean, clear-cut victories or defeats that characterize warfare. Nor are the "sides" at all clear. The identity of the enemy, if there is one, may be uncertain: "the conflict, not the belligerent parties, is the enemy."[144] In Rwanda, one Army officer said that "the enemy" was the death rate among refugees and that was what U.S. forces attacked. The objective of a peace operation is not victory, but *settlement*—creating conditions in which political and diplomatic efforts can proceed.[145] In short, the mission, the adversary, and the goal may be less than clear-cut. The outcome is almost certain to be less black-and-white than in more traditional military operations. Typically, some of an operation's goals (say, humanitarian relief) may be met, while others (political reconciliation) may not. This fuzzy end state makes it more difficult for U.S. political and military leaders to portray to the media and to the American public what the operation has accomplished. It is almost certain to lead to challenges from the news media about why, despite a large expenditure of resources, problems remain in the area where the operation took place.

Officials' and reporters' differing viewpoints on outcomes can be seen most clearly in the case of Somalia. Virtually all of the military, and even some of the political, officials I interviewed said that they felt Operation Restore Hope was a success, despite the twenty-eight U.S. combat deaths and other casualties, the failure to capture Aidid, and the summary U.S. withdrawal. They cited the accomplishment of saving hundreds of thousands of Somali civilians from starvation—people who almost certainly would have died if it were not for the intervention. The news media, and many politicians, have characterized Somalia simply as a failure, to the point of using "Somalia" as a shorthand for the folly of peace operations and the shortcomings of the United Nations.[146]

This gap in perceptions was evident when John McWethy, the ABC News correspondent, traveled to Somalia four months after the events of October 1993. Among the officers in Mogadishu, he encountered intense bitterness about reporters' portrayal of the Somalia operation as a failure. Gen. Montgomery and Col. Rausch, the U.S. military spokesman, asked McWethy to address a group of about fifty U.S. officers. Why does the press always describe this mission as a failure? they wanted to know. How do you describe it? McWethy responded. The officers said their mission, the safe withdrawal of U.S. combat troops by March 31, 1994, was going without a hitch. Yes, said McWethy, but the overall mission was a failure. "There was just a total disconnect between their perception of the kind of coverage we provided" and the way the officers saw the mission, McWethy said.[147] A Defense Department official said, "From the military's perspective, Somalia was a great success" because of the lives saved by the mission. But that was "a very difficult story to sell to the media."[148] In reality, the mission to Somalia was a mixture of success and heroism, as well as failures of strategy, communication, and understanding. But the tragic events of October 3–4, 1993, because of failures by the administration and the media to better inform, meant that the American public was deprived of a more balanced view of the Somalia intervention.[149]

The October 1993 images from Mogadishu came to represent the failure of the Somalia mission. According to White House spokesman McCurry, there were no images that were equally powerful in explaining the "systemic failure" of peacekeeping in the former Yugoslavia prior to the Dayton accords. This power of images to define, he suggested, has led to imbalances in the way the two missions have been characterized. McCurry suggested that the failures of UNPROFOR were the greater, evidence of an inability of the United Nations and NATO to work together harmoniously. But "[t]here were few vivid demonstrations of that." The failure was political, not military.[150] As in Somalia, many officials complained that the United Nation's humanitarian contributions in the former Yugoslavia were given short shrift, overshadowed in media reports by UNPROFOR's inability to bring peace to the region. The media, these officials said, often failed to point out that peace enforcement was never part of UNPRO-FOR's mandate.

But the principal problem, both in conducting a peace operation and in explaining it to the media and the public, is that it can be hard to know where to stop. "In war, we expect victory. But in peacekeeping and humanitarian operations, what do we expect?" asked Gen. Shalikashvili.[151] Sometimes it is hard to know when to declare victory and go home. This characteristic of peace operations, and Gallucci's injunction that "simple news is good news," have important implications. They reinforce the demands on policymakers and military commanders to set clear, definable goals for an operation and to constantly communicate not only those goals but how they are being achieved: "The media should see an identifiable end state and progress in moving toward it."[152] This end state should be changed only in extremis.

Summary

The conventional view of news media coverage of Somalia is that a graphic image of a dead American soldier being dragged through the streets of Mogadishu caused the collapse of public support for a continued U.S. military mission there. In this view, the images were the downward side of Rozanne Ridgway's CNN curve that began with images pushing the

United States to intervene in Somalia. We have now seen that on both sides of that curve—the *push* side and the *pull* side—the reality is far more complex and the media's role less than it seemed.

In this chapter and chapter 1, I have attempted to show that it is not the news media reports of U.S. casualties that determine public support for U.S. military operations. While cause and effect are difficult, if not impossible, to establish precisely, it might not be an exaggeration to say that the reverse is true. In other words, the existing level of public support, along with the stability of an administration's policy and its public communications, determine what the media's impact will be. These relationships have not changed from Vietnam through the Persian Gulf War to the present. This is evidence that the advancing powers of communications technology employed by journalists have not altered the basic equation by which the American public determines support for U.S. military operations, including peace operations. The one factor that *has* changed is the speed with which the media can highlight the gap between mission parameters and public support. For U.S. political and military leaders, this factor is well worth pondering. As one senior military officer noted, it took 52,000 combat deaths in Vietnam to upend public support; in Beirut in 1983, it took the deaths of 243 U.S. Marines; and, in Somalia, 18 casualties in a single day. "Somebody's learned something," the officer said. "I'm not sure it's the government."[153]

The argument here is not that the media have no impact on U.S. military operations. Rather, it is that the constant stream of images and written reports produced by CNN and other media outlets do not automatically result in the loss of policy control that has been associated with the CNN effect.[154] The media's impact can be very real; it was seen in three ways. First, because of their pervasiveness and speed, reporters had a significant impact on U.S. tactical military operations in Haiti and Somalia. Sometimes this impact aided commanders' mission goals; often it did not. In a second and related way, media reports at times put pressure on U.S. leaders to expand the scope of a mission that was already under way. This was seen in the U.S. role in stopping Haitian-on-Haitian violence during Operation Uphold Democracy and in the pressure exerted to expand or accelerate the relief operations in Somalia and Rwanda. To repeat, once U.S. troops have been deployed and a mission is under way, political and military leaders have subjected themselves to greater potential media effects.

Finally, while the news media was not the cause of decreased public support in Somalia, the October images did accelerate the Clinton administration's policy process, forcing the president and his senior aides to rapidly come up with a new policy course that met congressional demands.

The concept of a loss of policy control includes the notion that government policymakers are helpless in the face of a pervasive, technologically sophisticated media. Closer to the truth, it would seem, is that if policymakers allow the right conditions to come into play during a peace operation, the media—the reporters, the cameras, the persistent questions, the videotape—take on a suddenly altered, even menacing, role. The media's power is highly conditional. Two factors help determine that power.

First, the words and actions of the U.S. government when it dispatches American military forces overseas play a vital part. At the beginning of a mission, the president and his aides, even absent the binding Cold War glue of a "Soviet threat," have tremendous power to summon public support and frame an international crisis as they see it. This power declines once the mission is under way, owing to both the vagaries of the media and the particular nature of peace operations. Recalling the quote from "Winning CNN Wars" at the beginning of this chapter, the importance of not leaving a vacuum for media reports to fill is as vital, if not more so, in the *pull* phase of an operation as it is in the *push* phase. Filling a vacuum is what the media did in Somalia. Public opinion and the media give an administration little room to change the nature of a peace operation once it has begun. At the very least, such a transition demands the utmost attention from policymakers to the evolving situation on the ground and to communicating (or framing) developments to the audience at home. While the United States and other Western nations were heavily criticized for their minimal response to the slaughter in Rwanda, the Clinton administration outlined a limited mission there and stuck to it. If it had not—if the United States had intervened in the civil war—there is no evidence that the American public would have accepted the mounting costs in time and U.S. lives, and every evidence that the news media would have communicated those costs rapidly and graphically.

The second factor that affects the power of the news media is the nature of peace operations themselves, which was analyzed in the last half of this chapter. In a phrase, peace operations can be a difficult story for policymakers to tell. On one level, of course, the story that the U.S. leadership and the media communicate to the public is a direct one: the starvation in Somalia or, as was seen in Haiti, the brutal power of a dictatorship against helpless civilians, whom the U.S. military intervened to protect. Peace operations reflect the higher aspirations—what might be called the Wilsonian side—of Americans' role in the world. But beyond that, the challenge of communication becomes more difficult. The adversary, the "battlefield," the goals, and the desired outcome are less clear-cut in peace operations than in warfare, where national survival, or at the least maintenance of national status, prestige, or economic prosperity, is at stake. The environment in which U.S. troops find themselves can change rapidly. This change does not mean that it is impossible to communicate policy, that leaders must "tell no stories from the heart." But, like the end of the Cold War itself, the advent of the era of peace operations makes the task of leadership more difficult.

6

Assessing the Gap

Conclusions and Recommendations

> "We are, simultaneously, both your supporter
> and your detractor. By virtue of that
> characterization we will remain, under
> the best of circumstances, allies
> in separate trenches."
>
> —*U.S. Army Maj. David Stockwell
> on the media and the military*

T he news media have less influence over American foreign and military policy than many observers believe to be the case. Claims that this influence is growing do not hold up under scrutiny, and what at first appears to be media-driven policy eventually reveals a host of other determining factors. The media *can* exert influence on policy regarding peace operations, but whether they do depends on many factors, most of which are within government officials' power to control. The CNN effect is highly conditional. Images and written accounts of the horrors of the post–Cold War world that stream into the offices of government officials do not dictate policy outcomes. Sometimes they suggest policy choices, but there is ample reason to believe that officials can reject those choices if they feel it necessary. At other times, media reports become an ally for an entire administration, or individual members of it, seeking to pursue new policies.

The cases studied here provide little evidence of a *push* effect, in which responsibility for launching a peace operation belonged wholly, or even primarily, to the news media. Nor is there evidence of a *pull* effect, an *independent* media influence that forces the alteration or termination of a mission in conflict with factors such as administration policy preferences or public support. The cases, buttressed by historical evidence, indicate that levels of support for contemporary U.S. military operations are determined by factors other than the media—chiefly, the goals and costs of those missions, in part as explained by U.S. political leaders.

The role that the news media play in peace operations is more a function of the particular nature of these military missions than of the media's new capabilities. Put another way, the technology of the laptop computer and the satellite dish gives journalists the capability to report on events from every corner of the earth in real time. But it is the unique nature of peace operations—their openness, the lack of a defined enemy, the multiplicity of institutions involved, and the absence of vital national security stakes—that ultimately permits the type of coverage that exists and determines its effects on the audience.

The conclusion that the media do not independently affect levels of public support and that their impact is related to the nature of peace operations themselves demands one caveat. There is no existing case of the impact of the post-Vietnam news media, and particularly of real-time television, in a conventional war where popular support was high but U.S. military forces suffered large numbers of casualties that were quickly and vividly reported to the American public.[1] Fortunately, the Persian Gulf War involved relatively few U.S. casualties. Some observers have speculated that there would have been no "D-Day Plus One"—that the public would have turned against the war effort—had there been videocameras and satellite dishes in 1944 to capture the bloodshed at Normandy.[2] But the findings here suggest otherwise. An alternate conclusion was stated by the late Les Aspin:

> This skittishness does not hold across the whole spectrum of cases of U.S military use of force. If the American people believe that the military assets are being used to protect the security or the interests of the United States— even if Americans get killed—they will hang in there, they will stay with it. . . . Americans, I believe, will not be spooked automatically by the loss of life. (Some people have drawn the opposite conclusion from Somalia.) I think they will be spooked by the loss of life in pursuing values cases. We haven't got proof of that yet, so we will see as these examples play out.[3]

By "values cases," Aspin meant military operations that do not involve the direct interests or security of the United States but, rather, our values:

that people should not starve; that they should not be tortured, raped, or killed because of their ethnicity; that democratic governments should not be overthrown by force—in other words, the conditions that most frequently give rise to peace operations.[4]

The values cases examined here, from Somalia to Bosnia, indicate that there are real limits to the costs in terms of American lives and tax dollars that the American people are willing to pay to solve such problems in other countries. The absence of a Cold War adversary seems to have reestablished the high level of reluctance that existed little more than a half century ago to intervene in other nations' affairs. In general, the American public supported providing humanitarian assistance in northern Iraq, Somalia, Bosnia, and Rwanda but did not support any deeper intervention in those countries. The news media did not change the public's cost-benefit calculation. It merely made the costs transparent and immediate, eliminating the dimension of time and public acquiescence that governments have long relied on as they conduct wars.

The American people always will be sensitive to the loss of life in combat, so how will future administrations build and maintain support for peace operations that involve anything more than the relatively small level of risk represented by the tardy and brief U.S. intervention in Rwanda? Must American military force be limited only to the "big ones," foreign crises involving major U.S. national security interests in which American society can be mobilized and the news media controlled, either through formal restraints or the societal pressures that Hallin identified? Are more Somalias inevitable, if by "Somalia" we mean a mission whose humanitarian goals enjoy strong public support at the beginning, only to see the support dwindle as the mission grows more complex and unexpected costs mount—costs vividly portrayed in the news media? Does the combination of news media capabilities and the characteristics of peace operations, in fact, render officials completely vulnerable to the dictates of public opinion?

The answer to the last question must be, to some extent, yes. Peace operations "are carried out under the full glare of public scrutiny,"[5] and any hope of shielding the public from the costs and consequences of U.S. military action is misplaced. Yet, if properly understood and utilized, the very news media that at times seem to be the enemy of peace operations can help increase public understanding for an operation before and during its execution. Understanding this is vital for mission commanders, too, who are operating in a milieu where information is often more important than the number of soldiers and armaments they have at their disposal. In peace operations, information is wielded not just by two opposing governments with forces on the field, but by two or three or four different sides; international and nongovernmental organizations; factions, or factions within factions; unofficial, even self-appointed, mediators; and many others.

The practical questions of how to sustain support for peace operations in an information-rich environment will consume most of this concluding chapter. First, I will review briefly what the cases of northern Iraq, Bosnia, Somalia, Rwanda, and Haiti tell us about the push effect, which was covered in detail in chapters 2 and 4. Then I will look at how the pull effect works in peace operations. The remainder of the chapter contains recommendations to civilian and military leaders on how to deal with information and communications during peace operations. The chapter ends with a brief note about the future of the relationship between officials and reporters.

The Push Effect

In late 1995, President Clinton ordered the deployment of more than twenty thousand U.S. troops to Bosnia and neighboring countries to participate in the NATO-led Implementation Force, which would monitor and, if necessary, enforce compliance with the Dayton peace accords signed by the leaders of Bosnia, Croatia, and Serbia.

For more than four years, global television images, radio broadcasts, and newspaper accounts ensured that the war in the former Yugoslavia could not be ignored by the West's senior policymakers and their nations' publics. But, in the end, the news media did not have the power to push those nations into the Balkan conflict. Clinton dispatched troops for more fundamental reasons: he had repeatedly promised that U.S. troops would help support a peace agreement if one was reached; American credibility and leadership were on the line; the future of Europe and the U.S.-European partnership were at stake; and he believed the military's mission was limited and achievable.[6]

The president repeatedly used the television images—rather than being used by them—as a device to remind the public of the horrors of the

Bosnian war, seeking to invoke the public's memory of what had happened in the Balkans for the preceding four and a half years to build understanding and increase support.[7] In this way, Clinton emulated his predecessor, who used the images of human suffering in northern Iraq and Somalia to explain his actions to the American people.

By late 1995, Clinton faced no concerted pressure from the media or public, like that he and President Bush had faced earlier in the conflict, to take the particular course of action he did in Bosnia. The public was deeply divided over the president's Bosnia decision; those opposed to sending U.S. troops consistently outnumbered those in favor. The media reflected this lack of consensus about intervening in Bosnia. Clinton's November 27 address on national television may have helped explain the mission and build confidence in his handling of the situation, but it did not fundamentally alter public skepticism about the need for U.S. military intervention.[8] It would have been much more politically popular to keep the troops at home.

Clinton's dispatch of troops to Bosnia, like his deployment of forces to Haiti the year before, is continuing testimony to the power of the chief executive to lead, at least in the short run, in ways that are not automatically in tune with prevailing sentiment. The push in this case came not from the television-driven public opinion that so worries George Kennan and others, but from government leaders who chose to exercise that leadership at the expense of short-term popularity or political capital.

The interviews and findings in this study do not support the notion that U.S. policy decisions on whether to deploy American troops overseas are increasingly determined by the news media, especially television. If this media effect on policy exists at all, it is confined to situations of mass humanitarian tragedy, where officials see low costs and high benefits in an intervention. Even in such limited cases, the unique characteristics of these tragedies—especially officials' policy analyses of the situations—played an important role in the decision to intervene or not. And even the limited media power that seemed to exist may diminish over time—or, at least, *for a time*—by the numbing effects of repeated exposure to images of human suffering that viewers are only peripherally connected to and feel powerless to do anything about.

While it may seem self-evident, it is still worth noting that in no case do the news media have the power to actually decide policy. They can exert strong influence on the policymaking environment, pushing themselves into officials' deliberations; but in the end, leaders must choose.

For this very reason, as former secretary of state Lawrence Eagleburger stated, U.S. officials are wary of being pushed in the direction suggested by the news media, because they know that that same media will take no responsibility for the outcome of the policy. While the news media's role in foreign policy crises largely depends on government officials and other policy actors, as well as on events themselves, it is inherently weaker in pushing governments into a peace operation than pulling them out. The reason for this asymmetry is clear: before the intervention, American troops and prestige have not yet been put at risk, actions that in themselves heighten news media and public attention.

The media's push role can be summarized as follows:

- The cases of northern Iraq (Operation Provide Comfort), Somalia (Operation Restore Hope), and the later phases of Rwanda (Operation Support Hope) showed that news media reports, sometimes including dramatic real-time television images, can play a supplementary role in pushing policymakers into launching a peace operation to provide humanitarian relief.

  In each of these cases, however, officials addressed themselves to the narrow human dimensions of the tragedy, intending to avoid any role in solving the underlying ethnic or civil strife that contributed to the humanitarian crisis in the first place. As Eduard Shevardnadze noted, when television affects this area of policy, it encourages officials to "adopt humanitarian decisions and avoid political ones."[9]

- Generally speaking, humanitarian action has strong public support and direct intervention into another country's internal problems has weak public support.

- Even when the media did exert influence, it did not do so independently (that is, it was not the result of journalists' initiative in highlighting a region or problem). Instead, journalists reported on, and thus facilitated, others' agendas. This situation was seen most clearly in Somalia, where international and nongovernmental organizations played a central role in putting that nation on the agenda of the news media and thus on the government's and public's agendas. A loose coalition of these groups, midlevel U.S. government officials in charge of humanitarian relief policy, and concerned members of Congress used the media for their own (no doubt noble) goals. This testifies to the fact that, in this era of rapidly advancing telecommunications, access to the media's powers has spread far beyond the narrow realm of senior executive branch policymakers.

In northern Iraq, the legions of reporters in the region were unleashed not by some separate media agenda, but by the Persian Gulf War. President Bush helped make the fate of the Kurdish rebels an issue by calling on the Iraqi people to rise up against Saddam Hussein.

- The cases of northern Iraq and Somalia illustrate how the media follow government officials (especially the president) much more than they lead them. Increases in television coverage of Somalia followed Bush's actions to, first, initiate a humanitarian airlift and then send in U.S. ground forces. The cameras follow the troops—a truism seen in the media's behavior as U.S. troops were deployed to Bosnia in late 1995.

  A logical extension of this finding is that the smallest policy action on the part of officials can generate media attention, leading to pressures for the next, larger step. Part of this pressure is caused by the media's inevitable assessment of whether the first step succeeded or failed. This point brings up a cautionary note for senior U.S. officials contemplating even the most tentative act of intervention. Assistant Secretary of State Herman Cohen's description of how the United States got into Somalia is worth recalling here: "It started with government manipulating press and then changed to press manipulating the government."[10]

- A corollary of this finding is that the media can have a negative impact on intervention decisions. High-level government officials are acutely aware that military operations attract additional media scrutiny, possibly resulting in dramatic images of casualties or other setbacks that may affect their ability to continue a mission in which the United States already has invested its prestige. Fear of just such a backlash adds to the argument in favor of forgoing an intervention when vital national interests are not at stake.

- In each case where the United States chose intervention, unique strategic, diplomatic, and military factors played a role in the choice and had little or nothing to do with the news media. In Somalia, U.S. intervention alleviated intense and simultaneous pressure to act in Bosnia, which officials unanimously judged would be much riskier. It also responded to the argument, to which Scowcroft and other officials were sensitive, that U.S. foreign policy paid little attention to the plight of the developing world, Muslims in particular.

In Rwanda, Somalia, and northern Iraq, the U.S. military itself played a central role in setting the scope and size of the intervention. Particularly in the first two cases, officials said the decision to act was made when it was determined that there was a job that American armed forces—and only American armed forces—could do.

- The cases of Bosnia and, in its earlier phases, Rwanda offer further evidence of how the news media's effect on intervention decisions occurs in a narrow range of circumstances. These two cases, which involved horrific bloodshed depicted in intense television (and other media) coverage, reveal how the media have no power to force governments to intervene when the potential costs—especially the loss of American lives—are perceived to be high and national interests are perceived to be low.

Media reports did not substantially alter U.S. intervention policy in Bosnia or Rwanda when the civil conflicts in these countries were at their height. As former ambassador Warren Zimmermann put it: "It wouldn't have mattered if television was going twenty-four hours around the clock with Serb atrocities. Bush wasn't going to get in."[11]

An alternative explanation of why television's impact on its audience differed regarding Somalia and Bosnia focuses less on the perceived costs of intervention than on the public's judgment about the causes of suffering—whether the viewer judges that the victims of tragedy are truly innocent. Comparing the international responses to Ethiopia and the Lebanese civil war in the early 1980s, one author writes: "Where empathy fails to find the blameless victim—as in Lebanon—the conscience finds comfort in shallow misanthropy."[12]

- The news media did have a less tangible effect in cases such as Bosnia, however. Reports such as Roy Gutman's in *Newsday* and the ITN video clearly played some role in officials' policy calculations.

These reports' political impact, real and potential, on the public (and sometimes a personal impact on officials) could not be ignored. But the reaction did not involve truly media-induced policy change. In Bosnia, especially, officials seemed to deal with the reports in ways that suggested greater policy change than actually took place. This *minimalist response* relieved some of the pressures for action that officials keenly sensed and usually involved rhetoric or discrete acts of humanitarian assistance, neither of which represented serious risk or a change in the underlying stance of noninvolvement. The key in Bosnia, as a senior British official told Nik Gowing, "was to respond to limit the damage, and be seen to react without undermining the specific focus" of policy.[13] Or, as former Foreign Service officer George Kenney put it, official concern "only extended to the appearance of maintaining we were behaving responsibly."[14] Interestingly, the initial international media reports of large-scale atrocities in Bosnia in late summer 1992 represented such a threat to established policy that the first, short-lived response was to attempt to ignore them.

- The news media, especially television, do a poor job of providing early warning of ethnic conflict, famine, and other elements of post–Cold War humanitarian crises. Attempts to increase the use of the media as an early warning device are likely to have limited success and will perennially be at risk of a more newsworthy big story that—especially on television—pushes less immediate events to the side. While it helps, media attention is not a precondition for action. The willingness to act on early warning and to engage in preventive diplomacy are primarily matters of political will and thus leadership.

- The effect of real-time television (and news media reports in general) is directly related to the unity, coherence, and communication of existing policy. If there is a policy vacuum or if officials are searching for a new policy, media reports can have a decided effect. Conversely, media reports have little or no effect on a policy that is widely and strongly held within an administration, has been well communicated, and has congressional and public support. While real-time television reports can generate pressure for rapid response, several officials questioned whether the decisions reached were any different because of these pressures. Official spokesmen, most notably Richard Boucher and Kenneth Bacon, believed that government officials were becoming more sophisticated in dealing with these time pressures and could hold off demands for an instant response if they deemed it necessary.

The Pull Effect

The news media and the new technology that supports news gathering and reporting have not altered long-established patterns that determine whether the public and opinion makers support U.S. military operations or whether they will pressure the government for a new policy, possibly including withdrawal. The brief review of the media and Vietnam in chapter 1 showed that it was not the news media that eroded public support for that war. Much of the early reporting in Vietnam was far more favorable, or at least neutral, to the mission than is remembered. Television reporting was not dominated by gruesome scenes of American casualties, as is often assumed. Rather, the White House and the military misled Congress and the American public about the costs, length, and successes of the Vietnam War. This gap was dramatically pointed out by the media reporting of the Tet Offensive, which, while a failure for the enemy in purely military terms, made clear to the public and Congress that the conflict was nowhere near conclusion. As the country's consensus over the war collapsed, the tone of news media coverage shifted accordingly.

Somalia was almost identical to Vietnam in this respect. Support for Operation Restore Hope, which was relatively high at the beginning, eroded first in Congress, as costs mounted and the mission's goals shifted to ones lawmakers had not approved of. The public, apparently prompted by the debate in Washington, began to withdraw its support. This erosion in support took place in the absence of significant levels of media (especially television) coverage and before the dramatic, real-time images of two U.S. soldiers, one captured and one slain. These images merely provided the coup de grâce to a policy to which neither the public nor the Clinton administration was attached any longer and that the latter was already in the process of altering.

Of course, this does not mean that the modern news media—again, particularly real-time television—has no effect on peace operations once they are in progress. In an open reporting environment, the news media can dramatically and quickly highlight the costs of an operation. Because of their technological capability and the lack of media censorship and control, reporters can make the successes and failures of peace operations transparent in an unprecedented way. This fact is key to understanding the media's role in peace operations.

The words of the senior military officer who served in Somalia are worth recalling here. He noted that there were 52,000 casualties in Vietnam, but that it took the deaths of only 243 U.S. Marines in Beirut in 1983 and 18 casualties in Somalia in a single day to make the missions unsustainable. "Somebody's learned something," the officer said. "I'm not sure it's the government."[15] This observation does not mean that television has made the American public "more skittish" (using Secretary Aspin's phrase) about combat casualties per se. It docs mean that the American people and Congress will not stand still for long if they believe their sons' and daughters' lives are lost for vague or unworthy purposes. The news media can now reveal any gaps between reality and public preferences more quickly and urgently than ever before. In other words, the media make Clausewitz's trinity of people, military leaders, and government even more binding than before. Modern military operations simply cannot proceed for long without the vital ingredient of public support.

In the broadest sense, what occurred in Somalia suggests that the impact of televised images and other news media reports continues to be directly related to the level of preexisting support for the military mission. In World War II, particularly, news reports of casualties and other setbacks in the war effort strengthened the resolve of the American public in most instances. Even in the more ambiguous cases, such as the Korean conflict, Vietnam, or Somalia, there is evidence that, in some segments of public opinion, news that American forces had been harmed caused at least a short-term increase in support for escalation, not withdrawal.

In Somalia, news media reports of combat casualties in August, September, and October 1993 undercut support for U.S. forces' mission only in the sense that they revealed higher costs than the American people expected to pay to save innocents in the Horn of Africa. If anything, the media were slower than they might have been in reporting what was actually occurring in Somalia during the summer of that year. The primary effect of the images was to restart a slumbering policy debate in Washington. The media paid more attention to the debate among the executive branch, Congress, and various other opinion makers than to the deaths themselves.[16]

This finding is consistent with Hallin's observation that the news media's role is intimately related to the degree of social consensus on a given issue. If the consensus is strong (that is, there is overwhelming support for a course of action), the news media reinforce and extend this consensus. If segments of society are in dispute over a given issue, the "sphere of legitimate controversy" is expanded, allowing the media to report on issues that previously were either off limits or not newsworthy.[17]

Because media technology is now so advanced, pervasive, and rapid, the media reflect societal consensus even more directly than before. And because virtually every aspect of a peace operation is open to coverage by journalists, the relationship between public support and military operations is drawn more tightly than ever. Peace operations lacking public support cannot be sustained for long in the presence of rising casualties or other costs.

This finding, in turn, suggests that there were significant potential problems with the missions in Haiti and Bosnia, both of which were characterized by, at best, mixed public support and significant divisions in Congress as they began. The two cases, as was noted, show that strong leadership and communication can almost always overcome initial public and congressional reluctance to send U.S. troops overseas. Americans rally 'round the flag at a mission's outset, muting opposition somewhat. This situation occurred in late 1995, when Congress, despite many members' misgivings about sending troops to Bosnia, did not stop President Clinton from proceeding.

Yet the nation's leadership should not be lulled into thinking that, once intervention has gone forward, the nation will support whatever policy the leadership might want to pursue. The Haiti mission proceeded largely as it was explained to the American public. The mission in Bosnia, as of this writing, has not encountered significant unforeseen difficulties. However, the presence of U.S. troops has continued beyond the termination date originally set by President Clinton, a development that required him to explain the reasons why and secure congressional and public support once more. This study suggests that, given the low national priority accorded to Bosnia, American casualties or similar misfortunes would reinvigorate the Washington policy debate, most likely leading to calls to withdraw American troops. The House and Senate votes on Bosnia, while offering less than full-hearted support, gave the president some protection regarding his Bosnia policy; he had no such protection regarding Haiti.

The one way that the news media might appear to distort the costs of a peace operation is through their "roller coaster" news coverage—periods of intense scrutiny followed by inattention. This phenomenon is most pronounced in television coverage. Government officials express considerable frustration that after the initial, usually positive, rush of news coverage following the launching of a peace operation, the news media pay little attention to the rest of the mission unless something goes wrong. These officials believe their ability to retain or reinvigorate reporters' interest in the story is quite limited.

In terms of public support, the fact that after the initial phase of a peace operation the news media focus mainly on the mission's costs or setbacks rather than its successes might seem to distort public perceptions of costs and benefits, contributing to a pull effect. While this is certainly plausible, the level of media coverage does not seem to affect the public's view of the importance of an international problem. Nor is it clear that fluctuating levels of coverage change the public's all-important initial cost-benefit calculation about the sacrifices they are willing to bear to solve such a problem. In other words, "better" coverage (that is, more reporting on a mission's success and progress) probably will not insulate policymakers if the public perceives that the mission has become a folly.

As is the case with the push side of the media's influence on peace operations, it should be noted on the pull side that news media reports do not demand precise policy responses. In October 1993, the horrible images of a dead U.S. soldier being dragged through the streets of Mogadishu and a captured U.S. airman propelled an existing policy debate toward resolution. Congress, the American public, and the Clinton administration itself all wanted policy in Somalia changed. But the new policy was shaped by the circumstances as much as by political pressures fanned by the news media. As White House spokeswoman Dee Dee Myers put it, "It had to have something that had a reasonable chance of succeeding on the ground and also to respond to Congress."[18] The administration reviewed several policy options, including an escalation of the battle against Aidid. It chose the course it did after determining—belatedly—that there were no significant national security stakes to justify continued combat.

Finally, the cases that were examined provided evidence of what might be called "tactical" news media effects on peace operations, where the media affected how the mission was conducted on the ground (as opposed to "strategic" effects, which involve the media's impact on public support and the government's ability to continue the mission).

A massive news media presence usually occurs once U.S. troops have been deployed or news organizations are reasonably certain they are about to be. In Somalia, Rwanda, and Haiti, the news media's presence brought with it pressures on the military to expand the mission or shift resources to respond to reports of new or unfulfilled needs. This happened early in the Somalia mission, when media and NGO pressures accelerated the Marines' deployment to Baidoa. In Haiti, the media helped put greater attention on protecting civilians from beatings by paramilitary forces tied to the military junta.

These reports seem to have had the greatest impact when they occurred in a policy vacuum (that is, when they involved scenarios that the U.S. military had not planned for). While it is impossible to plan for every contingency, particularly in the fluid environment of peace operations, these findings further underscore the necessity of being thoroughly prepared for a wide variety of scenarios. In at least one incident—the CNN broadcast of the mass looting of a store in Port-au-Prince—military and civilian officials leavened what they saw on real-time television with intelligence information that told a different, less alarming story.

In general, none of these tactical effects seemed to have long-term impacts on public support for the mission. In primarily humanitarian operations, such as Rwanda or northern Iraq, officials were virtually unanimous in saying that reporters' presence, while a complicating factor for them, was vital in garnering public attention.

The next section contains recommendations for civilian and military leaders in dealing with the news media and other channels of information during peace operations, and in building and maintaining public support.

Recommendations for Policymakers and the Military

A lot had changed by the time Maj. David Stockwell returned to the United States in March 1994 after a year in Somalia. Landing at Andrews Air Force Base outside Washington, he was brusquely introduced to the Pentagon's new terminology. "You've been in an 'Operation Other Than War,'" he was told. Stockwell, hearing the phrase for the first time, thought, "No, more like an 'Operation Other Than Peace.'"[19]

Peace operations are both war and other than war. Conditions of combat, and all that goes with it, indeed occur during most peace operations. But when they occur, they take place in an environment quite different from that of most military operations of the past. There is no "enemy," except starvation, waves of refugees, economic degradation, or the conflict itself that peacekeepers have come to stop. The "belligerents" are hard to identify. Victory (or, in military parlance, the "end state") is less clear-cut and even less emotionally satisfying than in combat. Numerous civilian, military, and other international actors crowd the "battlefield." The public, while supportive at the outset, may be sensitive about casualties. The media's—and society's—attention may wander. Most important, peace operations take place in a fish tank of journalistic and public scrutiny. With the possible exception of questions of immediate military security, peace operations are transparent, and the instruments of communication become integral to their failure or success, which depends on the vital ingredients of local consensus and domestic support for the mission.

This book has attempted to demonstrate that there is nothing inevitable about the news media's ability, sometimes seemingly out of the blue, to alter plans and complicate policy. The CNN effect does not result in officials' loss of policy control. But the powers of CNN and other news media will manifest themselves if officials allow certain conditions—especially, a policy or communications vacuum—to develop. These powers can be real and are ignored at civilian and military leaders' peril. Moreover, communication is no longer a simple, two-way street. The most profound change that the revolution in communications technology has brought about is a democratization of information. Ethnic nationalists, guerrilla leaders, humanitarian-relief organizations, and freelance diplomats all potentially have as much ability to characterize a peace operation through the media or affect its outcome as do White House officials or a military commander on the scene. Properly understood, this power of information can be an important tool for leaders of a peace operation. Misunderstanding or inattention to its power can cripple a mission.

The following recommendations are based on the premise that attention to issues of public support, communication, and media relations are as important—and perhaps as difficult—as any other part of the mission and need to be integrated into the mission plan from the beginning. Commanders on the ground and officials in Washington must walk a fine line between legitimate communications activities and boosterism. These recommendations are not a call for "public relations" in the sense of trying to con reporters and the public (which both will see through sooner or later), but for an open and proactive communications strategy:

- For the reasons described above, peace operations demand constant, credible, and coherent communication from government leaders to Congress and the many other policy actors involved, the American people, and real or potential parties to a conflict. This effort should involve all phases of the operation: from predeployment decisions through the deployment, throughout the many stages of the mission, and right up to the exit. It should include explanation of the operation's goals, its risks, and, to the extent possible, the timetable for completion.

  These conditions are dictated by the limited and transparent nature of peace operations. The rules of wartime—where Congress, the public, and even the media suspend doubts for the greater national good—do not apply in the same way.

- Government officials should communicate openly with the American public about a prospective peace operation well in advance of the deployment decision. The instantaneity of communications means that public and congressional opinion before and during a peace operation can change more rapidly than before. If officials find themselves in the position of trying to catch up, the communications battle is already half lost. During the Persian Gulf War, the Bush administration managed to stay ahead of the congressional and public debate, but just barely. President Clinton waited too long to make his case for sending troops to Haiti. His single nationally televised speech on Haiti, given after months of debate in Washington, had little effect, and his last-minute attempts to demonize the Cédras regime were seen as such.

  However, because media and public interest are at their peak just before and during the first days of a U.S. troop deployment, officials are afforded a unique window of opportunity to conduct a communications strategy. The nation's attention inevitably will subside (to a degree depending on the importance accorded the foreign crisis and the risks to U.S. troops), making communication and support-building much harder later on. Congress and the public are likely to snap back to attention only if something goes wrong with the mission.

- Because of the fluidity of the peace operation environment, some modifications to the mission may be inevitable, but significant mission changes should be undertaken only if absolutely necessary. Changes in the goals, risks, or rules of engagement for U.S. troops should never be permitted to occur without full disclosure and communication by the administration and public discussion, as the mission in Somalia showed.[20]

However, any change in mission tasks is dangerous because of the roller-coaster of media and public attention that accompanies a peace operation. It may be difficult, if not impossible, for an administration to regain the media's attention to explain a mission's new course. As we have seen, senior administration officials felt that their efforts to stimulate media interest in the middle of a peace operation had little effect when the mission was going as planned. This "dangerous pause," when an ongoing military operation is not high on the public's agenda of concerns, is the worst time to alter a mission.

- Peace operations do not contain the tidy win-lose dichotomy that applies in wartime. While easing a region's mass suffering and setting it on a course toward reconstruction are the goals, a peace operation's final outcome is bound to include continuing problems and unfulfilled tasks. These leftover problems will undoubtedly attract criticism from political opponents of the mission and the news media, as happened when U.S. troops prepared to leave Haiti.

  Executive branch leaders need to explain fully and frankly the administration's goals, the progress it has made in achieving those goals, and what will be left undone or turned over to other organizations (whether military, civilian, or some combination) when U.S. troops leave the region. This communication should be directed not just toward the American public but toward inhabitants of the affected region (whose expectations of U.S. assistance naturally will be high) as well as private and international voluntary organizations, which should know what they can and cannot expect from their military colleagues.

- In the field, military commanders and their subordinates should be as open as possible with the news media. Part of the media contingent covering a peace operation will already have been in the region for months (or even years) and will have a detailed understanding of the situation and alternative sources of information. Others will have just arrived for a two- to three-week stay, having never been in the region before, and will depend on the military's assistance. Telling the military's story does not guarantee positive media coverage for the mission but almost always helps balance coverage. In the information-rich environment of peace operations, not telling the military's story guarantees that someone else's views will prevail in print and broadcast reports.

A key part of telling the military's story is to ensure that reporters have extensive and thorough access to individual military units as they perform their tasks, a strategy that was followed by and large in Haiti and Bosnia.[21] This strategy is not the same as staging press pools, which should be done only in discrete and limited circumstances. The U.S. military deployment to Bosnia has seen the implementation of an alternative concept called "embedded media," in which individual reporters integrate themselves into military units for a minimum of two weeks at a time.[22] This arrangement seems to signal a return to the more cooperative media-military relationship of the pre-Vietnam era.

The U.S. military—particularly the Marines, followed by the Army —seems to be slowly emerging from the one-dimensional view of the news media shaped by the experience in Vietnam and understanding the positive potential for media coverage of military operations. During the IFOR mission in Bosnia, formal restrictions on reporters have been limited to matters of intelligence collection, special operations, and details of casualties. Efforts have been made to ensure access to operations and individual troops.[23] In some instances, the military was ahead of civilian leaders in this regard. Strictly humanitarian-relief peace operations involve virtually no military restrictions on coverage.

These and other proactive media strategies can help build understanding and support among the American public for the complicated endeavors that constitute peace operations. However, there is no public affairs strategy intense or sophisticated enough to provide an insurance policy to insulate a mission with limited public support from the negative effects of large numbers of U.S. casualties or other significant setbacks.

- Reporters may at times seek or accept the U.S. military's protection. In return, they have a responsibility to understand military doctrine, operations, and equipment, and even to consider accepting a modicum of military training. As in any assignment, they should be prepared for the conditions of the modern peace operations "battlefield," including how to behave in a firefight or ambush and knowledge of rudimentary first aid.[24]

- Because of their mobility, reporters can be an important source of "open intelligence" for military commanders.[25] However, care needs to be taken so that journalists do not appear to be agents of the military. This is particularly true in cultures with little tradition of an adversarial press, where the news media are viewed as arms of the state.

- Public affairs cannot be a second- or third-tier priority (or worse, an afterthought) in peace operations, as it has been in too many recent military deployments. A media and public affairs plan needs to be in place well before the mission begins and should be integrated into the overall operational plan. The JIB or other public affairs contingent should have all the personnel and equipment it needs before the deployment begins, rather than waiting at the rear of the logistics line.

  Senior military commanders must learn how to be spokespersons for their mission and to interact with the news media on a regular basis. This interaction almost certainly will lead to criticism that commanders are becoming "politicized" or neglecting their principal duties, but it is part of the multifaceted nature of peace operations, which demands commanders who are well rounded and can serve as impromptu diplomats and politicians as well as war fighters.

  Above all, media relations should be proactive, not just defensive. Once on the defensive, it is exponentially more difficult for commanders (or anyone else) to make their case.

- Peace operations often involve more information warfare than conventional combat. Modern communications technology and the quasi-political nature of peace operations mean that parties to a conflict can use the media—both international and local—to affect the military mission and how it is perceived. This ability is more than an annoyance: it can destroy the brittle local consensus regarding troops' presence in a region. Mohamed Farah Aidid in Somalia and Lt. Gen. Raoul Cédras in Haiti showed some sophistication in using the media to achieve their political goals, with significant consequences for the U.S. mission and troop safety. Leaders of undeveloped or developing nations may not be particularly adept at manipulating U.S. public opinion yet, but there is every indication they will become more sophisticated over time.[26]

  Government-controlled news media may have helped create the conditions that necessitated the peace operation in the first place. In

Bosnia and Rwanda, factional leaders used television and radio to fan ethnic resentments and incite killings, in the former case beginning long before any peacekeepers arrived.

Military commanders need to be keenly aware of how other actors are attempting to portray the role and actions of peacekeeping troops. Charges that the troops are attempting to "occupy" the country or are biased in favor of a particular political faction could easily make soldiers subject to attack. From the beginning of the mission, commanders should implement aggressive, credible civil affairs and PSYOPS campaigns to explain their troops' actions to the local populace.

- Local news media are far more important in building support for a mission than generally realized. Top AID official Andrew Natsios was astounded at the power of the BBC's Somali-language news service and his ability to use it to send messages to influential village elders. Maj. Stockwell rapidly gained respect for Somali journalists, finding them far more sophisticated than he had expected. Before and during the U.S.-assisted withdrawal of UN peacekeepers from Somalia in March 1995 (Operation United Shield), the commander, Marine Lt. Gen. Anthony Zinni, made the local media a top priority to deliver the message that his troops meant no harm to Somalis but would respond with deadly force if attacked.

- In peace operations, the multiplicity of actors—peacekeeping units from various countries as well as nongovernmental and international organizations—complicates coherent communication to the American and other publics, the international community, and inhabitants in the area of operations.

Public diplomacy and media relations are easier when a single nation or organization (such as NATO) leads the mission in a "subcontract" with the United Nations, as during the U.S.-led UNITAF mission in Somalia. However, the benefits of such an arrangement need to be weighed against the greater support the U.S. public generally affords missions in which the burden is more evenly shared with other nations.

Radically different operating styles and mutual distrust limit the ability of the U.S. military and NGOs to work hand in hand. For good reason, NGOs are wary of being seen by the local populace as an arm of the military. The military, rightly, is focused on security and is wary of relinquishing control. However, the two institutions have made significant progress in recent years to overcome their once almost absolute unfamiliarity with each other. The CMOC proved to be a vital tool for coordinating the security, relief, and economic-assistance components of the operations in Rwanda and Somalia. All actors should at least explore whether it is feasible to replicate this cooperation in communications activities, with a combined JIB that would serve as a central clearinghouse for reporters covering a peace operation.

- To the extent that it will continue to play a significant role in peace operations, the United Nations urgently needs to improve its public affairs apparatus, both in New York and in the field. Every reporter interviewed for this study, as well as many civilian and military officials, harshly criticized the closed and inefficient manner in which the United Nations distributes information. With the exception of the Congo operation in the early 1960s, the United Nations traditionally has not had to confront intense, sustained scrutiny of its peacekeeping activities by the world media. UN officials seem to have only slowly and grudgingly adapted to the new environment of intense media interest.

  As with other UN activities, there are inherent difficulties in its media and public affairs operations. Member nations have sharply differing views about the news media and the dissemination of information generally. The organization is in perpetual financial crisis, and many member nations (including the United States) are reluctant to fund what their citizens might deem as public relations for the world body. But if concerned countries are to understand and support UN actions, it is vital that the organization's information functions be given a much higher priority, more professionalism, and at least moderately higher funding. Most of all, UN officials need to properly understand the impact of communication on the parties to a conflict and the population at large. Some progress along these lines was made in the course of the Rwanda mission, but much more needs to be done.

- Finally, both the military and the news media need to be wary of letting one peace operation become a straitjacket for the next. This is especially true for the media, which tended to explain the Haiti mission through the lens of Somalia and the Bosnia mission through the lens of all recent, failed attempts to bring peace to the Balkans.

While all actors in a peace operation obviously want to learn as they conduct these new types of missions, the danger is that they will draw too many parallels from what may have been a unique event. Each peace operation described here was unique in fundamental ways, hampering the search for broader conclusions about what works and what does not.

These recommendations should help ensure news media coverage of peace operations that is thorough, balanced, and accurate. They also should help ensure a deeper understanding about the goals of peace operations among members of the American public and numerous other constituencies. They will not insulate officials from public retribution if a peace operation with little support suddenly incurs unacceptable costs or develops different, ambiguous goals while the mission is well under way.

There is evidence that U.S. public support for peace operations always will be limited. Americans support their government's lending a hand when their television screens and newspapers tell them humanitarian disaster has struck overseas. The public will rally to support its troops anytime the president sends them into danger, but it is not willing to incur large costs in support of nation building or intervention in seemingly intractable ethnic warfare. From the Mexican-American War through Korea and Vietnam to the present, Americans have shown little patience for longer-than-expected wars when they do not perceive a vital national interest to be at stake.

In the distant past, it may have been possible to conduct unpopular wars with little or no regard for the citizenry's preferences. Since Clausewitz's time, the buffer has been eroding between leaders and the military on the one hand and the people on the other. The modern news media's mobility and speed have made it impossible to conduct military operations for any length of time without at least tacit public and congressional support.

A Note on the Future

The writing and research of this study took place during a period (1994–96) that saw truly awesome changes in how information is used and communicated in American society. These changes include the staggering growth of computer networks—elements of the Information Superhighway—as a means of exchanging data and conducting commerce; the melding of computer, telephone, and television services adumbrated in the Telecommunications Act of 1996; and the further expansion of global and regional television news services, many of them devoted to exclusive coverage of highly specialized topics.

The social and political ramifications of these changes remain to be seen and, in any case, go far beyond the scope of this study. It is worth noting, however, that various branches of the military and humanitarian-relief organizations now use the Internet for both internal and external communications. At the outset of the Bosnia mission, the Defense Department made briefing transcripts, maps, and other information available on the World Wide Web.

The findings here suggest that with each technological advance, some things change, yet others do not.

What *has* changed is the environment within which foreign policy and national security decisions are made. That new policymaking environment is characterized by the speed of information flows and a rapid democratization of access to the tools of communications, in which numerous actors outside the narrow confines of government can be heard and attempt to influence various publics. These changes are clearly disturbing to George Kennan and many others, who worry that American policies will be "controlled by popular emotional impulses, and particularly ones provoked by the commercial television industry."[27] Yet virtually every significant study of public opinion has concluded that, at least over the long term, the public is neither so irrational nor so whimsical as many government officials assume. Certainly, the argument can be made that in the cases studied here, the public's choices were, by and large, rational.

More pluralism in democratic institutions does not demand less leadership; if anything, it demands more. The modern news media have made governance more difficult and more "risky." But Kennan's fears about the obsolescence of official prerogatives are exaggerated at best. The new communications technologies examined in this study, and in all likelihood those of the future, open up new opportunities for leaders to communicate. (Indeed, during the Persian Gulf War, government leaders' use of these technologies prompted concerns in the news media and elsewhere about vastly increased executive power, a fear precisely opposite to Kennan's.) Yet paired with these new opportunities is an enhanced ability by the news media—and, through them, by many other actors—to influence outcomes rapidly when leadership is absent. In northern Iraq, Somalia, Rwanda, Haiti, and Bosnia, the news media were able to wield what influence they did when journalists discovered a policy or communications vacuum. At these critical points, the CNN effect suddenly came into play.

This is what has *not* changed: Policymakers retain the power to set the agenda, to make policy choices, and to lead. To do so, they need a sophisticated understanding, not simplistic descriptions, of the complex role of the news media in a democratic society.

Notes

Introduction

1. Although I was present that day, I rely on the superior memory of Cable News Network correspondent Ralph Begleiter. This reconstruction of events is based in part on an excerpt from Begleiter's address, "Media and International Affairs in the Satellite Age," presented at the Meridian International Center, Washington, D.C., April 24, 1995. The analysis of the incident is my own.

2. George F. Kennan, "Somalia, Through a Glass, Darkly," *New York Times,* September 30, 1993, A25.

3. Quoted in Johanna Neuman, *Ambassadors: Relics of the Sailing Ships? A Gentle Inquiry into the Diplomatic Trade in the Age of Cyberspace* (Washington, D.C.: Annenberg Washington Program in Communications Policy Studies of Northwestern University, 1995).

4. Remarks by UN secretary general Boutros Boutros-Ghali at the Freedom Forum Media Studies Center, New York, March 19, 1995.

5. This is Begleiter's definition.

6. For a more complete definition of the CNN curve, see Johanna Neuman, *Lights, Camera, War: Is Media Technology Driving International Politics?* (New York: St. Martin's Press, 1996), 15–16.

7. Steven Livingston and Todd Eachus, "Humanitarian Crises and U.S. Foreign Policy: Somalia and the CNN Effect Reconsidered," *Political Communication* 12, no. 4 (October–December 1995): 415.

8. See Frank J. Stech, "Winning CNN Wars," *Parameters* 24, no. 3 (Autumn 1994): 37–56.

9. Rick Inderfuth, quoted in Nik Gowing, *Real-Time Television Coverage of Armed Conflicts and Diplomatic Crises: Does It Pressure or Distort Foreign Policy Decisions?* Working Paper 94-1 (Cambridge, Mass.: Joan Shorenstein Barone Center on the Press, Politics, and Public Policy, Harvard University, June 1994), 20.

10. Telephone interview with James Baker, September 11, 1995.

11. See W. Lance Bennett and Jarol B. Manheim, "Taking the Public by Storm: Information, Cuing and the Democratic Process in the Gulf Conflict," *Political Communication* 10, no. 4 (October 1993): 343.

12. For more on this point, see Eric V. Larson, *Casualties and Consensus: The Historical Role of Casualties in Domestic Support for U.S. Military Operations* (Santa Monica: Rand Corporation, 1996), especially 99–103.

13. Bernard Cohen, *The Press and Foreign Policy* (Princeton: Princeton University Press, 1963).

14. Daniel C. Hallin, *The "Uncensored War": The Media and Vietnam* (Berkeley: University of California Press, 1986).

15. Ted Koppel, "The Global Information Revolution and TV News" (address to the United States Institute of Peace "Managing Chaos" conference, Washington, D.C., December 1, 1994); testimony of Koppel, Beschloss, and CNN Executive Vice President Ed Turner to the Committee on Foreign Affairs, U.S. House of Representatives, April 26, 1994, U.S. Government Printing Office Document 79-868.

16. U.S. Department of State, *The Clinton Administration's Policy on Reforming Multilateral Peace Operations*, Publication 10161, May 1994, p. 1, footnote.

17. Gowing, *Real-Time Television*, 3–4.

1. Fighting the Last War

1. For more on the Clausewitzian trinity, see Karl von Clausewitz, *On War*, ed. Michael Howard and Peter Paret (Princeton: Princeton University Press, 1976), especially p. 89.

2. On the U.S. Marines' more open (and more successful) media strategy during the Persian Gulf War, see Stech, "Winning CNN Wars": 47–48. For a critical assessment of the Army's public affairs policy and capabilities, see James L. Fetig, "Inside Fort Apache: The Army and the Media in the Persian Gulf" (unpublished manuscript, June 1992).

3. Douglas V. Johnson II, *The Impact of the Media on National Security Policy Decision-Making* (Carlisle Barracks, Penn.: U.S. Army War College, Strategic Studies Institute, October 1994), 7.

4. Quoted in Johnson, *The Impact of the Media*, 1.

5. Richard J. Barnet, *The Rockets' Red Glare: War, Politics and the American Presidency* (New York: Simon & Schuster, 1990), 127, 131.

6. Johnson, *The Impact of the Media*, 4–5.

7. H. Wayne Morgan, *America's Road to Empire: The War With Spain and Overseas Expansion* (New York: Alfred A. Knopf, 1965), 60.

8. Morgan, *America's Road to Empire*, 14.

9. For more on the value and costs of war, see Harry G. Summers, Jr., *On Strategy: A Critical Analysis of the Vietnam War* (Novato, Calif.: Presidio Press, 1982).

10. Hallin, *The "Uncensored War,"* 63–67.

11. Thomas A. Bailey, *A Diplomatic History of the American People* (New York: Appleton-Century-Crofts, 1958), 592–93.

12. Barnet, *The Rockets' Red Glare,* 157.

13. Cited in Hallin, *The "Uncensored War,"* 127.

14. David Stebenne, "The Military and the Media: The Gulf Conflict in Historical Perspective," in *The Media at War: The Press and the Persian Gulf Conflict,* ed. Craig LaMay, et al. (New York: Gannett Foundation Media Center, 1991), 11–12.

15. Cited in Richard Halloran, "Soldiers and Scribblers Revisited: Working With the Media," *Parameters* 21, no. 1 (Spring 1991): 10–20.

16. R. James Woolsey, "Eisenhower's Folly," *Washington Post,* June 8, 1994, A23.

17. Hallin, *The "Uncensored War,"* 130–31.

18. John E. Mueller, *War, Presidents, and Public Opinion* (Lanham, Md.: University Press of America, 1985), chapter 3.

19. Ibid., 51.

20. Ibid., 98–99; Benjamin C. Schwarz, *Casualties, Public Opinion, and U.S. Military Intervention: Implications for U.S. Regional Deterrence Strategies* (Santa Monica, Calif.: Rand Corporation, 1994), 9–10.

21. Mueller, *War, Presidents, and Public Opinion,* 103.

22. Quoted in Bernard C. Cohen, *The Public's Impact on Foreign Policy* (Boston: Little, Brown, 1973), 124.

23. Stebenne, "The Military and the Media," 12–13.

24. See Hallin, *The "Uncensored War,"* 127.

25. Don Oberdorfer, *Tet! The Turning Point in the Vietnam War* (New York: Da Capo Press, 1984), 247, 251.

26. Mueller, *War, Presidents, and Public Opinion,* 107.

27. See, for example, William Drozdiak, "For Europe, Haiti Confirms U.S. Hesitation," *Washington Post,* September 17, 1994, A12.

28. Mueller, *War, Presidents, and Public Opinion,* 107.

29. Ibid., 167. Italics are mine.

30. Edward N. Luttwak, "Where Are the Great Powers? At Home with the Kids," *Foreign Affairs* 73, no. 4 (July/August 1994): 23–28. Luttwak cites another cause for industrialized nations' aversion to casualties: the smaller number of children and the greater "emotional economy" poured into each child, transforming death of offspring on the battlefield from tragic to "fundamentally unaccept-able." Regarding Afghanistan, a Soviet Politburo member ordered, in writing, that the state-controlled media show "no more than one report of a death or wound per month among Soviet servicemen." David Remnick, *Lenin's Tomb: The Last Days of the Soviet Empire* (New York: Random House, 1993), 521.

31. James F. Hoge, Jr., "Media Pervasiveness," *Foreign Affairs* 73, no. 4 (July/August 1994), 141.

32. Mueller, *War, Presidents, and Public Opinion*, 60.

33. Schwarz, *Casualties, Public Opinion, and U.S. Military Intervention*, 23.

34. Lee Sigelman, et al., "As Time Goes By: Daily Opinion Change During the Persian Gulf Crisis," *Political Communication* 10, no. 4 (October 1993): 353–67.

35. Summers, *On Strategy*.

36. Oberdorfer, *Tet!*, 259–60.

37. Quoted in Hallin, *The "Uncensored War,"* 36.

38. Cohen, *The Press and Foreign Policy*.

39. Hallin, *The "Uncensored War,"* 63–75.

40. See Douglas Davis, *The Five Myths of Television Power* (New York: Simon and Schuster, 1993), 114–25.

41. Hallin, *The "Uncensored War,"* 116–18.

42. Interview with Frankel in Todd Gitlin, *The Whole World Is Watching: Mass Media in the Making and Unmaking of the New Left* (Berkeley: University of California Press, 1980), 205.

43. Oberdorfer, *Tet!*, 332–33.

44. Ibid., 83; Mueller, *War, Presidents, and Public Opinion*, 54–55.

45. Hallin, *The "Uncensored War,"* 169.

46. Quoted in Peter Andrews, "The Media and the Military," *American Heritage* 42, no. 4 (July 1991): 78–85.

47. Defense Secretary Caspar Weinberger's doctrine on use of U.S. military force is described in Woodward, *The Commanders*, 117. Gen. Colin Powell's views are summarized in "Why Generals Get Nervous," *New York Times*, October 8, 1992, A35. For the Clinton administration's more cautionary peace operations policy, see U.S. Department of State, *The Clinton Administration's Policy on Reforming Multilateral Peace Operations*, Publication 10161, May 1994.

48. Background interview with senior Clinton administration official, December 16, 1994.

49. Stephen S. Rosenfeld, "In the Gulf: The Wars of the Press," in *The Media and Foreign Policy*, ed. Simon Serfaty (New York: St. Martin's Press, 1991), 243.

50. Stebenne, "The Military and the Media," 15.

51. David R. Gergen, "Diplomacy in a Television Age," in Serfaty, ed., *The Media and Foreign Policy*, 57–58.

52. Louis J. Klarevas and Daniel B. O'Connor, "At What Cost? American Mass Public Opinion and the Use of Force Abroad" (paper presented at the annual meeting of the International Studies Association, Washington, D.C., March 31, 1994), 20.

53. Barnet, *The Rockets' Red Glare*, 383–84.

54. Gary C. Woodward, "The Rules of the Game: The Military and the Press in the Persian Gulf War," in *The Media and the Persian Gulf War*, ed. Robert E. Denton, Jr. (New York: Praeger, 1993), 8–9.

55. Ibid.

56. Gergen, "Diplomacy in a Television Age," 59.

57. Woodward, "The Rules of the Game," 10.

58. Ibid.

59. Rosenfeld, "In the Gulf," 244.

60. Woodward, "The Rules of the Game," 8.

61. Interview with Brent Scowcroft, February 7, 1995.

62. Lynn E. Gutstadt, "Taking the Pulse of the CNN Audience: A Case Study of the Gulf War," *Political Communication* 10, no. 4 (October 1993): 389–409.

63. *Public Papers of the Presidents of the United States, George Bush, 1991, Book I* (Washington, D.C.: U.S. Government Printing Office, 1992), 44.

64. LaMay, et al., eds., *The Media at War*, 16–17, 98–101.

65. Ibid., 18.

66. "Operation Desert Shield Ground Rules and Supplementary Guidelines, Revised 14 January 1991," in ibid., Appendix B.

67. Ibid., 20.

68. Rosenfeld, "In the Gulf," 254–55.

69. LaMay, et al., eds., *The Media at War*, 88.

70. Figures compiled by ADT Research, reprinted in ibid, p. 47.

71. Andrew Kohut and Robert C. Toth, *The People, The Press, and the Use of Force* (Washington, D.C.: Times-Mirror Center for the People and The Press, 1994), 3.

72. Michael Morgan, et al., "More Viewing, Less Knowledge," in *Triumph of the Image: The Media's War in the Persian Gulf—A Global Perspective*, ed. Hamid Mowlana, et al. (Boulder, Colo.: Westview Press, 1992), 229.

73. Ibid., 222.

74. Hallin, *The "Uncensored War"*; Cohen, *The Press and Foreign Policy*.

75. Richard C. Vincent, "CNN: Elites Talking to Elites," in Mowlana, ed., *Triumph of the Image*, 181–200.

76. W. Lance Bennett and Jarol B. Manheim, "Taking the Public by Storm": 343.

77. Telephone interview with James Baker, September 11, 1995.

78. Gladys Engel Lang and Kurt Lang, "The Press as Prologue: Media Coverage of Saddam's Iraq, 1979–1990," and William A. Dorman and Steven Livingston, "News and Historical Content: The Establishing Phase of the Persian Gulf Policy Debate," in Bennett and Paletz, eds., *Taken by Storm.*

79. Dorman and Livingston, "News and Historical Content." The authors show that the analogy did not originate with Bush, but was used earlier that summer by newspaper columnists, lawmakers, and senior Israeli officials. A wider search found 1,170 mentions of Saddam and Hitler. LaMay, et al., eds., *The Media at War,* 42.

80. Baker made the statement in Hamilton, Bermuda, on November 13, 1990.

81. Woodward, *The Commanders,* 315–16.

82. Warren Strobel, "Bush Drops Ball in Keeping Congress Informed on Gulf," *Washington Times,* November 20, 1990, A9.

83. Background interview with former Bush administration official, January 18, 1995.

84. Jarol B. Manheim, "Strategic Public Diplomacy: Managing Kuwait's Image during the Gulf Conflict," in Bennett and Paletz, eds., *Taken by Storm.*

85. W. Lance Bennett, "The News about Foreign Policy," in Bennett and Paletz, eds., *Taken by Storm.*

86. CBS/*New York Times* poll cited in Kohut and Toth, *The People, the Press, and the Use of Force,* 6.

87. Ibid., 6–7.

88. Rosenfeld, "In the Gulf," 241.

89. Michael Hedges, "Desert Diary: Anxiety, Loneliness Engulfed Life on Front," *Washington Times,* March 22, 1991, H6.

90. Daniel C. Hallin, quoted in LaMay, et al., eds., *The Media at War,* 66.

91. LaMay, et al., eds., *The Media at War,* 53. Newspapers studied were the *Atlanta Constitution, Chicago Tribune, Los Angeles Times, New York Times,* and *Washington Post.* On the *New York Times'* editorials, see also Bennett and Manheim, "Taking the Public by Storm."

92. Bennett and Manheim, "Taking the Public by Storm," 344.

93. Marvin Kalb, "A View from the Press," in Bennett and Paletz, eds., *Taken by Storm.*

94. LaMay, et al., eds., *The Media at War,* 83.

95. Ibid., 93.

96. Pete Williams, "Let's Face It, This Was the Best War Coverage We've Ever Had," *Washington Post,* March 17, 1991, D1.

97. Peter Arnett, *Live from the Battlefield: From Vietnam to Baghdad* (New York: Simon & Schuster, 1994), 406–10.

98. Kohut and Toth, *The People, the Press, and the Use of Force*, 21.

99. Schwarz, *Casualties, Public Opinion, and U.S. Military Intervention*, 20.

100. See, for example, Jim Hoagland, "A Too-Perfect Victory," *Washington Post*, July 7, 1994, A19.

101. See, for example, Noam Chomsky, "The Media and the War: What War?" in Mowlana, ed., *Triumph of the Image*.

102. Richard Zoglin, "It Was a Public Relations Rout Too," *Time*, March 11, 1991, 56-57.

2. Driving Fast without a Road Map

1. James Reston, *The Artillery of the Press* (New York: Council on Foreign Relations, 1966), 48–51.

2. Background telephone interview with senior White House official, October 1995. In April 1995, a prime-time news conference by Clinton was carried live by only one of the three major broadcast networks (CBS). John F. Harris, "The Snooze Conference: Networks, Viewers Not Tuned into Clinton," *Washington Post*, April 20, 1995, D1, D2.

3. Bernard Gwertzman, "Memo to the *Times* Foreign Staff," *Media Studies Journal* 7, no. 3 (Fall 1993): 33–34.

4. Ibid., 34–35.

5. Everette E. Dennis, "Life without the 'Evil Empire': New Ways to Make Sense of the World," in Freedom Forum Media Studies Center, *The Media and Foreign Policy in the Post–Cold War World* (New York: Freedom Forum Media Studies Center, 1993), 8–10.

6. The specially marked bag in which exposed film is rushed via airplane to a television network's editing and broadcast facilities.

7. In a typical poll, 83 percent of respondents cited television as their primary source for national and international news. Times-Mirror Center for the People and the Press, *America's Place in the World* (Washington, D.C.: Times Mirror Center for the People and the Press, November 1993).

8. See, for example, Cohen, *The Press and Foreign Policy*, 74–75.

9. Freedom Forum Media Studies Center, *The Media and Foreign Policy*, 28–29.

10. Kennan, "Somalia, Through a Glass, Darkly." See also Warren P. Strobel, "TV Images May Shock But Won't Alter Policy," *Christian Science Monitor*, December 14, 1994, 19.

11. Comments of British foreign secretary Douglas Hurd, quoted in Nicholas Hopkinson, *The Media and International Affairs after the Cold War,* Wilton Park Paper 74 (London: HMSO, August 1993), 11.

12. Ed Turner, statement to the Committee on Foreign Affairs, U.S. House of Representatives, April 26, 1994, U.S. Government Printing Office document 79-868, p. 9.

13. Telephone interview, January 20, 1995.

14. Cohen, *The Press and Foreign Policy,* 13. Italics are in the original.

15. Ted Koppel, statement to the Committee on Foreign Affairs, U.S. House of Representatives, April 26, 1994, U.S. Government Printing Office document 79-860, pp. 5–6.

16. Telephone interview with senior Clinton administration official, January 24, 1995.

17. See, for example, Richard Harwood, "An America of Niches," *Washington Post,* September 10, 1994, A23.

18. Survey by the Times-Mirror Center for the People and the Press, quoted in Howard Kurtz, "O. J. Squeezes the News: Poll Finds the Public Ignores Other Stories," *Washington Post,* April 6, 1995, B1.

19. Davis, *The Five Myths of Television Power,* 30–32. Davis's larger point is the human ability, over time, to control and indeed *use* technological innovations such as TV, rather than succumb to them.

20. Howard Kurtz, "Bosnia Overload: Is The Public Tuning Out?" *Washington Post,* September 13, 1993, D1, D3. See also Gowing, *Real-Time Television,* 6.

21. Center for Media and Public Affairs, "1994—The Year in Review," *Media Monitor* 9, no. 1 (January/February 1995): 3.

22. Discussion with Lawrence T. McGill, director of research and administration, Freedom Forum Media Studies Center at Columbia University, New York, November 15, 1994.

23. For a more detailed analysis of changes in foreign affairs coverage, see Stephen Hess, *International News and Foreign Correspondents* (Washington D.C.: Brookings Institution, 1996).

24. Quoted in Jon Vanden Heuvel, "Looking at a World in Motion" in Freedom Forum Media Studies Center, *The Media and Foreign Policy,* 20.

25. Interview with Bernard Gwertzman, November 15, 1994.

26. Louis D. Boccardi, "Redeploying a Global Journalistic Army," *Media Studies Journal* 7, no. 4 (Fall 1993):45–46.

27. Ibid., 44–45.

28. Koppel, "The Global Information Revolution and TV News," 10.

29. Brent MacGregor, "'Our Wanton Abuse of Technology': Television News-gathering in the Age of the Satellite," *Convergence* 1, no.1 (Spring 1995): 88.

30. Interview with NBC News vice president Bill Wheatley, November 21, 1994.

31. Freedom Forum Media Studies Center, *The Media and Foreign Policy*, 45, 50.

32. Ibid., 18–19.

33. This can be a problem even in formal news-sharing arrangements, although it may diminish over time as the two organizations understand each other's standards and needs.

34. Jacqueline Sharkey, "When Pictures Drive Foreign Policy," *American Journalism Review* (December 1993): 17.

35. John R. MacArthur, *Second Front: Censorship and Propaganda in the Gulf War* (New York: Hill and Wang, 1992).

36. These figures were compiled and relayed over the telephone by Andrew Tyndall of ADT Research, New York. They represent stories in which the correspondent or anchor was reporting from overseas.

37. MacGregor, "'Our Wanton Abuse of Technology'": 89.

38. Telephone interview with Andrew Tyndall, February 6, 1995.

39. Interview with Sir Brian Urquhart, November 15, 1994.

40. Gutstadt, "Taking the Pulse of the CNN Audience," 389–399; Paul Farhi, "When No News Is Bad News: CNN's Ratings Tumble As Events Fail to Capture the TV-Viewing Public's Attention," *Washington Post*, June 10, 1994, F1.

41. Walter Lippmann, *Public Opinion* (New York: Harcourt, Brace and Co., 1922), 364.

42. Cohen, *The Press and Foreign Policy*, 99. Italics are mine.

43. John Rielly, ed., *American Public Opinion and U.S. Foreign Policy 1995* (Chicago: Chicago Council on Foreign Relations, 1995), 9–10.

44. Times-Mirror Center for the People and the Press, *America's Place in the World*; see also Rielly, *American Public Opinion*; and Al Richman, "American Public's Attitudes toward U.S. International Involvement in the Post–Cold War Era" (paper prepared for the 1994 annual meeting of the International Studies Association, Washington, D.C., March 29, 1994).

45. Times-Mirror Center for the People and the Press, *America's Place in the World*, 19.

46. Center for Media and Public Affairs, "1994—The Year in Review."

47. John Carmody, "The TV Column," *Washington Post*, February 3, 1995, D4.

48. Koppel, "The Global Information Revolution and TV News."

49. Wheatley interview.

50. Bernard Kalb, "In the Days of Carrier-Pigeon Journalism," *Media Studies Journal* 7, no. 4 (Fall 1993): 73–79.

51. Ibid., 75–76, 78.

52. Barrie Dunsmore, speech for seminar of North Atlantic Treaty Organization permanent representatives, Norfolk, Virginia, June 24, 1994.

53. Ibid.

54. MacGregor, "'Our Wanton Abuse of Technology'": 85.

55. Turner, statement to the House Committee on Foreign Affairs, 11–12.

56. MacGregor, "'Our Wanton Abuse of Technology'": 87.

57. Dunsmore speech.

58. Elihu Katz, "The End of Journalism? Notes on Watching the Persian Gulf War," *Journal of Communication* 42, no. 3 (Summer 1992): 26–41.

59. Koppel, "The Global Information Revolution and TV News," 9.

60. Brent MacGregor, *Live, Direct, and Biased? Making Television News in the Age of the Satellite* (London: Arnold, 1997), 195.

61. Ibid. See also Gowing, *Real-Time Television*, 3.

62. Mort Rosenblum, *Who Stole the News? Why We Can't Keep Up with What's Happening in the World and What We Can Do about It* (New York: John Wiley & Sons, 1993).

63. Reston, *The Artillery of the Press*, 83.

64. Ibid., viii.

65. Eric V. Larson, "U.S. Casualties in Somalia. Vol. 1: The Media Response and the Myth of the 'CNN Effect'" (unpublished manuscript, March 1995), 20–21.

66. Koppel, "The Global Information Revolution and TV News," 10.

67. Cohen, *The Press and Foreign Policy*, 219–220; Martin Linksy, *Impact: How the Press Affects Federal Policymaking* (New York: W.W. Norton, 1986), 117.

68. Gowing, *Real-Time Television*, 3.

69. Ibid., especially pp. 1–30.

70. Ibid., 21–23.

71. Interview with J. Brian Atwood, October 14, 1994.

72. For more on the role of U.S. government press offices, see Stephen Hess, *The Government/Press Connection: Press Officers and Their Offices* (Washington: Brookings Institution, 1984).

73. Interview with Jeremy Rosner, February 7, 1995. For another example, see Steve Vogel, "Army 'Fire Department' Keeps Watch on World," *Washington Post*, August 25, 1995, A21.

74. Interview with former White House spokeswoman Dee Dee Myers, February 27, 1995; Rosner interview. See also Elizabeth Drew, *On the Edge: The Clinton Presidency* (New York: Simon & Schuster, 1994), especially 317.

75. Madeleine K. Albright, remarks to the CNN World Contributors Conference, Atlanta, Georgia, May 2, 1994, 3.

76. Gowing, *Real-Time Television*, 1. Bernard Cohen found a similar distrust of the press among many of the State Department officials he interviewed.

77. This statement is based on interviews with numerous officials who worked with Tutwiler, as well as my tenure covering the State Department.

78. Michael R. Beschloss, *Presidents, Television, and Foreign Crises* (Washington, D.C.: Annenberg Washington Program, 1993), 6.

79. Myers interview.

80. Interview with Brent Scowcroft, February 7, 1995.

81. Baker interview.

82. Quoted in Beschloss, *Presidents, Television, and Foreign Crises*, 10.

83. Background interview, December 16, 1994.

84. Scowcroft interview.

85. Background interview, December 16, 1994.

86. Interview with Richard Boucher, June 29, 1995.

87. Interview with Kenneth Bacon, May 31, 1995.

88. Ibid.

89. Interview with Margaret Tutwiler, July 13, 1995.

90. Bacon interview.

91. Background interview, August 2, 1995.

92. The station owners were told *after* the technical arrangements had been made. Beschloss, *Presidents, Television, and Foreign Crises*, 14–15.

93. Ibid., 12.

94. Scowcroft interview.

95. Baker interview. The author was present at Ta'if that day.

96. "CNN Diplomacy?" *Washington Post*, January 31, 1995, B2.

97. Background interviews.

98. Boucher interview.

99. See, for example, President Clinton's Rose Garden statement on the Dayton peace agreement, White House press release, November 21, 1995.

100. Baker interview.

101. Background interview.

102. Boucher interview.

103. Background interview with senior U.S. intelligence official, November 14, 1995.

104. Atwood interview.

105. Tutwiler interview.

3. Reporting the New Story

1. By this, I mean operations outside the traditional parameters of UN peacekeeping, in which all sides in the conflict accept, more or less, the peacekeepers' presence.

2. Howard Kurtz, "TV Viewers Join Military Critics of Media Spectacle on Beach," *Washington Post*, December 10, 1992, A33.

3. Ibid. See also Jonathan Yardley, "In Somalia, a Picture-Perfect Military Maneuver," *Washington Post*, December 14, 1992, B2.

4. Interview with Keith Richburg, January 17, 1995.

5. Michael R. Gordon, "T.V. Army on the Beach Took U.S. by Surprise," *New York Times*, December 10, 1992, A18.

6. John L. Hirsch and Robert B. Oakley, *Somalia and Operation Restore Hope: Reflections on Peacemaking and Peacekeeping* (Washington D.C.: United States Institute of Peace Press, 1995), 54, footnote.

7. This account is based on interviews with State and Defense Department officials. See also Howard Kurtz, "Administration Acts to Soothe News Media," *Washington Post*, September 16, 1994, A30; Gen. John Shalikashvili, chairman of the Joint Chiefs of Staff, speech to George Washington University conference on "The Media, Military, and Humanitarian Crises," National Press Club, Washington, D.C., May 4, 1995.

8. Background interview.

9. Richburg interview.

10. Interview with Barry Willey, February 17, 1995.

11. Willey interview.

12. Interview with Steven Rausch, March 30, 1995.

13. Cohen, *The Press and Foreign Policy.*

14. See LaMay et al., eds., *The Media at War*, 2.

15. Charles W. Ricks, *The Military–News Media Relationship: Thinking Forward* (Carlisle Barracks, Penn.: U.S. Army War College, Strategic Studies Institute, December 1993), 11.

16. U.S. Army Peacekeeping Institute, *Support Hope After-Action Review* (Carlisle Barracks, Penn.: U.S. Army Peacekeeping Institute, October 20–21, 1994). The CMOC approach was used earlier by the United States in Somalia. See Hirsch and Oakley, *Somalia and Operation Restore Hope*, 67.

17. The U.S. Army's after-action report concluded that the United States was slow and ambiguous in responding to requests for aid from the UNHCR and that it did not follow through on promises made by senior Defense Department officials to repair Kigali's water system and establish a radio station. It also found that the military gave UN agencies little advance notice of its pullout, hampering coordination for the handover to relief agencies. See U.S. Army Peacekeeping Institute, *Support Hope After-Action Review*, 18; R. Jeffrey Smith, "U.S. Mission to Rwanda Criticized," *Washington Post*, September 5, 1994, A1.

Given what had happened in Somalia, representatives of the NGO coordinating group InterAction were told by a U.S. congressman not to expect U.S. troops to return to Africa for years. They were thus surprised at and unprepared for the American military presence. Some relief officials were thankful that the U.S. military left Rwanda when it did, fearing that if the military incurred casualties following the experience in Somalia, it would never come to their aid again.

18. Interview with official of InterAction, April 6, 1995. See also U.S. Army Peacekeeping Institute, *Support Hope After-Action Review*, especially pp. 6, 12.

19. Daniel C. Hallin, "The Media and War" in *International Handbook of Media Research*, ed. John Corner, Philip Schlesinger, and Roger Silverstone (London: Routledge, forthcoming).

20. Ed Turner, statement to the Committee on Foreign Affairs, U.S. House of Representatives, April 26, 1994, U.S. Government Printing Office document 79-868, p. 8.

21. Quoted in Hallin, "The Media and War."

22. Warren Strobel, "U.S. Had, but Lost, the Chance to Lead," *Washington Times*, May 19, 1993, A1.

23. Predrag Simic, "Instant Publicity and Foreign Policy," *Media Studies Journal* 7, no. 4 (Fall 1993): 154. Gutman interview.

24. Gutman's work is collected in *A Witness to Genocide: The Pulitzer Prize-winning Dispatches on the "Ethnic Cleansing" of Bosnia* (New York: Macmillan, 1993). Other examples include Tom Gjelten, *Sarajevo Daily* (New York: HarperCollins, 1995) and the ABC News documentary "While America Watched: The Bosnia Tragedy," which first aired on March 17, 1994.

25. Gjelten, informal discussion at the United States Institute of Peace, Washington, D.C., March 22, 1995.

26. Background interview, November 14, 1994.

27. For example, see Anthony Lewis, "The Price of Weakness," *New York Times*, June 21, 1993, A19.

28. Background interview, November 14, 1994.

29. Gjelten, *Sarajevo Daily*, 117. This charge was reported by many in the European and U.S. media, this author included. Some UN officers still argue this was the case. See Andrew Borowiec, "Bosnians Stage Sacrifices, Peacekeeping Officer Alleges," *Washington Times*, February 21, 1995, A14.

30. Gjelten, informal discussion.

31. "UN Peacekeepers Keep the Press Out," *Time*, May 23, 1994, 18.

32. Roger Cohen, "In Bosnia, the War That Can't Be Seen," *New York Times*, December 25, 1994, 4E.

33. Interview with Gutman. See also Roy Gutman, "Bosnia Outrage: Ex-prisoners Say UN Troops Sexually Assaulted Detainees," *Newsday*, November 1, 1993, 3.

34. Interview with Maj. Gen. Maurice Baril, military adviser to the UN under-secretary general for peace operations, November 21, 1994.

35. Cohen, "In Bosnia, the War That Can't Be Seen."

36. Cohen, *The Press and Foreign Policy*, 19–47.

37. Quoted in ABC News, "While America Watched."

38. *Sarajevo: A Portrait of the Siege* (New York: Warner Books, 1994), 118–19.

39. Gjelten, informal discussion.

40. Richburg interview.

41. For criticism of Rwanda coverage, see James MacGuire, "Rwanda Before the Massacre," *Forbes MediaCritic* (Fall 1994): 44–45.

42. Peter Brock, "Dateline Yugoslavia: The Partisan Press," *Foreign Policy* 93 (Winter 1993–94): 152–72.

43. Roger Cohen, "C.I.A. Report Finds Serbs Guilty in Majority of Bosnia War Crimes," *New York Times*, March 9, 1995, A1.

44. Interview with UNHCR official, October 14, 1994.

45. Robert I. Rotberg and Thomas G. Weiss, *The Media, Humanitarian Crises, and Policy-Making*, WPF Report no. 7 (Cambridge, Mass.: World Peace Foundation), 5.

46. Larson, "U.S. Casualties in Somalia. Vol. 1," xix.

47. Rotberg and Weiss, *The Media, Humanitarian Crises, and Policy-Making*, 11.

48. Interview with officer of InterAction, April 6, 1995; Hirsch and Oakley, *Somalia and Operation Restore Hope*, 39–40.

49. Interview with Andrew Natsios, May 8, 1995.

50. Interview with officer of InterAction.

51. Quoted in CROSSLINES Global Report (October 1994).

52. Ibid.

53. Richburg interview.

54. Gutman interview.

55. InterAction officer interview.

56. David Wood, memo to Army Lt. Col. Michael H. Wood, deputy director, Plans Directorate, Office of the Secretary of Defense (Public Affairs), October 4, 1994; interview with David Wood, April 12, 1995.

57. U.S. Army, *Peace Operations*, Field Manual 100-23, December 30, 1994, v.

58. Wood interview.

59. U.S. Army, *Peace Operations*, 47–48; Stech, "Winning CNN Wars," 37–51.

60. Ricks, *The Military–News Media Relationship*, especially p. vi.

61. Willey interview.

62. Background interview, December 16, 1994.

63. Stech, "Winning CNN Wars," 50.

64. Ibid., 39–42, 44–45.

65. Ibid., 47; Ricks, *The Military–News Media Relationship*, 8; comments by Barry Zorthian and retired Vice Adm. William Lawrence at the symposium "Media Perspectives Twenty Years After the End of the Vietnam War," The Freedom Forum, Rosslyn, Virginia, April 21, 1995.

66. Background interview, April 6, 1995.

67. Ricks, *The Military–News Media Relationship*, 2.

68. U.S. Army, *Peace Operations*, v, 1; Willey interview.

69. Stech, "Winning CNN Wars," 37–38.

70. Ricks, *The Military–News Media Relationship*, 18; Willey interview. The Pentagon has been working on a rapid-deployment public affairs unit, known popularly as "JIB in a box." See Ricks, *The Military–News Media Relationship*, 18, footnote.

71. Wood, memo to Lt. Col. Wood.

72. Stech, "Winning CNN Wars," 43–44.

73. U.S. Army, *Peace Operations*, 17; Air Land Sea Application Center, *Multi-Service Procedures for Humanitarian Assistance Operations*, final draft, March 1994, pp. 3-16–3-17.

74. George J. Church, "In And Out With The Tide," *Time*, October 25, 1993, 26–32.

75. See, for example, Lt. Col. G. Peterson, "Psyops and Somalia—Spreading Good News," *Australian Defense Force Journal* 104 (January–February 1994), 38–40.

76. Air Land Sea Application Center, *Multi-Service Procedures for Humanitarian Assistance Operations*, 3-16–3-17.

77. U.S. Army, *Peace Operations*, 48.

78. Francois Misser and Yves Jaumain, "Death by Radio," *Index on Censorship* 4/5 (1994): 73–74; John-Thor Dahlburg, "Why the World Let Rwanda Bleed," *Los Angeles Times*, September 10, 1994, A2; Christopher Hanson, "Courting Disaster," *Columbia Journalism Review* (September–October 1994), 49.

79. Telephone interview, May 11, 1995.

80. U.S. Army Peacekeeping Institute, *Support Hope After-Action Review*, 12–13.

81. Baril interview.

82. Hirsch and Oakley, *Somalia and Operation Restore Hope*, 54, 58.

83. Ibid., 61–63, 85. The radio could not reach much of the Somali interior, a problem since Somalia is a highly oral culture. The newspaper had a circulation of about twenty thousand in ten cities, but because it was posted in public places it was read by many more.

84. Natsios interview.

85. Hirsch and Oakley, *Somalia and Operation Restore Hope*, 116–18, 153 (footnote).

86. Natsios interview.

87. Howard Kurtz, "Deaths Spur Media Retreat from Somalia," *Washington Post*, July 17, 1993, A11; Howard Kurtz, "No American Journalists Reporting From the Scene," *Washington Post*, October 6, 1993, A13.

88. Telephone interview with Roy Gutman, April 26, 1995.

89. *Journalists Survival Guide: The Former Yugoslavia* (New York: Committee to Protect Journalists, October 1994).

90. Interview with Laura Logan, April 6, 1995.

91. Gowing, *Real-Time Television*, 34–37. As Gowing notes, many other journalists were killed in and around Mostar.

92. Ibid., 48. The remainder of my description of this episode is based on interviews with Logan.

93. Kurtz, "No American Journalists"; Ricks, *The Military–News Media Relationship*, 7.

94. Wood, memo.

95. Hallin, "The Media and War."

96. Telephone interview, October 28, 1994.

97. Jacqueline Sharkey, "When Is a Picture Too Graphic to Run?" *American Journalism Review* (December 1993), 18.

98. Gutman interview. Vulliamy is quoted in Gowing, *Real-Time Television*, 40.

99. Keith Richburg, "Pests Amid Famine: In Somalia, News Crews Are on the Job and in the Way," *Washington Post*, October 13, 1992, E1.

100. Richburg interview.

4. The Push

1. *Public Papers of the Presidents of the United States, George Bush, 1991, Book I* (Washington, D.C.: U.S. Government Printing Office, 1992), 321.

2. Ibid., 378.

3. Haass and Wolfowitz are quoted in Beschloss, *Presidents, Television, and Foreign Crises*, 25. For another account of the television images' effect on Bush, see "Knee-deep in the Big Muddy," *U.S. News & World Report*, April 29, 1991, 24–26.

4. Senior British official quoted in Gowing, *Real-Time Television*, 38.

5. Margaret Tutwiler, remarks at the Meridian International Center, Washington, D.C., May 1, 1995.

6. Interview with Margaret Tutwiler, July 13, 1995.

7. Alan Elsner, "Baker Spends Seven Minutes at Site of Kurdish Refugee Tragedy," Reuters, April 8, 1991. The author was among the journalists accompanying Baker. At the time, Baker aides cited security concerns in explaining the brevity of the visit, saying they feared the secretary might be harmed as thousands of refugees pressed around him to plead for help. According to Tutwiler, it snowed the night Baker left, and thirty-seven people died there the following day.

8. Tutwiler, remarks at Meridian International Center.

9. Natsios interview.

10. Quoted in Beschloss, *Presidents, Televsion, and Foreign Crises*. Italics are mine.

11. Natsios interview; "The Pentagon Chief's Fear: The Specter of a Quagmire," *U.S. News & World Report*, April 15, 1991, 31.

12. *Newsweek*/Gallup poll, April 1991, cited in Klarevas and O'Connor, "At What Cost?"

13. *Public Papers of the Presidents of the United States, George Bush, 1991, Book I*, 361.

14. Probably the best contemporary account of the decision-making process is Don Oberdorfer, "The Path to Intervention: A Massive Tragedy 'We Could Do Something About,'" *Washington Post*, December 6, 1992, A1. I also rely on U.S. Agency for International Development, Bureau for Legislative and Public Affairs, "Chronology of U.S. Government Assistance to Somalia."

15. CNN data are from Livingston and Eachus, "Humanitarian Crises and U.S. Foreign Policy."

16. Natsios interview; Oberdorfer, "The Path to Intervention." Excerpts from Hempstone's cable were published as "Dispatch From a Place Near Hell," *Washington Post*, August 23, 1992, C1.

17. Herman J. Cohen, "Intervention in Somalia," *The Diplomatic Record 1992–1993* (Boulder, Colo.: Westview Press), 60.

18. Livingston and Eachus, "Humanitarian Crises and U.S. Foreign Policy," 425.

19. Interview with Herman Cohen, June 1, 1995.

20. Cohen, "Intervention in Somalia."

21. Natsios interview.

22. Jonathan Mermin, "Television News and American Intervention in Somalia: The Myth of a Media-Driven Foreign Policy" (paper delivered to the New England Political Science Association annual meeting, Portland, Maine, May 5–6, 1995). Mermin provides a detailed examination of Congress's role in setting television's agenda. He concludes: "Somalia emerged as a political liability in August, and a threat to the president's place in history in November, not because television made it an issue, but because American politicians made it an issue."

23. I thank Steven Livingston for first pointing this out to me. Livingston and Eachus ("Humanitarian Crises and U.S. Foreign Policy") quote Natsios as suggesting that a principal motive for the airlift was *to generate more media attention to Somalia.*

24. Cohen, "Intervention in Somalia," 63–64.

25. See, for example, Richburg, "Pests Amid Famine," and Michael Maren, "Feeding a Famine," *Forbes MediaCritic* (Fall 1994): 35.

26. Scowcroft interview. See also Hirsch and Oakley, *Somalia and Operation Restore Hope,* 42; Oberdorfer, "Path to Intervention."

27. Quoted in Cohen, "Intervention in Somalia," 54.

28. Maren, "Feeding a Famine."

29. Interview with Lawrence Eagleburger, February 1, 1995.

30. Interview with Robert Gallucci, May 31, 1995.

31. "Operation Restore Hope," *U.S. News & World Report,* December 14, 1992, 26–30.

32. Larson reaches the same conclusion; see his "U.S. Casualties in Somalia. Vol. 1," 72.

33. Scowcroft interview.

34. Eagleburger interview.

35. Scowcroft interview.

36. Cohen interview. At this point, the State Department was recommending that the United States support an expanded UN force in Somalia under UN command.

37. Hirsch and Oakley, *Somalia and Operation Restore Hope,* 42.

38. Oberdorfer, "The Path to Intervention."

39. Scowcroft interview.

40. For Bush's responses to questions on his Somalia policy from the Refugee Policy Group, see John G. Sommer, *Hope Restored? Humanitarian Aid in Somalia 1990–1994* (Washington, D.C.: Refugee Policy Group, November 1994).

41. Natsios interview.

42. *Public Papers of the Presidents of the United States, George Bush, 1992–93, Book II* (Washington, D.C.: U.S. Government Printing Office, 1993), 2174.

43. Mermin, "Television News and American Intervention in Somalia."

44. Scowcroft interview.

45. Eagleburger interview.

46. Gallucci interview.

47. Background interview, October 25, 1994.

48. Atwood interview. Atwood said his policy views on Rwanda, transmitted by television from Goma, had more impact on U.S. policymaking than they would have if he had been arguing his position by telephone to Washington.

49. Background interview, November 17, 1994.

50. Background interview, December 15, 1994.

51. Julia Taft, remarks at the conference on "Media, the Military, and Humanitarian Crises: New Relations for New Challenges," George Washington University, Washington, D.C., May 5, 1995.

52. On the evolution of the new policy, see Ivo H. Daalder, "Knowing When to Say No: The Development of U.S. Peacekeeping Policy in the 1990s," in *UN Peacekeeping, American Policy, and the Uncivil Wars of the 1990s*, ed. William Durch (New York: St. Martin's Press, 1996).

53. Dahlburg, "Why the World Let Rwanda Bleed."

54. U.S. Department of State, *The Clinton Administration's Policy on Reforming Multilateral Peace Operations*, 5.

55. Background interview, July 10, 1994.

56. Ibid.

57. See Gutman's dispatches in his *A Witness to Genocide*.

58. Said Gutman: "That gave it a brand new life, because the pictures told a zillion words." See also the comments by *Guardian* correspondent Ed Vulliamy, who accompanied the ITN team, in Gowing, *Real-Time Television*, 40. Gutman and his colleague, freelance photographer Andree Kaiser, had not been permitted to visit Omarska, although they had been given a circumscribed tour of another camp, at Manjaca, two weeks earlier. At that site, Kaiser furtively shot still photos of Muslim men obediently waiting to have their heads shaved, while Gutman conducted supervised interviews with detainees. Away from camp officials' watchful eyes, he also interviewed men who had been released recently. Gutman's August 2 account of conditions at Omarska and Brcko was based on interviews in Zagreb, Croatia, with former detainees. According to Gutman, the emaciated prisoners videotaped at Trnopolje by ITN actually had been moved a day or two earlier from Omarska, which had been closed.

59. Scowcroft interview.

60. Eagleburger interview.

61. Interview with Warren Zimmermann, June 8, 1995.

62. Eagleburger interview.

63. Gutman, *A Witness to Genocide*, xii.

64. Private journal entry, dated August 9, 1992, provided by Don Oberdorfer.

65. Interview with George Kenney, January 26, 1995.

66. Tutwiler interview. Kenney, who was responsible for providing daily "press guidance" on Bosnia to Tutwiler in anticipation of reporters' questions at her midday press briefing, gave a similar account: Tutwiler "was a dissident in trying to quietly gin up the press," and her actions met with resistance from the department's careerists.

67. Quoted in Don Oberdorfer, "Week of Publicity and Policy-Making Started Off with a Chilling Headline," *Washington Post*, August 9, 1992, A26.

68. Ibid.

69. Oberdorfer journal.

70. Quoted in Gowing, *Real-Time Television*, 42–43.

71. Eagleburger interview.

72. Quoted in Don Oberdorfer, "State Department Backtracks on Atrocity Reports: Calls for Action on Serb Camps Rise," *Washington Post*, August 5, 1992, A1.

73. Zimmermann interview.

74. Interview on ABC News, "While America Watched: The Bosnia Tragedy."

75. Interview and June 28, 1995 e-mail correspondence. Kenney said he went through two "what did we know and when did we know it" exercises after Boucher's statement. Boucher's office photocopied his personal file of Bosnia reports, while he and Maggie Pearson, the European Bureau's public affairs officer, went through the same material with a highlighter. Kenney added that if the U.S. government had addressed the reality of the camps more forthrightly in public, it would have been able to put the issue into perspective and leave an accurate historical record. He now argues that there was no "Genocide with a big 'G'" in Bosnia and that the figure of 200,000 dead in the war, which journalists had gotten from various sources and used without checking, is vastly inflated. See George Kenney, "The Bosnia Calculation," *New York Times Magazine*, April 23, 1995, 42–43.

76. Gowing, *Real-Time Television*, 40–41.

77. *Public Papers of the Presidents, George Bush, 1992–93, Book II*, 1320.

78. On August 14, Bush announced Operation Provide Relief, the military airlift to Somalia.

79. Background interview.

80. Kenney interview. Gutman reaches the same conclusion—that Bush and Eagleburger did the "absolute minimum." See Gutman, *A Witness to Genocide*, xxxii.

81. Gowing, *Real-Time Television*, 18.

82. Gutman interview.

83. Ibid.

84. Interview with Strobe Talbott, March 13, 1995.

85. Interviews with three people present in Munich; Richard Cohen, "Flights of Fancy," *Washington Post*, February 8, 1994, A19.

86. Albright, remarks to CNN World Contributors' Conference.

87. CBS and NBC led their broadcasts that night with a different story: events surrounding U.S. figure skater Tonya Harding.

88. My findings in this regard are generally in agreement with Gowing's. For his analysis, see Gowing, *Real-Time Television*, 69–76.

89. Myers interview.

90. Elaine Sciolino and Douglas Jehl, "As U.S. Sought a Bosnia Policy, The French Offered a Good Idea," *New York Times*, February 14, 1994, A1.

91. Drew, *On The Edge*, 410–12. Drew's account differs slightly from that of Sciolino and Jehl.

92. Background interview, February 3, 1995.

93. Unless otherwise noted, this account of the U.S. decision-making process is drawn from Sciolino and Jehl, "As U.S. Sought a Bosnia Policy."

94. While Bosnian Serbs charged that the shell was fired by the Bosnian government itself to generate international sympathy and action, no evidence has surfaced to confirm this. On Friday, February 4, the day before, three shells fell on the Sarajevo neighborhood of Dobrinja, killing ten people. Military experts were able to quickly assign responsibility to the Bosnian Serbs. See John Kifner, "To Sarajevans, Shells Came from the Hills, but the Serbs Deny It," *New York Times*, February 10, 1994, A14. A detailed account of the United Nations' inconclusive investigation of the February 5 shelling can be found in David Binder, "Anatomy of a Massacre," *Foreign Policy* 97 (Winter 1994–95), 70–78.

95. Elaine Sciolino, "Clinton Aides Seek Approval by NATO on Bosnia Air Raids," *New York Times*, February 8, 1994, A1.

96. Ibid.

97. Gowing, *Real-Time Television*, 71.

98. Interview with Michael McCurry, May 15, 1995.

99. Background interview.

100. Linsky, *Impact*, 87.

101. Background interview.

102. Drew, *On the Edge*, 411.

103. See, for example, John Walcott, "The Tracks of Our Tears, Then and Now," *U.S. News & World Report*, February 21, 1994, 10.

104. Background interview, November 17, 1994.

105. Telephone interview with McCurry, August 30, 1995.

106. Boutros Boutros-Ghali, *An Agenda for Peace* (New York: United Nations, 1992).

107. Rotberg and Weiss give some attention to this question in *The Media, Humanitarian Crises and Policy-making.*

108. James MacGuire, "Rwanda Before the Massacre," *Forbes MediaCritic* (Fall 1994): 39–46.

109. Richburg interview.

110. Data are from the Television News Archives at Vanderbilt University.

111. For example, see Kurtz, "O. J. Squeezes the News."

112. Cohen, *The Press and Foreign Policy*; Reston, *The Artillery of the Press.*

113. Cohen, *The Press and Foreign Policy,* 101.

114. Andrew S. Natsios, "Illusions of Influence: The CNN Effect in Complex Emergencies?" (unpublished manuscript, March 1995).

115. Ibid., 7.

116. Quoted in Livingston and Eachus, "Humanitarian Crises and U.S. Foreign Policy," 417.

117. Natsios, "Illusions of Influence," 10.

118. Roger Winter, "The Year in Review," *World Refugee Survey 1995* (Washington, D.C.: U.S. Committee for Refugees, 1995).

119. Livingston and Eachus, "Humanitarian Crises and U.S. Foreign Policy."

120. Eagleburger interview. In this context, Eagleburger mentioned President Bush's reaction to the widely televised Chinese government attack on students in Tiananmen Square in June 1989. Bush felt strongly that relations with China should not be severed. He preserved them as much as possible but enacted limited sanctions to appease Congress and the media.

121. Jonathan C. Randal, "Donors Desert Rwandan Orphanage: Contributions for Children Drop When TV Cameras Leave," *Washington Post,* February 20, 1995, A20.

5. The Pull

1. Text of Clinton's address, *Washington Post,* October 8, 1993, A21.

2. See, for example, Sharkey, "When Pictures Drive Foreign Policy."

3. Background interview.

4. *Public Papers of the Presidents of the United States, William J. Clinton, 1993, Book I* (Washington, D.C.: U.S. Government Printing Office, 1994), 565.

5. For example, see the president's news conference of June 17, 1993, shortly after hostilities began between UNOSOM II and the forces of Mohamed Farah

Aidid. At least three times, the president told reporters that how Aidid was dealt with was up to the United Nations, not the United States. *Public Papers of the Presidents of the United States, William J. Clinton, 1993, Book I*, 867–75.

6. UN Security Council Resolution 814 (March 26, 1993).

7. Quoted in John R. Bolton, "Wrong Turn in Somalia," *Foreign Affairs* 73, no. 1 (January/February 1994): 62.

8. Hirsch and Oakley, *Somalia and Operation Restore Hope*, 111, 115.

9. For a cogent look at this problem, see Thomas L. Friedman, "Round and Round," *New York Times*, April 2, 1995, A15.

10. Larson, "U.S. Casualties in Somalia. Vol. 1," 52–56.

11. UN Security Council Resolution 837 (June 6, 1993).

12. Interview with Samuel R. Berger, August 2, 1995.

13. See, for example, President Clinton's Saturday morning radio address of June 12, 1993.

14. PBS's *MacNeil/Lehrer NewsHour* was an exception, devoting considerable attention to the May handoff from UNITAF to UNOSOM II. Larson, "U.S. Casualties in Somalia. Vol. 1," 20–21.

15. Interview with UNITAF's chief spokesman, Marine Col. Fred Peck, July 25, 1995.

16. Interview with U.S. Army Major David Stockwell, June 20, 1995.

17. There were restrictions on access to, and photography of, UNOSOM compounds, as well as a requirement that journalists' armed guards (a necessity in Mogadishu) have a weapons authorization card—probably a first in the history of media-military relations. See *UNOSOM II: United Nations Operations in Somalia, Rules for Media*. In May 1992, the Defense Department and major media representatives had agreed on nine principles of combat coverage, the first of which stated that "[o]pen and independent reporting will be the principal means of coverage of U.S. military operations." Pentagon Press Release 241-92, May 21, 1992. The Pentagon later took the position that these rules did not apply to Somalia, because it was technically a UN relief operation. Howard Kurtz, "No American Journalists Reporting from the Scene," *Washington Post*, October 6, 1993, A13. Reporters were not permitted to accompany the Ranger/Delta teams who in late August began missions to capture Aidid and his top lieutenants. This was in keeping with long-standing Pentagon rules regarding special operations. The Rangers had no separate public affairs contingent.

18. Kenneth Allard, *Somalia Operations: Lessons Learned* (Washington, D.C.: National Defense University Press, 1995), 86.

19. This was the unanimous assessment of at least four individuals I interviewed.

20. Peck interview.

21. Stockwell interview. Reporters had to be careful to avoid the appearance of collusion with the U.S. military. If Aidid's forces thought a reporter was passing useful intelligence to the United States merely in the course of doing his or her professional work, that reporter's life could very well have been endangered. Thus, several media organizations turned down a UNOSOM offer to stay on the main UN compound. CNN, after some internal deliberations, moved its operations onto the compound in early September, shortly before it evacuated Mogadishu. Reuters also accepted the offer.

22. David Stockwell, "'Perception Warfare': How the Media Covers the Military" (unpublished essay, U.S. Marines Corps School of Advanced War-Fighting, Quantico, Virginia, July 3, 1995); Stockwell interview.

23. This was not the only time the news media had videotape or other evidence that clashed with the official version of events. For another, involving an otherwise routine patrol, see Michael Maren, "The Tale of the Tape," *Village Voice*, August 24, 1993, 23.

24. Stockwell, "'Perception Warfare'"; Sommer, *Hope Restored?*, 41.

25. For example, see the comments of Senator John McCain in Lloyd Grove, "The Fog of War—and Words," *Washington Post*, October 17, 1993, C1.

26. Patrick Sloyan, "Hunting Down Aidid; Why Clinton Changed Mind," *Newsday*, December 6, 1993, 7.

27. Stockwell interview. See also Keith Richburg, "Aidid's Urban War, Propaganda Victories Echo Vietnam," *Washington Post,* October 6, 1993, A12.

28. Larson, "U.S. Casualties in Somalia. Vol. 1," 68.

29. Telephone interview with Michael Maren, August 18, 1995.

30. Journalists became far more wary after July 12, when SNA officials promised reporters protection if they would come witness what U.S. helicopter gunships had done to the Aidid command center, a raid that killed many of Aidid's top lieutenants and was a turning point in the conflict. However, the SNA could not protect journalists from the angry crowd and four were killed.

31. Maren, "The Tale of the Tape."

32. Richburg interview.

33. Hirsch and Oakley, *Somalia and Operation Restore Hope*, 123.

34. Background interview.

35. See, for example, Eric V. Larson, "U.S. Casualties in Somalia. Vol. 2: The Public Response—A Grief and Rage" (unpublished manuscript, March 1995).

36. Keith Richburg, "In War on Aidid, UN Battled Itself," *Washington Post*, December 6, 1993. Quoted in Hirsch and Oakley, *Somalia and Operation Restore Hope*, 121.

37. Maren interview. See also Michael Maren, "A Pound of Flesh," *Village Voice*, August 17, 1993, 19.

38. Maren and Stockwell interviews.

39. Richburg and Maren interviews; background interviews.

40. Jacqueline Sharkey, "Determined to Get the Evidence," *American Journalism Review* (December 1993).

41. Stockwell interview; background interview. Paul Watson, who took the still photographs, brought Stockwell some articles that identified the dead soldier, an identity which neither Stockwell nor the Pentagon has divulged. Mary Cleveland of Portsmouth, Virginia, saw Watson's photograph in the *Norfolk Virginian-Pilot* and identified it as that of her son.

42. Myers interview.

43. Background interview.

44. Drew, *On the Edge*, 317; Lee Michael Katz, "Graphic Photos from Somalia Gave 'Urgency,'" *USA Today*, October 13, 1993, 8A.

45. An October 5 Gallup poll found that nearly 60 percent of respondents recalled seeing the image.

46. Sharkey, "When Is a Picture Too Graphic To Run?" A survey of thirty-four major daily newspapers found that eleven used Watson's picture on the front page, fifteen used it inside the paper, and eight did not use it.

47. Berger interview.

48. Myers interview.

49. David W. Moore, "Public: 'Get Out of Somalia,'" *Gallup Poll Monthly* (October 1993); "Effect of Slain Soldier's Photo," *USA Today*, October 7, 1993, 7A.

50. Myers interview.

51. Berger interview.

52. Drew, *On the Edge*, 329.

53. Background interview.

54. Myers interview.

55. Rosner interview.

56. Daalder, "Knowing When to Say No."

57. Drew, *On the Edge*, 322.

58. Larson, "U.S. Casualties in Somalia. Vol. 1," 31–43.

59. Sloyan, "Hunting Down Aidid."

60. Berger interview.

61. Stech, "Winning CNN Wars," 43.

62. Background interview.

63. Quoted in "Somalia: Inattention Led to U.S. Deaths," *Washington Post*, October 17, 1993.

64. Patrick Sloyan, "Somalia Mission Control: Clinton Called the Shots in Failed Policy Targeting Aidid," *Newsday*, December 5, 1993, 7.

65. Rosner interview.

66. On this point, see Hirsch and Oakley, *Somalia and Operation Restore Hope*, 150, and Lake's comments in Katz, "Graphic Photos from Somalia."

67. Rosner interview.

68. Background interview.

69. John Lancaster, "Aspin Outlines Goals in Somalia," *Washington Post*, August 28, 1993.

70. Gallup poll of October 8–10, 1993, cited in Larson, "U.S. Casualties in Somalia. Vol. 2," 65. Larson argues (p. 66) that it was not the change in objectives per se that affected the public commitment, but the fact that ends other than the public preference (humanitarian) had become prominent in administration policy.

71. Background interview.

72. Background interview.

73. McCurry interview.

74. Under the Constitution, U.S. military forces always remain under the *command* of the president. At times, *operational control* of U.S. forces can be given to military commanders of other nations, as happened in World War II and Operation Desert Storm.

75. This was graphically illustrated in a four-part series on the Somalia decision-making process by Patrick Sloyan, published in *Newsday*, December 5–8, 1993, as "Mission in Somalia." It is in agreement on this point with the accounts by Drew, *On the Edge*, and by Hirsch and Oakley, *Somalia and Operation Restore Hope*.

76. Background interview.

77. Hirsch and Oakley, *Somalia and Operation Restore Hope*, 154, footnote.

78. See Thomas Friedman, "Dissing The World," *New York Times*, February 19, 1995.

79. Hirsch and Oakley, *Somalia and Operation Restore Hope*, 153.

80. Maren interview; background interview.

81. Quoted in Sloyan, "Somalia Mission Control."

82. Hirsch and Oakley, *Somalia and Operation Restore Hope*, 129; Drew, *On the Edge*, 335.

83. Reuters transcript of the first presidential debate between President Clinton and Senator Dole, October 7, 1996.

84. Clinton's remarks at a White House press conference, May 8, 1994. *Public Papers of the Presidents of the United States, William J. Clinton, 1994, Book I*, 859–63.

85. Quoted in Elaine Sciolino et al., "Haitian Impasse—A Special Report. Failure on Haiti: How U.S. Hopes Faded," *New York Times*, April 29, 1994, A1.

86. On this point, see Ted Koppel, "The Perils of Info-Democracy," in *Managing Global Chaos: Sources of and Responses to International Conflict*, ed. Chester A. Crocker and Fen Osler Hampson with Pamela Aall (Washington, D.C.: United States Institute of Peace Press, 1996).

87. Telephone interview with Stanley Schrager, April 19, 1995.

88. Prior to former president Jimmy Carter's visit to Port-au-Prince, 88 percent of network evening news sources voiced criticism of Clinton's policies. See "1994—The Year in Review," *Media Monitor* 9, no. 1 (January/February 1995). Print examples include Jim Hoagland, "Don't Do It," *Washington Post*, September 15, 1994, A17.

89. "Haiti: Consensus and Consent," *Washington Post*, September 14, 1994, A20; "Congress Must Vote on Haiti," *New York Times*, September 13, 1994, A22.

90. ABC News poll of July 17, 1994, reported as "Americans Favor Haiti Invasion to Stop Refugees," Reuters, July 26, 1994.

91. Text of Clinton's address on Haiti, *Washington Post*, September 16, 1994, A31.

92. ABC News/*Nightline* poll, September 15, 1994.

93. Background interview, October 25, 1994.

94. Helen Dewar and Kevin Merida, "Opposition to Invasion Appears Unswayed by Address," *Washington Post*, September 16, 1994, A30.

95. ABC News poll of September 18, 1994; CBS–*New York Times* poll of September 19, 1994.

96. See Elaine Sciolino, "Invasion of Haiti Would Be Limited, Clinton Aides Say," *New York Times*, September 13, 1994; Michael Gordon, "Pentagon's Haiti Policy Focuses on Casualties," *New York Times*, October 6, 1994.

97. United Nations Association of the United States of America, *A Report on the Fourth Annual Peacekeeping Mission* (Washington, D.C.: United Nations Association, August 1995), 22.

98. Numerous interviews; Sciolino, "Invasion of Haiti." For an operational comparison of the two, see Robert Oakley and David Bentley, "Peace Operations: A Comparison of Somalia and Haiti," *Strategic Forum* 30 (May 1995).

99. Senior State Department official quoted in Howard Kurtz, "Administration Acts to Soothe News Media," *Washington Post*, September 16, 1994, A30.

100. Gen. John Shalikashvili, speech to George Washington University conference on "The Media, the Military, and Humanitarian Crises," National Press Club, Washington, D.C., May 4, 1995.

101. Interview with John McWethy, June 28, 1995. McWethy's report aired on *ABC World News Tonight* on October 13, 1994.

102. Background interview, October 25, 1994.

103. Talbott interview.

104. John F. Harris and Ruth Marcus, "U.S. Sends Military Police: Scenes of Violence Prompt a Shift in Troop Policy," *Washington Post*, September 22, 1994, A31.

105. Bacon interview.

106. Schrager interview; second telephone interview with Schrager, September 12, 1995.

107. Quoted in David C. Unger, "Taking Haiti," *New York Times Magazine*, October 23, 1994. See also the comments of Gen. Shalikashvili at a Pentagon news briefing, Department of Defense transcript, October 4, 1994.

108. Talbott interview.

109. Myers interview.

110. Interviews with members of the U.S. public broadcast on National Public Radio's *Morning Edition*, September 23, 1994, transcript no. 1440-9.

111. Remarks by Secretary of State Warren Christopher in Jim Hoagland, "Why Clinton Improvises," *Washington Post*, September 25, 1994, C1.

112. Willey interview.

113. Opinion polls compiled by Eric V. Larson.

114. Gen. Shalikashvili, speech to George Washington University conference (see note 100).

115. Peck interview.

116. Natsios interview.

117. Canadian Maj. D. M. Last and Done Vought, *Interagency Cooperation in Peace Operations: A Conference Report* (Fort Leavenworth, Kans.: U.S. Army Command and General Staff College, November 24, 1994).

118. Ibid.

119. Ibid.

120. Interview with Gary Anderson, August 1, 1995.

121. Interview.

122. Lippmann, *Public Opinion.*

123. On this last point, see U.S. Army, *Peace Operations*, 12.

124. Kohut and Toth, *The People, the Press, and the Use of Force,* 14.

125. Regarding Somalia, see Larson, "U.S. Casualties in Somalia. Vol. 1," 73. Larson cites similar findings regarding media coverage of Vietnam (p. 5).

126. Background interview, July 10, 1995.

127. Howard Kurtz, "As Landing Delivers Dearth of Drama, Only CNN Stays with Coverage," *Washington Post*, September 20, 1994, A16.

128. Gallucci interview.

129. Talbott interview.

130. Willey interview.

131. Schrager interview.

132. Background interview.

133. Kohut and Toth, *The People, the Press, and the Use of Force*, 14.

134. Ibid., 11.

135. Larson, "U.S. Casualties in Somalia. Vol. 1," 52–56.

136. See Larson, "U.S. Casualties in Somalia. Vol. 2."

137. Larson, "U.S. Casualties in Somalia. Vol. 1," 55.

138. Kohut and Toth, *The People, the Press, and the Use of Force*, 24.

139. Background interview.

140. Larson, "U.S. Casualties in Somalia. Vol. 2," 96.

141. Ibid., 95.

142. *Public Papers of the Presidents, George Bush, 1992–93, Book II*, 2174–75.

143. Background interview, December 16, 1994.

144. U.S. Army, *Peace Operations*, v–vi.

145. Ibid.

146. On this point, see the special report *Restoring Hope: The Real Lessons of Somalia for the Future of Intervention* (Washington, D.C.: United States Institute of Peace, July 1994).

147. Interview.

148. Remarks by Defense Department official at George Washington University conference (see note 100).

149. United States Institute of Peace, *Restoring Hope*.

150. McCurry interview.

151. Shalikashvili remarks at George Washington University conference (see note 100).

152. *Joint Task Force Commander's Handbook for Peace Operations* (Ft. Monroe, Va.: Joint War-Fighting Center, February 28, 1995), 26.

153. Background interview.

154. Livingston and Eachus, "Humanitarian Crises and U.S. Foreign Policy."

6. Assessing the Gap

1. See Kohut and Toth, *The People, the Press, and the Use of Force*, 21.

2. The opposite case was argued by Gen. Norman H. Schwarzkopf in "CBS Reports: D-Day," which first aired May 26, 1994.

3. Les Aspin, "Challenges to Values-Based Military Intervention," address to the United States Institute of Peace "Managing Chaos" conference, Washington, D.C., November 30, 1994.

4. Ibid.

5. U.S. Army, *Peace Operations*, 47.

6. President Clinton, Address to the Nation on Bosnia, White House press release, November 27, 1995.

7. Ibid.; President Clinton, Rose Garden statement, November 21, 1995.

8. Louis Harris and Associates poll, November 30–December 3, reported as "Poll Shows Opposition to U.S. in Bosnia," United Press International, December 4, 1995; AP poll of the same dates, reported as "Skepticism Persists about Obligation to Bosnia," Associated Press, December 5, 1995; ABC News poll, November 29, reported as "Support for Clinton's Bosnia Policy Drops in Poll," Reuters, December 1, 1995.

9. Speech to the Royal Institute of International Relations, London, February 16, 1995. See chapter 4.

10. Cohen interview.

11. Zimmerman interview.

12. Michael Ignatieff, "Is Nothing Sacred? The Ethics of Television," *Daedalus* 112 (Fall 1985): 69.

13. Gowing, *Real-Time Television*, 18.

14. Kenney interview.

15. Background interview.

16. Larson, "U.S. Casualties in Somalia. Vol. 1," 44, 74–75.

17. Hallin, *The "Uncensored War,"* 116–18.

18. Myers interview.

19. Telephone interview with Stockwell.

20. See, for example, United States Institute of Peace, *Restoring Hope*, 2, 17.

21. On Bosnia, see Tony Capaccio, "Army Gets Smart in Bosnia, Opens Up to News Media," Hearst Newspapers, New York Times News Service, January 17, 1996.

22. Ibid.

23. Ibid.

24. David Wood, memo.

25. Stockwell, "'Perception Warfare,'" 2.

26. See Koppel, "The Global Information Revolution and TV News."

27. Kennan, "Somalia, Through a Glass, Darkly."

Index

ABC News
    danger to reporters in Bosnia, 123
    effect of camera on reporting, 125
    foreign news coverage, 68–72
    on military mission in Haiti, 189
Adams, Eddie, 36
Addis Ababa agreements, 119
Agency for International Development,
    77, 105, 106, 135, 143
AID. *See* Agency for International
    Development
Aidid, Mohamed Farah, 85, 116, 118–119,
    169, 171, 173–174, 181–182, 229
Akashi, Yasushi, 102
Albright, Madeleine K., 57, 79, 154, 155,
    168, 173
Amanpour, Christiane, 192
Anderson, Col. Gary, 196
Anderson, Terry, 120
Annan, Kofi, 102
AP. *See* Associated Press
Arafat, Yasser, 143
Arbatov, Georgi, 57
Aristide, Jean-Bertrand, 93, 185, 199
Arnett, Peter, 41, 52, 116
The Artillery of the Press (Reston), 76
Aspin, Les, 181, 212
Associated Press, 67
Attachés, 191
Atwood, J. Brian, 77, 89, 143–144

Bacon, Kenneth, 82, 191, 219
Baker, James A., III
    attempt to obtain Russian support
        for Arab-Israeli negotiations, 1–2
    Kuwait comments, 48
    messages to Saddam Hussein, 84
    on benefits of television, 86
    on CNN reports, 80
    on effects of communications tech-
        nology, 7
    on press after the Gulf War, 19
    use of news media during Persian
        Gulf War, 46–47
    visit to Kurdish refugee camps, 129
Bangladesh, 196–197
Barre, Mohamed Siad, 160
BBC. *See* British Broadcasting
    Corporation
Begin, Menachem, 81
Begleiter, Ralph, 85
Berger, Samuel "Sandy," 169, 177–178
Bessmertnykh, Aleksandr, 1–2
Binder, David, 102, 104
Birtley, Tony, 121–123
Boccardi, Louis D., 67
Boomer, Lt. Gen. Walter, 114
Bosnia
    conflict between news media and
        UN, 98–102
    danger to reporters, 119–124

Bosnia *(cont.)*
    effect of camera on reporting,
      124–125
    embedded media, 228
    impact of real-time television,
      153–159
    influence on policy in Somalia,
      137–139
    news coverage of, 202
    news media's effect on intervention
      decisions, 218–219
    public opinion of mission, 222
    role of international troops, 13
    role of television, 146–153
    struggle for objectivity in reporting,
      102–105
    Vance-Owen proposal, 155
Boucher, Richard, 81–82, 87, 149–150,
    162, 219
Boutros-Ghali, Boutros, 4, 101, 137–138,
    159, 179
Bowen, Jeremy, 121
Boyd, Shannon, 101
British Broadcasting Corporation, 68,
    123, 171, 230
Brock, Peter, 105
Brokaw, Tom, 92
Burns, Jonathan F., 99
Burundi, 159–160
Bush administration
    Bosnia policy, 147–153
    challenges in communicating
      policies, 58
    "Day in Hell" cable, 132
    InterAction letter asking for aid in
      Somalia, 106
    Iraqgate, 53
    messages to Saddam Hussein, 84
    Panama invasion, 40–41
    peace operations in northern Iraq,
      127–131
    policy in Somalia, 131, 136–141, 181
    Saddam Hussein and, 47–49
    use of news media during Persian
      Gulf War, 6, 42–47, 49–52
Byrd, Sen. Robert, 179
Byrne, Jay, 78

Cable News Network. *See* also Real-time
    television
    CNN curve, 4–5, 206
    CNN effect, 4–6, 79, 162, 175, 207,
      211, 225
    coverage of Panama invasion, 40
    coverage of Persian Gulf War, 41,
      44–47
    effect of technology on government
      officials, 76–90
    foreign news coverage, 70
    foreign policy and, 3
    as global news organization, 98
    impact on public opinion concerning
      Somalia, 173–176
    role in Somalia, 131–137
    tele-diplomacy, 84
    use as weapon in peace operations,
      116–119
    use of stringers, 69
Cable Satellite Public Affairs Network, 78
Cameras, effect on peace operations,
    124–125
CARE, 141
Carter, Jimmy, 85, 111, 179, 188
Castro, Fidel, 84
Casualties, impact on public opinion,
    30–31, 55–56
CBS News
    coverage of relief operations, 197
    foreign news coverage, 68–72
    Vietnam War coverage, 29
Cédras, Lt. Gen. Raoul, 94, 111, 116–117,
    185, 229
Censorship
    Grenada invasion and, 39
    Korean War and, 28
    Persian Gulf War and, 43
    World Wars and, 25–26
Central Intelligence Agency, 88
Chancellor, John, 37–38
Cheney, Richard, 19, 38, 43
China, 27
Christian, George, 29
Christopher, Warren, 155–157, 179, 180
CIA. *See* Central Intelligence Agency
Citizens for a Free Kuwait, 49

Civil-military operations centers, 97, 231
Clifford, Clark, 37
Clinton administration
    challenges in communicating
      policies, 58
    demand for action in Bosnia, 150
    description of Bosnian conflict, 99
    effect of news coverage on policy
      decisions, 100, 116–117
    emphasis on UN role in Somalia,
      168, 183–184
    foreign policy, 63–64
    Haiti policy, 185–194
    media response to message on Haiti
      mission, 202
    military-media relations in Haiti,
      113
    policy on peace operations, 38
    pressure from Congress to end
      Somalia mission, 178–180
    public opinion on Somalia mission,
      203
    response to Durant video, 176–177
    response to Sarajevo marketplace
      massacre, 154–158
    Rwanda policy, 143, 146
    shift from military to political strategy
      in Somalia, 182
    Somalia policy, 167
    treatment of news media during mis-
      sion to Haiti, 20
    use of television in building support
      for Bosnia mission, 214–215
CMOCs. *See* Civil-military operations
    centers
CNN. *See* Cable News Network
Cockburn, Alexander, 102
Cohen, Bernard, 9, 33, 62, 70, 103
Cohen, Herman, 132, 135, 141, 217
Cold War, impact on news media, 9–10,
    33, 57–59, 88–89
Communications technology
    effect on foreign correspondents and
      government officials, 76–88
    impact of increased speed of com-
      munication, 6–7
    spatial effects, 7

temporal effects, 7
use as weapon in peacekeeping
    operations, 115–119
Congress
    opposition to Haiti invasion, 188
    pressure to end Somalia mission,
      178–180
Congressional Black Caucus, 185
Contact Group, 154
Coughlin, Rep. Lawrence, 52
Croats, 99, 105, 147, 150, 154
Cronkite, Walter, 29, 35
Crowe, Adm. William, 81
C-SPAN. *See* Cable Satellite Public
    Affairs Network
Cuba, 22
Cuban Missile Crisis, 79, 80–81, 84
Cyclone Marian, 196

Dallaire, Maj. Gen. Roman, 196
Dallas Morning News, 67
"Day in Hell" cable, 132
Dayton peace accords, 146, 214
D-Day, 26, 212
Defense Department, 92–93
de Laski, Kathleen, 184
Deputies Committee, 106, 140, 180
Doctors without Borders. *See* Médecins
    sans Frontières
Dole, Sen. Robert, 156
Donovan, Hedley, 35
Doyle, Mark, 171
Drug interdiction, 12
Dunsmore, Barrie, 73, 74
Durant, Michael, 120, 166, 171, 176

Eagleburger, Lawrence, 132, 138–142,
    148, 150, 152, 216
Early warning, 159–161
Eckhard, Fred, 101
Eisenhower, Gen. Dwight D., 26
El Salvador, 12
Elsner, Alan, 129
Embedded media, 228
Espionage Act, 25

Falklands War, 39

Fatigue factor, 65
Federal News Service, 83
Fleishman-Hillard, 113
Foreign Policy, 105
Foreign policy. *See* also Peace operations
    effect of technology on reporters and
        government officials, 72–88
    effect of television on reporting,
        60–61
    impact of media, 3–5, 33–34
    news reporting during Cold War,
        57–59
    news reporting since Cold War,
        60–88
    role of media during Vietnam War,
        37
Fourth Estate, 24
Fox, John, 151
France, 157
Frankel, Max, 35
FRAPH. *See* Front Révolutionnaire
        pour l'Avancement et le Progrès
        d'Haïti
Friendly fire, 182
Front Révolutionnaire pour l'Avancement
        et le Progrès d'Haïti, 191

Galbraith, Peter, 195
Gallucci, Robert, 138–139, 142, 198
Gallup polls, 36
Gandhi, Rajiv, 196
Gergen, David, 93
Germany, 24, 25
Gjelten, Tom, 99, 100, 103–104
Glaspie, April, 48
Global news organizations, 98
Gosende, Robert, 174
Government officials. *See* U.S. gov-
        ernment
Gowing, Nik, 14, 77, 152, 219
Gray, William, III, 185
Grenada, 39, 41
The Guardian, 125, 171
Gutman, Roy, 91, 99, 101–104, 110,
        120, 125, 147–149, 151–153, 162,
        218
Gwertzman, Bernard, 58–59, 66

Haass, Richard, 128, 130
Haiti
    behavior of news media, 94
    impact of news coverage, 184–194,
        196, 197–202
    military-media relations, 110–111,
        113
    public opinion of mission, 222
    request for no television lights during
        invasion, 93–94
Hallin, Daniel C., 9, 32, 34–35, 50
Hamilton, Rep. Lee, 156
Hearst, William Randolph, 22
Hempstone, Smith, 132
Hill and Knowlton, 49, 69
Hirsch, John, 118–119
Holliman, John, 41
House Select Committee on Hunger, 136
Howe, Adm. Jonathan, 169, 174, 183
Huband, Mark, 171
Humanitarian-relief operations. *See* also
        Nongovernmental organizations;
        Peace operations
    relationship of organizations with
        news media, 105–110
Hurd, Douglas, 155
Hurtic, Zlatko, 151
Hussein, Saddam, 44, 47–49, 84, 127–131
Hutus, 143

ICRC. *See* International Committee of
        the Red Cross
IFOR. *See* Implementation Force
Implementation Force, 146, 214, 228
Independent Television News, 69, 70, 77,
        125, 147, 151
Information Superhighway, 232
Information warfare, 116–119, 229
INMARSAT satellite system, 74
Inner-perimeter security, 191
InterAction, 106–107, 110, 140, 144
International Committee of the Red
        Cross, 107, 110
Internet, 8, 233
Iraq, 41–43, 45–49, 127–131, 182, 194,
        216, 217
Iraqgate, 53

Israel, 45
ITN. *See* Independent Television News
Izetbegovic, Alija, 116

Japan, 25
Jennings, Peter, 154
Jeremiah, Adm. David, 140
JIB. *See* Joint Information Bureau
Johnson, Lyndon B., 29, 32–33, 36
Johnson, Ralph, 149
Johnson, Tom, 176
Johnston, Lt. Gen. Robert B., 168
Johnston, Phil, 141
Joint Chiefs of Staff, 32
Joint Information Bureau, 43, 98, 229
Juppé, Alain, 155, 157

Kaiser, Andree, 125
Kalb, Bernard, 72–73
Kalb, Marvin, 68
Kansteiner, Walter, 106
Kaplan, David, 121, 123
Karazdic, Radovan, 116
Kassebaum, Sen. Nancy, 135–136
Kennan, George F., 4–5, 233
Kennedy, John F.
    Cuban Missile Crisis, 80–81, 84
    Vietnam dilemma, 32–33
Kenney, George, 149, 151–153, 219
Khrushchev, Nikita, 84
Kigali, Rwanda, 143
Koppel, Ted, 63, 72, 76, 92
Korean War, 26–28, 30–31
Kunder, Jim, 135
Kurds, 127–131, 195
Kuwait, 43, 45, 47–49

Lake, Anthony, 155, 176
Lebanon, 182
Lewis, Anthony, 100
Libutti, Brig. Gen. Frank, 93
Limited wars
    Korean War, 26–28
    problems of, 32–33
    Vietnam War, 29
Lippmann, Walter, 70, 197
Local news media, 230

Logan, Laura, 121–123, 125
Lorch, Donatella, 107, 110
Luttwak, Edward, 30

MacArthur, Gen. Douglas, 27–28
MacArthur, John R., 102–103
MacKenzie, Brig. Gen. Lewis, 99, 100, 101
MacNeil/Lehrer NewsHour. See News-Hour with Jim Lehrer
Major, John, 128
Maren, Michael, 173, 175
Marshall Plan, 34
Mass media, 64
McCaffrey, Gen. Barry, 140
McCurry, Michael, 78, 157–159, 183, 206
McIntyre, Jamie, 83
McKinley, William, 21–23
McNamara, Robert, 37, 79, 80–81
McWethy, John, 189, 205
Médecins sans Frontières, 107, 164
Media control. *See* Censorship
Microwave dishes, 94
Military
    analysis of news media, 38
    Civil Affairs units, 117
    communications strategy, 225–228
    conflicts with civilian and relief
        organizations, 97–98
    cooperation with media during
        World War II, 25
    dependence on news media, 54
    deterioration of relationship with
        press during Vietnam War, 37–38
    invitation to media to cover Somalia
        landing, 92–93
    management of news media, 38–42
    media pressures, 224
    media relations, 110–115
    operations other than war, 12
    Psychological Operations units, 117, 118
    relationship with NGOs, 230–231
    role in setting size and scope of inter-
        ventions, 218
    wartime restrictions on news media, 20

Minimalist response, 163, 219
Mogadishu, Somalia
    danger to reporters, 120
    impact of news media on public
        support for relief operations,
        169–177
    use of television lights during mili-
        tary landing, 92–93
Mohamed, Ali Mahdi, 173
Mohamoud, Hassan, 176
Montgomery, Maj. Gen. Thomas, 170,
    171, 205
Morillon, Gen. Philippe, 121–122
Mozambique, 12
Mueller, John E., 30
Multilateralism, 96
Multinational Force, 191
Murtha, Rep. John, 192
Muslims, 105, 137, 147, 150
Myers, Dee Dee, 80, 155, 176–178, 186,
    192, 223

Namibia, 12
National Public Radio, 99
NATO, 154
Natsios, Andrew, 106–107, 118–119, 130,
    132, 135, 141, 161, 195, 230
NBC News, 68–72
Network news, 68–72. *See also* specific
    news organization by name
Newhouse News Service, 110
News broadcasts, 65
Newsday, 147, 148, 150, 151
NewsHour with Jim Lehrer, 76, 143
News media. *See also* Newspapers;
    Real-time television; Television
    censorship during Korean War, 28
    censorship during World Wars I
        and II, 25–26
    changes in coverage of foreign news,
        65–72
    cooperation of the military during
        World War II, 25
    danger to reporters, 119–124
    deterioration of relationship with
        military during the Vietnam War,
        37–38

    effect of technology on foreign corre-
        spondents and government offi-
        cials, 72–88
    effect of Vietnam War, 51
    effect on public opinion, 55
    foreign policy reporting during Cold
        War, 57–59
    foreign policy reporting since Cold
        War, 60–88
    freedom of peace operations com-
        pared to wartime restrictions,
        95–98
    impact on events in Mogadishu,
        169–177
    impact on foreign policy, 3–5,
        33–34
    impact on interventions, 127–164
    impact on public opinion, 166–196
    management of, 38–42
    military-media relations, 110–115
    pressures on military, 224
    relationship with government, 8
    relationship with relief organizations,
        105–110
    relationship with UN in Bosnia,
        98–102
    reporting on peace operations,
        91–125
    responsibilities of reporters, 228
    role during Spanish-American War,
        21–23
    role during Vietnam War, 35–37
    role during World Wars I and II,
        23–26
    role in Persian Gulf War, 49–52
    role in Somalia, 141–142
    role in Vietnam War, 33–37
    struggle for objectivity in Bosnia,
        102–105
    sustaining support for peace opera-
        tions, 196–204
    wartime restrictions, 20
Newspapers
    censorship during Korean War, 28
    compared to television, 15
    coverage of Persian Gulf War, 45
    effects of real-time television, 87

Newspapers *(cont.)*
    focus of, 8
    foreign news reporting, 66–67
    as the Fourth Estate, 24
    role during Spanish-American War,
        22–23
New World Order, 53
New York Times, 14, 32–33, 35, 51, 58, 66,
    87, 99, 100, 186
NGOs. *See* Nongovernmental organiza-
    tions
Nightline, 63, 72, 76
Niles, Thomas, 150
Nongovernmental organizations. *See* also
    InterAction
    criticism of actions in Mogadishu,
        172
    relationship with military, 230–231
    relationship with news media, 105–110
    role in Somalia, 216–217
    support for news media's presence, 95
Noriega, Manuel, 40
NPR. *See* National Public Radio
Nunn, Sen. Sam, 111

Oakley, Robert, 118–119
Oberdorfer, Don, 149, 150
Objectivity in reporting, 102–105
OFDA. *See* Office of Foreign Disaster
    Assistance
Office of Foreign Disaster Assistance,
    106, 130, 132, 135, 161
"Official news," 8
Open intelligence, 229
Operation Just Cause, 40
Operation Provide Comfort, 128, 194,
    195, 216
Operation Provide Relief, 131, 136, 138,
    195
Operation Restore Hope, 92–93, 106,
    118, 120, 136, 139, 168, 202, 205,
    216
Operation Sea Angel, 196
Operation Support Hope, 97, 144, 216
Operation United Shield, 230
Operation Uphold Democracy, 207
Oslobodenje, 104

Outer-perimeter security, 191
Owen, David, 100

Pakistani peacekeepers, 169
Palestine Liberation Organization, 143
Palmer, Frederick, 25
Palm-tree journalism, 75
Panama, 39–41
Panamanian Defense Forces, 40
Panic, Milan, 121
Parachute journalism, 68, 92
PBS. *See* Public Broadcasting System
Peace operations
    building support for future opera-
        tions, 213
    Clinton administration's policy, 38
    compared to restrictions on news
        media during wartime, 95
    danger to reporters, 119–124
    definition, 11–12
    determining outcome of operation,
        204–206
    effect of cameras, 124–125
    impact of news media on public
        support, 166–196
    Iraq, 127–131
    phases of, 11
    role of news media, 3, 5–6, 10, 54,
        91–125
    sustaining support in the news
        media, 196–204
    use of communications technology
        as weapon, 115–119
Pearl Harbor, 25
Peck, Col. Fred, 170–171, 195
Pell, Sen. Claiborne, 196
Pentagon pools. *See* Press pools
Perlez, Jane, 132
Perot, H. Ross, 4, 87
Perry, William, 83, 154
Persian Gulf War
    Bush administration's use of the
        media, 6
    CNN coverage of, 41–42
    Iraqgate, 53
    management of news media, 20,
        41–44

Persian Gulf War *(cont.)*
  role of news media, 49–52
  role of Saddam Hussein, 47–49
  television coverage of, 44–47
  use of stringers, 69
Peyronnin, Joe, 93, 198
Philadelphia Inquirer, 151
Phnom Penh, 12
Port-au-Prince, Haiti
  behavior of news media, 94–95
  criticism of news reporting, 191–192
Powell, Gen. Colin, 111, 139–140
Powell Doctrine, 38
The Press and Foreign Policy (Cohen), 8,
    33, 62
Press briefings, 62
Press pools
  future of, 115
  during Persian Gulf War, 42–43
  Sidle Panel, 39–40
Preventive diplomacy, 159–161
Private voluntary organizations, 105,
    110
Psychological Operations, 117, 118
PSYOPS. *See* Military, Psychological
    Operations units
Public affairs, 78, 229
Public Broadcasting System, 76
Public opinion
  decline in support for Somalia mis-
    sion, 203
  impact of casualties, 30–31, 55–56
  impact of news media on support for
    peace operations, 166–194
  increased opposition to U.S. involve-
    ment in Vietnam, 36
  interest in foreign news, 71
  during Korean War, 27
  management of news media, 39–42
    during Spanish-American War, 22
    during World Wars I and II, 24
Public relations, 113
Pulitzer, Joseph, 22
Pulitzer Prizes, 67, 99
Pull effect, 11, 165–209, 220–224
Push effect, 11, 21, 127–164, 214–219
PVOs. *See* Private voluntary organizations

QRF. *See* Quick Reaction Force
Quick Reaction Force, 168, 183
Quindlen, Anna, 138

Radio
  Korean War coverage, 28
  World War II coverage, 26
Radio Mille Collines, 117–118, 144
Radio Mogadishu, 119, 169
Radio Moscow, 84
Rather, Dan, 92, 111
Rausch, Col. Steven F., 95, 205
Reagan, Ronald
  influence on shelling in Beirut, 81
  management of news media during
    Grenada invasion, 39
  Saddam Hussein and, 47
Real-time television. *See also* Cable News
    Network
  coverage of Persian Gulf War, 44–47
  definition, 14–15
  effect on foreign news coverage,
    72–76
  effect on government officials, 76–90
  effect on peace operations, 220
  effects on newspaper reporting, 87
  impact of, 6–7
  impact on policy in Bosnia, 153–159
  role during Persian Gulf War, 42
Relief operations. *See*
    Humanitarian-relief operations
Reston, James, 58, 76
Reuters, 69, 98
Richburg, Keith, 93, 94, 104, 110, 125,
    138, 159–160, 174
Ridgway, Rozanne, 4, 206
Rieff, David, 104
Robinson, Randall, 185–186
"Roller coaster" news coverage, 222
Roosevelt, Franklin D., 26
Rose, Lt. Gen. Sir Michael, 101
Rosner, Jeremy, 78, 178, 181
RPF. *See* Rwanda Patriotic Front
Russia, 1
Rwanda
  effect of television coverage, 159,
    163–164, 194

Rwanda *(cont.)*
    information warfare, 117–118
    media's push role, 216, 218
    role of television, 143–146
    volunteer relief efforts, 13
Rwanda Patriotic Front, 118, 143

Sarajevo, Bosnia
    danger to reporters, 121
    marketplace massacre, 153–159
    news media's struggle for objectivity
        in reporting, 102–105
Sarajevo Daily (Gjelten), 104
Saudi Arabia, 42, 48
Sawyer, Diane, 84
Schrager, Stanley, 186, 191, 199
Schwarzkopf, Gen. Norman, 51–52
Scowcroft, Gen. Brent, 41–42, 80, 81,
        137, 139–142, 147–148
Security Council. *See* UN Security
    Council
Sedition Act, 25
Senate Foreign Relations Committee, 135
Serbs, 99, 105, 137, 147, 149–152, 154,
        156–159
Sesno, Frank, 176
Shalikashvili, Gen. John, 189, 190, 194,
        206
Shaw, Bernard, 41
Shelton, Lt. Gen. Hugh, 110–113
Shevardnadze, Eduard, 45, 127, 163, 216
Shiites, 129
Sidle, Maj. Gen. Winant, 39–40
Simon, Sen. Paul, 135
Simpson, Sen. Alan, 52
Simpson trial, 71–72
SNA. *See* Somali National Alliance
Somalia
    danger to reporters, 119–120
    decline in public support, 203–204,
        220
    determining outcome of operation,
        205
    effect of policy in Bosnia, 137–139
    impact of news coverage, 3–4, 11, 95,
        166–184, 195
    impact of television, 221
        information warfare, 118–119
        media's push role, 216–217
        news coverage of, 197–202
        reasons for action, 139–141
        role of television, 131–137, 141–142,
            221
        similarities with Vietnam, 9
        use of stringers, 69
        use of television lights during mili-
            tary landing, 92–93
Somali National Alliance, 169, 171,
        172–175
Spangler, Scott, 135
Spanish-American War, 21–23
Srebrenica, Bosnia, 121–123
Stack, John, 107
State Department
    press briefings, 62
    use of television, 79
Stech, Frank J., 113–114, 116, 165
Stockwell, Maj. David, 170–173,
        175–176, 183, 211, 224
Strategic media effects, 223
Stringers, 68–69
Structural effects of technology, 77
Sudan, 61
Summers, Col. Harry, 31

Tactical media effects, 223
Taft, Julia, 144
Talbott, Strobe, 153, 190–192, 197, 199
Task Force Ranger, 170, 172, 181
Technology. *See* Communications
    technology
Teeter, Robert, 48
Telecommunications Act of 1996, 233
Tele-diplomacy, 84
Television. *See also* Real-time television
    compared to newspapers, 15
    early warning, 159–161
    effect of technology on foreign corre-
        spondents, 76–88
    effect on foreign policy reporting,
        60–61
    news broadcasts, 65
    Persian Gulf War coverage, 41–42,
        44–47

Television *(cont.)*
  preventive diplomacy, 159–161
  role in Bosnia, 146–153
  role in Rwanda, 143–146
  role in Somalia, 131–137, 141–142
  use by relief organizations, 105–106
  Vietnam War coverage, 28–30
Tet Offensive, 29, 182, 220
Thatcher, Margaret, 39
Time Inc., 35
Toronto Star, 120, 175
Total wars, 23–26
TransAfrica, 185
Truman, Harry S., 27–28
Turkey, 130
Turner, Ed, 92
Turner, Ted, 3, 44. *See also* Cable News
  Network
Tutwiler, Margaret, 79, 83, 129–130, 149
"Two-way" dialogues, 75
Tyndall, Andrew, 69

UNAMIR. *See* UN Assistance Mission
  in Rwanda
UN Assistance Mission in Rwanda,
  117–118, 196
The "Uncensored War" (Hallin), 9
UNHCR. *See* UN High Commissioner
  for Refugees
UN High Commissioner for Refugees,
  105–106, 110, 143
Unilaterals, 43
UNITAF. *See* United Task Force
United Nations. *See also* UN Security
  Council
  Children's Fund, 163
  Correspondents Association, 102
  Development Program, 172
  public affairs, 231
  relationship with news media in
    Bosnia, 98–102
  Undersecretary General for Peace-
    keeping Operations, 102
United Task Force, 168, 195, 230
UNMIH. *See* UN Mission in Haiti
UN Military Observer mission, 101–102,
  122

UN Mission in Haiti, 199
UNMO. *See* UN Military Observer
  mission
UN Operation in Somalia, 119, 139, 168,
  170–172, 175, 183
UNOSOM. *See* UN Operation in
  Somalia
UNPROFOR. *See* UN Protection Force
UN Protection Force, 99, 101, 157, 206
UN Security Council
  authorization of force against Iraq, 49
  criticism of Somalia policy, 137–138
  Resolution 688, 128
  Resolution 770, 152
  Resolution 837, 180
Urquhart, Sir Brian, 69–70
U.S. government
  communications strategy, 225–228
  effect of technology on officials,
    76–88
  interaction with media during peace
    operations, 96–98
  relationship with news media, 8
  as sources for journalists, 34
  use of news media during Vietnam
    War, 35
  wartime restrictions on news media,
    20
U.S. Information Service, 94
USIS. *See* U.S. Information Service
USS *Harlan County,* 116–117
USS *Vincennes,* 81

"Values cases," 212–213
Vance, Cyrus, 100
Videocameras, 59, 73–74
Vietnam War
  deterioration of relationship between
    press and military, 37–38
  effect on news media, 51
  government's public opinion con-
    cerns, 32–33
  impact of casualties on public opin-
    ion, 30–31
  news media's role, 33–37, 220
  role of television, 30
  similarities with Somalia, 9

Vietnam War *(cont.)*
    Tet Offensive, 29, 182, 220
    Vietnam Syndrome, 28
Village Voice, 175
VOA. *See* Voice of America
Voice of America, 84
Voice of Free Iraq, 129
Vulliamy, Ed, 125

Washington Post, 14, 100, 138, 149, 186
Watson, Paul, 120, 124, 175
Weinberger Doctrine, 38
Wheatley, Bill, 71, 72
Willey, Col. Barry E., 95, 113, 115, 189,
    191, 193, 196, 199

Williams, Pete, 40, 42–43, 52, 93
Wilson, Woodrow, 24
Wolfowitz, Paul, 128
Wood, David, 110–111, 115, 123–124
Woodruff, Judy, 85
World Wars I and II, 23–26
World Wide Web, 233

Yellow press, 21–22

Zaire, 107
Zimmermann, Warren, 148, 150–151,
    218
Zinni, Lt. Gen. Anthony, 230

United States Institute of Peace

The United States Institute of Peace is an independent, nonpartisan federal institution created by Congress to promote research, education, and training on the peaceful resolution of international conflicts. Established in 1984, the Institute meets its congressional mandate through an array of programs, including research grants, fellowships, professional training programs, conferences and workshops, library services, publications, and other educational activities. The Institute's Board of Directors is appointed by the President of the United States and confirmed by the Senate.

Chairman of the Board: Chester A. Crocker
Vice Chairman: Max M. Kampelman
President: Richard H. Solomon
Executive Vice President: Harriet Hentges

Jennings Randolph Program for International Peace

This book is a fine example of the work produced by senior fellows in the Jennings Randolph Fellowship Program of the United States Institute of Peace. As part of the statute establishing the Institute, Congress envisioned a program that would appoint "scholars and leaders of peace from the United States and abroad to pursue scholarly inquiry and other appropriate forms of communication on international peace and conflict resolution." The program was named after Senator Jennings Randolph of West Virginia, whose efforts over four decades helped to establish the Institute.

Since 1987, the Jennings Randolph Program has played a key role in the Institute's effort to build a national center of research, dialogue, and education on critical problems of conflict and peace. More than a hundred senior fellows from some thirty nations have carried out projects on the sources and nature of violent international conflict and the ways such conflict can be peacefully managed or resolved. Fellows come from a wide variety of academic and other professional backgrounds. They conduct research at the Institute and participate in the Institute's outreach activities to policymakers, the academic community, and the American public.

Each year approximately fifteen senior fellows are in residence at the Institute. Fellowship recipients are selected by the Institute's board of directors in a competitive process. For further information on the program, or to receive an application form, please contact the program staff at (202) 457-1700.

Joseph Klaits
Director

Warren P. Strobel is the White House and former State Department correspondent for the *Washington Times*. During 1994–95, Strobel was a senior fellow in the Jennings Randolph Fellowship Program at the United States Institute of Peace. His analyses of the news media and peace operations have appeared in the *American Journalism Review* and *Managing Global Chaos: Sources of and Responses to International Conflict* (U.S. Institute of Peace Press).

Late-Breaking Foreign Policy

This book is set in the typeface Minion; the display type is Twentieth Century. Hasten Design Studio, Inc. designed the book's cover, and Joan Engelhardt and Day W. Dosch designed the interior. Helene Y. Redmond of HYR Graphics did the page makeup. Graphics were done by Kenneth P. Allen.